Culture, Stratification and Development

Culture, Stratification and Development

K.L. Sharma

RAWAT PUBLICATIONS
Jaipur • New Delhi • Bangalore • Hyderabad • Guwahati

ISBN 978-81-316-0400-7

Published by
Prem Rawat for **Rawat Publications**
Satyam Apts., Sector 3, Jawahar Nagar, Jaipur 302 004 (India)
Phone: 0141 265 1748 / 7006 Fax: 0141 265 1748
E-mail: info@rawatbooks.com
Website: www.rawatbooks.com

New Delhi Office
4858/24, Ansari Road, Daryaganj, New Delhi 110 002
Phone: 011-23263290

Also at *Bangalore, Hyderabad* and *Guwahati*

Typeset by Rawat Computers, Jaipur
Printed at Chaman Enterprises, New Delhi

Contents

Acknowledgements

The author is grateful for permission accorded by the concerned authorities to publish the following papers in this book. Necessary editorial changes and modifications have been carried out while recasting the papers for re-publication:

1. "The Changing Structure and Process of Social Transformation in Contemporary India", earlier published in *Social Sciences: Communication, Anthropology and Sociology* by Yogendra Singh (ed.), 2010, Longman/Pearson, New Delhi, under the title "Caste, Class and Ethnicity: Continuities and Emerging Trends", pp. 351–61.
2. "Caste, Class and Globalisation: Continuity and Change", earlier published in *Globalisation, Governance Reforms and Development in India* by Kameshwar Chaudhary (ed.), 2007, New Delhi, Sage Publications, pp. 241–58.
3. "Caste and Peasantry: Some Questions and Clarifications" was presented as a keynote address at a seminar held at University of Rajasthan.

4. "Why there is only Caste and not Caste System in India?" is based on my current interest on revisiting caste in India.
5. "Gender and Social Stratification in Contemporary India" is reproduced from *Social Stratification in India: Issues and Themes*, by K.L. Sharma, 1997, New Delhi, Sage Publications, pp. 133–56.
6. "The Tamil Diaspora, Ethnicisation and State in Contemporary Sri Lanka", earlier presented at a seminar, held at the School of Social Sciences, JNU, New Delhi.
7. "Interlinking Culture and Development: A Case of Chanderi in Madhya Pradesh", earlier presented at a seminar, held at College de France, Paris.
8. "The Social Organisation of Urban Space: A Case Study of a Small Town in Central India", earlier published in *Contributions to Indian Sociology* in 2003.
9. "Some Reflections on Higher Education, State and Social Hierarchy in India", earlier presented at an International Conference of Vice-Chancellors in Brazil in 2004.
10. "A Note on Modernity and Post-Modernism", earlier delivered as an inaugural address at the University of Rajasthan at an Indo-Canadian Conference in 2004.
11. "Explicating Amartya Sen's Concept of 'Social Opportunity', earlier presented at a seminar in New Delhi, organised jointly by FIICI and SCIRHR in 2003, in honour of Amartya Sen, and later on published in *Development as Freedom: An India Perspective*, by J.S. Sodhi (ed.), 2004, under the heading "Amartya Sen's Concept of Social Opportunity", New Delhi, Shri Ram Centre for Industrial Relations & Human Resources, pp. 50-73.
12. "Society, State and Development: The Indian Dynamics", earlier delivered as the valedictory address, at the All-India Sociological Conference, held at Srinagar in October 2009.

Preface

The papers included in this book have been written over a period of nearly ten years from 2000 to 2010. The topics and themes discussed in these papers have a wide range, covering caste, class and change, social stratification, ethnicity, gender, culture, education, development, etc. However, my main concern is to explain the different aspects of structure, culture and process with regard to caste/community, rural and urban people, and women in particular. I have also reflected on the ongoing debates on caste-class nexus, education, state and social hierarchy, modernity, post-modernism and development, Amartya Sen's concept of 'social opportunity', Indian diaspora in Sri Lanka, and culture and change in the context of a small town.

I am aware that there is some overlapping in the two papers on a small town, however, two different aspects have been highlighted—one refers to urban space and social status, and the other brings out relationship between culture and economy. It is hoped that the book would encourage further debates and discussions and will promote research, which would explain interlinking of structure, culture and development.

I express my affection and thanks to my nephew Subhash Sharma, his wife Seema and their three sons for providing me all the comforts during my stay at Jaipur with them in the summer of 2006, when I was working on some papers included in this volume. These papers were later completed during my tenure as Vice-Chancellor at the Jaipur National University. I am grateful to Mr Sandeep Bakshi, Chancellor of the University for extending me all the possible support in my academic endeavours.

Finally, I am grateful to Rawat Publications for bringing this book well in time.

Introduction

Caste is no more an all-encompassing system as it supposedly used to be in the pre-independence era. In a way, today, caste is being surrounded by contemporary polity and economy to a considerable extent. In the present book, I have tried to explain the intertwining of caste, class, gender, education, social opportunity, country-town nexus, ethnicity and diaspora, peasantry, culture and development. Some of the papers have already appeared in volumes and journals. However, by putting these papers together in this book, I have threaded them by interlinking culture, stratification and development. Some salient points emanating from these papers may be highlighted here.

I have argued that social stratification refers to high and low positions/groups or individuals, but these ranked entities are not necessarily based on the principle of pure and impure or higher and lower castes, as determined by birth. Social inequality is ubiquitous, and caste-based inequality is particularly specific to Indian society in the present form, and also it was so in the past. But even birth-based caste system was not absolutely inequalitarian. There were provisions and mechanisms to resolve disputes and redress grievances through mediatory devices.

Today, the two extreme approaches, namely, the Marxist and the culturological ones, do not offer satisfactory explanations of the present social reality. "Social difference" and "power" have become two important focal points in the discourse on social stratification. Ritual hierarchy is no more coterminous with the hierarchies of power and wealth. Caste is not yet out, it may not be so for an indefinite period of time. But it is not the same today as it was in the past, and it would not be the same tomorrow as it is today. Caste was a bedrock of social relations among different groups in the past. Today, it has become a discrete phenomenon, and in future, it may acquire a new form and substantive character, depending upon new dynamics of society, economy and polity. Family and individual have gained a considerable significance in status determination, relegating caste in the background. There is a perceptible delegitimisation of the "essential" of the caste system. Everyday life is now governed by salaried jobs, status and power, education, mobility, etc. Since studies on caste and stratification have been influenced by the Marxian and Weberian approaches in particular, I have reflected on these two major viewpoints and the studies which have been guided by them.

While analysing caste as a system or a phenomenon or a state of mind and identity, I have ventured to interlink caste and class in terms of their nexus, continuity and change, and specifically in the context of globalisation. I have discussed time and again that caste and class are not polar opposites and antithetical to each other. The two are inseparable as one can be transposited into the other by way of appropriation of caste for economic/political gains, and class can be used for social superiority and cultural enhancement. In this context, I have found P. Bourdieu's concept of "capital" quite relevant in the interlinking and transposition of caste, class and power. However, there is no uniform country-wide congruence between caste and class. Caste is seeking new grounds in non-conventional spheres, and class is rapidly becoming a social phenomenon, a status-determinant. Caste is becoming a new political creation, a state of mind, more or less the way it was treated by British colonialism. In this process of transformation, middle classes have not only enlarged, but have also changed the urban landscape and the country-town nexus. Apart form the contemporary provisions enacted by the Indian State, education, globalisation, etc., have also changed the form and functioning of the middle classes, particularly in urban India. Professionals, including engineers, managers and service-providers, have acquired the centre stage of the Indian economy, and have impacted economy of the USA, in particular. New references of status and inequality are emerging, such as very rich, rich, well-off, not-so-poor and poor, in place of the caste-determined social and cultural ranks. Individual is becoming an effective unit of social standing alongwith his/her family.

Globalisation has enhanced the significance of the concepts, such as "individual", "development", "freedom", "opportunities", "market", "state", etc., in regard to status-determination. I have also discussed in this context the notions of "social opportunities" and "freedoms" and "unfreedoms" as explained by Amartya Sen. A race for seeking higher and better status can be seen in both urban and rural settings. People are no more complacent about their pre-given caste-based positions.

Based on my study of the Shekhawati region in Rajasthan, I have examined the questions of caste and peasantry and the nexus between the two. Since caste and peasantry were closely interlinked in terms of ranking and status, we have asked: Can peasantry be treated as a class, a constructed stratum? Is peasantry synonymous with caste? Does differentiation of peasantry reflect caste stratification? Is peasantry an isolated entity? In the pre-independence period, the Jats of Shekhawati constituted the principal agricultural castes. Other castes were not so predominant in agriculture. After India's independence, the former peasant castes have highly diversified their economic pursuits. Direct dependence on agriculture has also reduced to a perceptible extent.

I have debated in one of the papers in this volume: whether there is "caste system" or there is only "caste" in India today? Caste is a reality today, but of a different kind than what it was before 1947. It is being appropriated as a means of social and political mobilisation by the vested interests. In the last two decades, it is being used for (1) reservations in jobs and educational institutions; and (2) seeking support in elections; and (3) for aggrandisement through the connived institution of *Khanp*. These are not in coherence with the caste system as a bedrock of social relations between the castes and within the castes. Hence, there is a need for questioning these tendencies as elements of the caste system, and for reconceptualising caste, granting due significance to family and individual in the emerging pattern of social stratification.

The role of Indian State is paradoxical in relation to the caste system. The Constitution of India does not grant any space to the caste-based inequalities on the one hand, and grants caste-based reservations, on the other. Even the cruelties of the *Khanp* remain unchecked by the state/government. Some political parties use caste idioms in their pronouncements and manifestos, and, in fact, their political bases largely remain confined to specific castes and communities. The proposed caste-based census of 2011 reminds us of the colonial censuses of 1881, 1891, 1901 and 1931, in which caste was eulogised in multiple ways to restrain resistance against the British rule in India.

Caste is rapidly transforming itself, not because of the conscious efforts by the state or NGOs or anti-caste movements. Education, modern occupations, migration and mobility have weakened the caste rigidities and strings of rules and regulations. Who is bothered about the principle of pure and impure in India's metropolises? Caste is a matter of reckoning. It is there in villages in a mutilated form. Extra-caste alliances and relations are quite pronounced. To a large extent, in everyday life, caste-based rituals and practices are paid a lip-service. Thus, caste is a phenomenon, and not a system.

In one paper, I have pleaded for inclusion of gender as an independent variable, alongwith caste, class, power, ethnicity, etc., in the theory of social stratification. Among several relevant questions, two are quite pertinent here: (1) Why women are continually seen as objects? (2) What are the visible and invisible aspects in everyday life of a woman which make her subordinate to a man? Answers to these questions lie in the gendering of our social fabric. The institutions of patriarchy, marriage, dowry, property and inheritance, subordination and gendered division of labour provide ground for considering gender as a factor in social stratification. There is "male reason" in all situations. "Female reason" remains dormant or suppressed. Because of such a mindset, feminity remains weak and subordinate in actual life. There is also stratification among women as an entity, like caste, class and power hierarchies. It seems that there is nothing gender-neutral. Gender inequality has deep roots in India's socio-cultural fabric. Even education and modern occupations have not helped women considerably in having equality with men.

In another paper, the question of ethnicity and the role of state has been discussed in the context of the Tamil diaspora in contemporary Sri Lanka. The state and society created social divides and ethnicisation in Sri Lanka, between the Tamils and the Sinhalese. Immediately after Sri Lanka's independence from colonial yoke in 1948, one could sense ethnic conflict emanating from the deprivation of Tamils by the Sinhalese with the support of the state and its institutional apparatuses. The formation of several Tamil political parties and the demand for creation of a Tamil nation sprang up in the 1950s. The ethnic conflict was, in fact, more of a structural character, but its expression was mainly through cultural idioms. It may also be noted that though Sri Lankan Tamils formed only 11 per cent of the population at the time of independence, they were far ahead of the Sinhalese in professions and civil services, who were nearly 70 per cent of the total population. Sri Lankan Tamils were having English education, and were entrenched into universities, administration and professions. This was not taken kindly by the majoritarian Sinhalese.

In this way, it was articulated how a minority of Tamils could rule over the Sinhalese by occupying dominant positions in a newly born independent Sri Lanka? Intense rivalry ensued because of such bitter feelings rooted in ethnic divide. Religion, that is Hinduism and Buddhism, and language, that is, Tamil and Sinhala, have been ethnicised and politicised. The ethnic strife has ended with the downfall of the leader of the LTTE, but ethnic accommodation and reconciliation seem to be a difficult task.

An empirical exposition of culture, in conjunction with economy and polity, space and status, private and public life, is discussed in two papers, based on our field data about Chanderi, a small weavers' town in Ashok Nagar district of Madhya Pradesh. Some aspects of culture, such as image and reality of culture, culture and community, culture and livelihood, culture as space, etc., have been taken up to relate culture with development. Culture's centrality to development or underdevelopment is the main issue in the one thousand years' old town of Chanderi. "Culture of silence" rather than that of "protest" has become a sort of creed in the weavers town. People have capital, but no capitalism. There are entrepreneurs/master weavers, but no directly employed workers/wage-earners. Chanderi has industry (sari manufacturing), but no industrialisation. Chanderi looks like a "pre-industrial city", having "proto-industrialisation". There is hardly unemployment in Chanderi, but prosperity eludes the people in this town, which is gifted with beautiful natural surroundings and magnificent architecture and historical monuments. Its old market is a hub of social relationships, alongwith a place for economic activities.

In another paper on Chanderi, I have emphasised on a shift in conceptualisation because people consider social space and status more than their material conditions. Material objects and events are transformed into social space and status. Space-status nexus is clearly evident in the ordering and managing of *mohallas* and *galis*. The fact is that geographical space indicates the space of social relations. The people in Chanderi have accepted modernity, without dismantling tradition, existing hierarchies and multiculturalism. Chanderi combines the ideal and the actual social worlds in the enactment of socio-cultural activities. Space-segregation and social distance remain an open fact as new classifications of social classes, divisions and institutions have not yet replaced the persisting ones.

Higher education is generally considered both an agency of social change and a factor in persisting inequalities in society. Society in India is characterised by a complex of collectivities, differentiations, inequalities and specificities. Can education transform such a society? While reflecting upon the Marxist and the functionalist viewpoints on education, I have discussed that education is both a means of social change and a status stabiliser. As such, it is an ambivalent and paradoxical mechanism. It is both "reproduction" and "enlightenment", but it is reproduction for the entrenched sections, and it is enlightenment for the first generation learners. In a real sense, education must be emancipatory, it must bring a new awareness of self, a sense of dignity, a new hope, conscientisation, critical awareness and radicalism. Higher education suffers from several maladies, including its vulgar marketisation, neo-imperialism and a means of status and power rather than that of reflection and enlightenment.

To understand the dynamics of culture, stratification and development, it is necessary to know the concepts of "modernity" and "post-modernism". When we talk of modernity, we refer to a new man, a modern man, a citizen of the new state, a man in the era of science, an industrial man, etc. Rationality and consciousness are the core elements of modernity of a man. How do we consider a society a modern one? Generally, a society is considered "modern" in the wake of advancements in industry, trade and commerce. In such a situation, tradition encounters an onslaught of change. Indian tradition is viewed as resilient and adaptive. Another view is that India has witnessed a synthesis of both ontogenetic and heterogenetic changes at cultural and structural levels.

However, modernity is mistaken with westernisation and material advancement and possession of assets. Modernity is a course of social change, a way of life and mode of thinking. Post-modernism implies coming out of the syndrome of consumption and commodification. Getting away from limitations of modernity leads us towards post-modernism. Thus, post-modernity implies reconstruction, and inclination towards art, literature, cinema, music, fashion, communication, etc. A new meaning of progress and development is basic to the idea of post-modernity.

In the last two papers, I have discussed the concept of "social opportunity" as given by Amartya Sen and the interlinking of state, society and development. Sen looks at "freedom" as an instrument of action for development. Development implies removal of various types of unfreedoms that leave people with little choice and little opportunity of exercising their reasoned agency. Freedom is social, and it is required for education, health care, employment, etc., for the deprived groups and individuals. Freedom in one field is related to freedom in other field. Freedom is also a yardstick of progress and development. Unfreedom is inequality. Caste, gender and marginalisation often become hindrances in freedom, development and progress.

In the last paper, while analysing the viewpoints of D.P. Mukerji, Frantz Fanon and Paulo Freire, relating to relationship between man and society, oppression by the state, and the culture of oppression, I have argued that India is a distinct civilisation, and a quite different socio-political and economic formation, compared to Africa and Latin America. In this paper, I have provided an overview of the studies done by Charles Battelheim, Gunnar Myrdal, John Stuart Mill, Rudolph and Rudolph, Paul R. Brass, Jean Dreze and Amartya Sen, Pierre Bourdieu, Ram Chandra Guha, Dipankar Gupta, etc., on state, society and development. I have summed up the discussion by saying that categories such as caste, ethnicity, religion, ritual distance, etc., have lost their significance in understanding the interlinking of state, society and development. The categories, namely, rich and poor, strong and weak, privileged and deprived, resourceful and resourceless, etc., have gained significance as they are not tied to a caste, community, religion, language and region. A paradigm shift is needed to see the dynamics of development in relation to the complex nature of Indian society.

1

The Changing Structure and Process of Social Stratification in Contemporary India

I

How men and women are shaped and reshaped in terms of socio-cultural and economic and political considerations? What evaluative criteria to determine status take precedence over others at a given point of time in a society? How criteria of ranking of individuals, families and groups undergo a considerable change? An explication of these questions would require an in-depth understanding and analysis of the entire gamut of social inequality. The privileged on the one hand, and the underdog on the other, along with several individuals, families and groups in-between the two poles, constitute the structure of social stratification in all human societies. Anti-change and pro-change processes and factors are at work at any time vis-à-vis the system of social stratification.

The nature of formation of Indian society reflects the structure of inequalities or equalities in different domains of social life. Prior to independence, the colonial/feudal formation structured social relations and positions. A challenge to such a structuring emanated from India's independence in the form of values of equality and democracy.

Social stratification refers to the structure and process of allocation and distribution of resources, and to the rationale of decision-making about structuring of high and low positions. Based on such an understanding of human society, Marx and Engels (1975: 41) have observed that almost everywhere, a complicated arrangement of society into various orders, a manifold gradation of social ranks, existed in the earlier periods of history (prior to capitalism). And, this is why, Marx and Engels mention about divisions of society into freeman and slave, guild-master and journeyman, oppressor and oppressed as the contending classes (ibid.: 40). According to Marx and Engels, the present capitalist mode of production has put an end to all feudal and patriarchal relations. The bourgeoisie has reduced men as paid wage-earners. Not necessarily following the Marxist thesis, nevertheless, the question is to know the nature and composition of the Indian society in terms of high and low groups, families and individuals before independence, and their transformation into new status groups, classes and actors after independence till date.

II

Inequality is thus created by structural (ranked) differences, powerlessness and victimisation of the lowly ranked people. On the contrary, equality refers to unranked differences as well as egalitarianism in social roles. However, cultural values remain active in shaping of inequality/equality in a given society. In the context of Indian society, Gerald D. Berreman (1979) refers to institutionalised inequality which entails suffering of those who are at the bottom of caste hierarchy. Berreman equates the systems of stratification in India, the United States, Japan and the Rwanda in Africa at the same level and with the same yardstick. One may disagree with such a thesis which places India, the United States, Japan and Africa at par in terms of the suppressed position of the people at the bottom in these societies. Chris Samaje (2000: 1–4) also considers both caste and race as 'natural hierarchies', hence, caste and race look as similar systems of social stratification. For us, the question is: Can we treat the two as one and the same?

Berreman's view on caste, as a generalised aspect of social stratification, may not be a serious bone of contention. His objection to Louis Dumont's view is on caste as an 'institutionalised hierarchy', rather than opposite of 'equality'. Dumont's view on caste as an 'institutionalised inequality' is unacceptable to Berreman because Dumont considers the caste hierarchy as an essentially religious system. Pauline Kolenda (1984), while commenting on Berreman and Dumont, mentions that we have two different meanings of inequality: (1) depreciation and suffering of the inferior (Berreman); and (2) all-inclusive hierarchy. No doubt, Dumont refers to inequality based on ritual pollution-purity, but he also accepts interdependence of the ritually ranked unequal groups (castes). The question is: How 'binary opposition' would have complementary organic ties at the same time? The notion of 'power' is also quite prominent in Dumont's thesis in terms of the 'pure' having supremacy over the 'impure', in the form of the 'encompassing' and the 'encompassed'. The point is: Whether one thinks of a society which has 'high' and 'low' people, the latter being at the receiving and; or one takes into account in a positive sense the hierarchically arranged groups of people having organic interdependence.

Another point emanating from Dumont's thesis is that absence of individualism as an ideology in India has resulted into structured and hierarchical inequality. Dumont transforms equality into individualism, and individualism is very much an ideology that developed in Western Europe with the concepts of economics and economic systems (ibid.). One more related point is: Was there no equality in India and no inequality in West Europe? Whether India has been a 'just society' or not—is a debatable question. A 'just society' provides equal access to different occupations and positions and also equal shares of resources (Rawls, 1999: 3–15). And such a society does not ignore the special contributions of some members on the one hand, and welfare of the worst-off sections of the society on the other. I have argued elsewhere that there was no absolute inequality in the caste system and there was no absence of individual and economic and political considerations in Indian society (Sharma, 1999: 4).

Social inequality is a perennial phenomenon because it entails high and low positions, and this is caused by some given principles which society upholds as essential and sanctified. It is ubiquitous (Sharma, 1997: 17–24). Ralph Dahrendorf (1969: 17) poses four questions about inequality. These are: (1) Why is there inequality among men? (2) Where do its causes lie? (3) Can it be reduced, or even abolished altogether? (4) Do we have to accept it as a necessary element in society? Natural distinctions as well as social criteria are mentioned by Dahrendorf as relatively significant in different contexts, situations, and over a period of time. As such, inequality is a multifaceted and dynamic phenomenon. The so-called non-social criteria (age, sex and kinship) may not be so decisive in the advanced societies, but may be significant determinants of social status in pre-industrial societies (Smith, 1964: 141–76). On the contrary, in the latter, the criteria and notions of property, land, education, modern occupations, etc., might be quite insignificant determinants in shaping of social stratification.

Both equality and inequality are relative phenomena, and therefore, no debate on either equality or inequality can ignore the presence of the one in the other. The basic structural change in social stratification in India has been caused by derecognition and delegitimation of the value system, which sanctified power and privileges based on birth and caste rank. Such a normative change has created a sense of equal citizenship and equality of opportunity. I have observed in some other context: "Encouragement to the sections aspiring for equality to demand their share in national resources has brought about a new social language of interaction between the traditionally privileged and the emergent new strata" (Sharma, 1997). Birth and caste rank no doubt continue in some way as status considerations, but compared to the new economic and political imperatives of status determination, they have become considerably weak criteria in the present situation. The historical truth is that social inequality is constantly structuring and restructuring. "Inequality is not opposite of equality theoretically as well as empirically" (ibid.). Being a 'relational' phenomenon, it is to be seen in terms of its non-monolithic nature and at the levels of its presence with regard to individuals, families, and groups. Inequality remains a fact of life to evaluate ranks and positions of individuals, families and groups based on both sets of criteria, namely, age, sex and kinship on the one hand, and income, education, occupation and office, on the other.

III

Approaches to the study of social stratification in the Indian context are rooted into the cognitive-ideational realm as well as the structural-existential conditions of the people. However, such a distinction is more heuristic than substantive. The ideational-cognitive approach leads to the understanding of the real world, and the structural-existential approach contributes to the construction of the world of ideas and thought processes. Let us begin with the view that the existential conditions determine hierarchy and inequality. Marx and Engels (1968: 36) write: "As individuals express their life, so they are. What they are, therefore, coincides with their production both with *what* they produce and with *how* they produce." Based on such a thinking, Marx and Engels recognise existence of the bourgeoisie and the proletariat as antagonistic classes in the capitalist formation. The bourgeoisie behaves as a patriarchal master in the garb of the great industrial capitalist. He treats masses as slaves, hence despotism of the master. With increased use of machine, age and sex become instruments of appropriation, and women supersede men in factory. Working hours go up. Further, the manufacturer behaves as the landlord, the shopkeeper, the pawnbroker, etc. Marx and Engels (1975: 51) also observe existence of the lower strata of the middle class—the small trades people, shopkeepers, retired tradesmen, handicraft men and peasants, but they observe that all of them would sink gradually into the proletariat because of their diminutive capital and competition. Thus, social stratification is production and reproduction of a value system and structural forces at a given point of time in a society. Marx and Engels (1968: 32) observe that men as real beings reproduce themselves in a definite form of life through a definite mode of life on their part.

Can we understand the Indian social stratification with the Marxian frame of reference? Caste has become a different sort of system of social relations. I have stated in another publication: "What was considered as immutable and rigid has become quite flexible, and what was considered as an inevitable part of the system (caste) has become optional or it has disappeared. New dimensions have been accredited to it mainly because of some unintended and unanticipated consequences of both structural and ideological changes" (Sharma, 1997: 21). Incorporation of economic and political considerations in the caste framework implies diminution of 'culturalism' and structuralist stances, namely, pollution-purity, commensality and connubiality. Some of the structural changes have led to the emergence of a new middle class, which is disproportionate to the upper and the lower classes. Today, due to changes in the value system and social relations, individuals, families and groups are being replaced and reproduced in the Indian society. What has happened to Indian society, economy and polity which has resulted into restructuring of social life? What is the emergent mode of social relations? What units (individuals, groups, classes and collectivities) are being produced as a result of the present-day economy and polity? What is the nature of social interaction between the new units produced through the post-independence process?

Marx and Engels are right to the extent that structural forces determine the class character of a given society, but it is not correct to accept that there would be two classes only, and the lone structural-existential factor is 'economic'. The role of socio-cultural and political factors cannot be undermined, and the differentiation of class structure with burgeoning middle class reduces considerably the significance of the Marxist gospel.

These basic questions remain relevant in the Indian society because of its persisting semi-feudal, 'semi-capitalist' social and political relations (ibid.). Perhaps answers to these questions lie in this proposition: "Each generation continues the traditional activity in completely changed circumstances, and modifies the old circumstances with a completely changed activity" (ibid.).

IV

A number of studies (e.g., Beteille, 1966; Bhatt, 1975) have been influenced by multidimensional nature of social reality and man's rationality regarding distinction between economic, social and political aspects of social life. In case of Marx and Engels, economic determinism is key to social reality, and contrary to this, 'political and military materialism' is central to

Max Weber's approach to the study of social stratification (Gerth and Wright Mills, 1970: 46–50). Weber (1970: 180–95) considers classes, status groups and political parties as phenomena of the distribution of power. In Marx, 'collectivity' is the real unit of social rank; in Weber, 'individual' becomes an actor in a social situation to realise power. More significant is non-reducibility of economic, social and political orders to one another because of 'rationality' of man as the basic element in decision-making in a given situation. The myth of caste as an encompassing system or that of the determinism gets exploded when Weber argues that the "economically conditioned power is not, of course, identical with power as such" (ibid.: 180). Power may be valued for its own sake. Striving for power may be conditioned by the 'social honour' it entails, and not all power entails social honour (ibid.).

Following Weber's approach, distinctions and interrelations between caste, class and power have been reported in a couple of studies on social stratification. Points relating to rationality, subjectivity, historical specificity, cultural moorings, etc., need to be studied carefully keeping in view the Western experience, which is in the backdrop of Weber's *verstehen*, and the Indian society which has holism, collectivism and transcendence as the main principles of its tradition (see Singh, 1973).

The multidimensional studies of social stratification (see for example, Mukherjee, 1957; Beteille, 1966; Sharma, 1974), though lay emphasis upon caste, class, power, ethnicity and gender, do not give enough attention to culture as a significant determinant of social stratification. For example, Pierre Bourdieu (1991: 168) argues that symbolic productions are nothing but instruments of domination. However, it is an established fact that given symbolic productions serve the interests of the dominant class. A new dominant class is in the offing in India which has challenged the persisting hierarchisation and socio-cultural arrangements. This class is certainly a post-independence phenomenon. The beneficiaries of economic gains and political advantages have succeeded in carving out their respective identities and socio-political space. Intermediate castes and communities in particular are constantly replacing the entrenched upper and upper middle castes. Obviously, such a process of creation of identities and social spaces implies ordering and reordering of social groups, families and individuals. Further, such a change results into distribution and redistribution of people and resources, including making of choice and availing of opportunity. Thus, the system of social stratification as of now would require a new conceptualisation to understand the changed contents and contexts of caste, class and power. Instead of ritual hierarchy and segregation, today 'social difference' and 'power' have become new focal points of discourse on social stratification (Sharma, 1997: 22–23). Mobilisation for a specific purpose, including elections, and then the net result, would determine ranks of the groups and individuals in terms of loosers and gainers, successful and unsuccessful ones. Certainly, such a situation brings in resource mobilisation by way of appropriation of primordial ties, economic standing, networks, etc. Competition becomes the hallmark among individuals, families and groups.

V

Caste is significantly present today, but not by way of connubiality and commensality (inter-caste relations) based on the ascription of caste rank by birth. Caste is projected today as a perceived 'interest group' rather than a system characterised by pollution-purity, caste endogamy, and organic ties among different castes. A particular caste is propagated as an imaginary collective entity, so that its members, even while ignoring intra-caste differences, can come together for a supposed cause which is being advanced by a select group of people in their own interests. A private trouble is projected as a 'public issue'. It is not a situation of intra-caste fraternity or of encompassing of the pure by the impure. Moreover, the pollution-purity dimension of caste is not monolithic as it has regional variations based on rigidity-flexibility continuum (ibid.). McKim Marriott (1965) uses the term 'elaboration' in his study of five regions of India and Pakistan to work out such a continuum. The regional variations are also linked with ethnic differentiation of caste, hence economic and political factors play a notable role in status determination (Quigley, 1995). Even in ancient India, invasions and migrations changed the composition of society. There were 'mixed castes'. The 'ritual status' varied from the 'actual status'. It was not a rigidly structured and frozen society (Thapar, 1974). There were clearly distinct domains of power, ritual and economy (see, for example, Chakravarti, 1985; Thapar, 1974; Kosambi, 1958). Economy along with caste contributed to the making of the Indian society (Habib, 1995: 161–79). My study of six villages in Rajasthan shows that a socially patterned taxation system, systems of land control and land grants determined considerably the status distinctions in the village community (Sharma, 1989). Caste rank was a relative phenomenon. The notion and practice of 'contra-priest' signified co-existence of inequality and equality, ritual and actual statuses, and caste ranks as relative phenomena.

The question is: Why Louis Dumont and some others are in defence of caste as a ritual system? Dumont considers inequality as opposite of equality in the systemic sense. According to him, caste is a system of 'ideas and values' not only in theory but also in practice. Hierarchy is both a value and a fact for Dumont. Pure is superior, and therefore, priest is higher than king (ruler). The pure encompasses the impure (Dumont, 1970: 143; also see Sharma, 1997, for a brief critical appraisal of Dumont's understanding of caste). Similar was the approach and understanding of M.N. Srinivas (1952,1989) in his analysis of 'dominant caste' and 'sanskritisation'. Family, and not caste, plays the active part in the reproduction of inequality, observes Andre Beteille (1994: 235–51). The reproduction of the service class from one generation to another, and the unequal distribution of life chances or access to it are not automatically determined by caste. Bourdieu (1996) also considers family as repository of social and cultural capital through the process of socialisation of its members.

Caste is not yet out. It has cognitive continuity and change, though in transformed forms (Sharma, 1997: 31–33). Caste has been unable to check differentiation of property, technological change and occupational mobility. However, it has survived and even penetrated into non-traditional and new spheres of life (ibid.). At the same time, there is the 'double-headed' caste hierarchy, for example, in the Newar society in Nepal (Quigley, 1995: 298–327). "Claims to high status in complex caste hierarchies are based on multiple criteria which are contested and evaluated differentially" (ibid.). Quigley observes: "In Newar society there is ample scope for opposing view and contested rankings between castes of similar status"(ibid.). Within castes too, the ranking of lower order groups is also contested (ibid.). Similar was the situation in the princely Rajasthan where the king was not inferior to the priest, in some important contexts. Castes are also ranked differently and treated differently in different contexts and locations. Hence, sub-regional hierarchies and rigidity-flexibility or elaboration of caste are a stark reality of the system of social stratification. Without any doubt, it has been reported that inequalities are based on structural criteria, such as status, economic difference and power, and a lower rank in any one of these spheres may not be congruent with the remaining domains. Structural incongruities have become order of the day. Caste has renewed nexus with economy, polity, religion, region, migration, etc. Hence, restructuring of caste and role reversal.

VI

Social inequality is unevenly structured. One can see social stratification in diverse forms in different structural and historical contexts. These include physical force and economic power, distribution of material resources and power (Klass, 1980), multidimensional determination and multiple approaches to social stratification (Marriott, 1959). Migration, feuds, competition, bargaining, occupational choice, education, power, style of life, ownership, control and use of land are some of the important aspects which are operative at the levels of individual and family rather than caste (Beteille, 1994; Sharma, 1974). This is how Dipankar Gupta (2000) interrogates caste, and argues for its discrete nature. Yogendra Singh's review of the studies on social stratification brings out this point in a succinct manner. He observes that the sociology of social stratification is concerned mainly with the nature of social order, social equality and inequality, social justice, power and the nature of man (Singh, 1974). In another subsequent survey, Singh (1985) reports new substantive concerns in the stratification studies, which can be explained in terms of fruitful convergence of multidisciplinary interests, both substantive and theoretical. In the third survey, Sharma (1997) reports that the debate on social stratification centres around: (a) whether changes in caste and class are transformational or structural; (b) whether caste is closed and class is open; (c) whether caste is organic and class is segmentary; and (d) whether caste is being replaced by class and political power or not. The implicit multidimensional studies of social stratification as outlined above would focus upon the following points (ibid.):

1. Traditional pattern of stratification
2. Conceptual problems in defining caste and class
3. Continuous hierarchies and discrete castes
4. Caste and politics
5. Caste, class and power: Nexus, continuity and change

6. Agrarian classes, mobilisation and change
7. Weaker sections and social mobility
8. Professions and social stratification
9. State, society and social stratification

VII

Recently, while attempting "Conceptualisation of Caste-Class Nexus as an Alternative to Caste-Class Dichotomy", and "Rethinking Inter-caste Relations as the Basis of Social Stratification" (ibid.), I have observed that caste is increasingly becoming a matter of interpretation rather than substantialisation. Caste refers to a purposive rationality, and at the same time, it provides a description and explanation of the pathologies of modern polity and economy (ibid.). It is no more an absolutised system characterised by ostracisation and social neglect. Occasional outbursts, by way of killing and torture of the 'violators' of caste ethics, are incongruent anachronisms in the times of the dwindling of the organic character of the caste system.

Today, castes are discrete categories. The inter-caste relations, which were the bedrock of the caste system, have disappeared. Jajmani has become defunct. Family and individual have replaced caste in everyday life. Caste is becoming a desideratum, a state of mind, a plastic and malleable institution. No more hypersymbolisation is manifest to express caste differences and typifications on a continuing basis. Though there is a process of delegitimisation of the 'essential' of caste, yet the sporadic appearance of caste-based decisions, and articulation of religious and metaphysical interpretations of caste and its divinity, pose a serious challenge to the secularised understanding of social reality (ibid.). Politico-economic interpretations of caste, relating to different epochs in Indian history, indicate that the caste system remained an important pillar of the system of class exploitation (Habib, 1995), social distance and rivalry (Risley, 1969), an instrument of power (Sharma, 1998), social injustice (Blair, 1980: 64–74), etc. Clustering of castes as categories, such as 'forwards', 'upper backwards', 'lower backwards', 'dalits' etc., implies political mobilisation for power, employment and sharing of resources (Sharma, 1997: 107–32). Improvement in economic standing and political power has also added the dimension of dignity and honour to the system of social stratificaton (Kolenda, 1989: 1833–38). Equal etiquette and equal rights, inter-caste marriage and utility of the caste system have become the new points in the discourse on caste. Violation of caste endogamy is being accepted, and not considered as a 'grave' crime. Commensal violations have become quite frequent.

My own study shows that in everyday life issues relating to salaried government jobs, status and power, education, mobility, etc., have become mundane and caste is found as a feeble point for discourse, except during elections. Summation of statuses is key to a given rank in the system of social stratification, and this is not a static phenomenon. In the fifties, caste was an overriding determinant of social status. In the seventies, economic standing along with caste rank determined social status, and today the element of power has become quite significant factor. Even caste as an institution is appropriated for power. This is how summation of statuses has become the main yardstick of the reality of the system of social stratification. A value change is quite perceptible in the emerging pattern of social stratification.

References

Berreman, Gerald D., 1979, *Caste and Other Inequalities,* Meerut: Folklore Institute.

Beteille, Andre, 1966, *Caste, Class and Power*, Bombay: Oxford University Press.

——, 1994, "The Family and the Reproduction of Inequality", in Patricia Uberoi (ed.), *Family, Kinship and Marriage in India*, Delhi: Oxford University Press.

Bhatt, Anil, 1975, *Caste, Class and Politics*, Delhi: Manohar Publications.

Blair, Harry, 1980, "Ruling Kulaks and Backward Classes in Bihar: Social Change in the Late 1970's", *Economic and Political Weekly*, Vol. 5, No. 2

Bourdieu, Pierre, 1991, *Language and Symbolic Power*, Cambridge: Polity Press.

——, 1996, *The State Nobility: Elite Schools in Field of Power*, Cambridge: Polity Press.

Chakravarti, Uma, 1985, "Towards a Historical Sociology of Stratification in Ancient India: Evidence of Buddhist Sources", *Economic and Political Weekly*, Vol. XX, No. 9.

Dahrendorf, Ralph, 1969, "The Origin of Inequality among Men", in Andre Beteille (ed.), *Social Inequality*, New Delhi: Penguin Books.

Dumont, Louis, 1970, *Homo Hierarchicus*, London: Paladin Granda Publishing Ltd.

Gerth, H.H. and C. Wright Mills, 1970, "Intellectual Orientations", in Max Weber, *From Max Weber: Essays in Sociology*, London: Routledge & Kegan Paul.

Gupta, Dipankar, 2000, *Interrogating Caste: Understanding Hierarchy and Difference in Indian Society*, New Delhi: Penguin Books.

Habib, Irfan, 1995, *Essays in Indian History: Towards a Marxist Perception*, New Delhi: Tulika.

Klass, Morton, 1980, *Caste: The Emergence of the System in South Asia*, Philadelphia: Institute for the Study of Human Issues.

Kolenda, P., 1989, "Micro-ideology and Micro-utopia in Khalapur: Changes in the Discourse on Caste Over Thirty Years", *Economic and Political Weekly*, Vol. XXIV, No. 32.

Kolenda, Pauline, 1984, *Caste in Contemporary India: Beyond Organic Solidarity*, Jaipur: Rawat Publications.

Kosambi, D.D., 1958, *An Introduction to the Study of the Indian History*, Bombay: Popular Book Depot.

Marriott, McKim, 1959, "Interactional and Attributional Theories of Caste Ranking", *Man in India*, Vol. 34, No. 2.

——, 1965, *Caste Ranking and Community Structure in Five Regions of India and Pakistan*, Poona: Deccan College.

Marx, Karl and Frederick Engels, 1968, *The German Ideology*, Moscow: Progress Publishers.

——, 1975, *Manifesto of the Communist Party*, Moscow: Progress Publishers.

Mukherjee, Ram Krishna, 1957, *The Dynamics of Rural Society*, Berlin: Academic Verlag.

Quigley, Declan, 1995, "Conclusion: Caste Organisation and the Ancient City", in David N. Gellner and Declan Quigley (eds.), *Contested Hierarchies*, Oxford: Clarendon Press.

Rawls, John, 1999, *A Theory of Justice* (Rev. edn.), Oxford: Oxford University Press.

Risley, H.H., 1969, *The People of India* (2nd edn.), Delhi: Orient Books. First published in 1908 from London.

Samaje, Chris, 2000, *Natural Hierarchies: The Historical Sociology of Race and Caste*, Oxford: Blackwell Publishers.

Sharma, K.L., 1974, *The Changing Rural Stratification System*, New Delhi: Orient Longman.

——, 1989, *Caste, Feudalism and Peasantry: The Social Formation of Shekhawati*, New Delhi: Manohar.

——, 1997, *Social Stratification in India: Issues and Themes*, New Delhi: Sage Publications.

——, 1998, *Caste, Feudalism and Peasantary: The Social Formation of Shekhawati*, New Delhi: Manohar.

——, 1999, "Introduction: Some Reflections on Caste and Class in India", in K.L. Sharma (ed.), *Caste and Class in India*, Jaipur: Rawat Publications.

——, 2001, *Reconceptualising Caste, Class and Tribe*, Jaipur: Rawat Publications.

Singh, Yogendra, 1973, *Modernization of Indian Tradition*, New Delhi: Thomson Press.

——, 1974, "Sociology of Social Stratification: A Trend Report", in *A Survey of Research in Sociology and Social Anthropology*, Vol. I, ICSSR, Bombay: Popular Prakashan.

——, 1985, "Sociology of Social Stratification", in *A Survey of Research in Sociology and Social Anthropology*, Vol. II, ICSSR, Bombay: Popular Prakashan.

Smith, M.G., 1964, "Pre-industrial Stratification Systems", in S.M. Lipset and N.J. Smelser (eds.), *Social Structure and Mobility in Economic Development*, London: Routledge & Kegan Paul.

Srinivas, M.N., 1952, *Religion and Society Among the Coorgs of South India*, Bombay: Oxford University Press.

——, 1989, *The Cohesive Role of Sanskritization and Other Essays*, Delhi: Oxford University Press.

Thapar, Romila, 1974, "Social Mobility in Ancient India", in R.S. Sharma (ed.), *Indian Society: Historical Probings*, New Delhi: Peoples Publishing House.

Weber, Max, 1970, *From Max Weber: Essays in Sociology*, London: Routledge & Kegan Paul.

2

Caste, Class and Globalisation

Continuity and Change

I

Though caste has been questioned from time to time as a holistic system of stratification, however, it has functioned more or less as an encompassing arrangement of social groups (castes and sub-castes). Dynamics and ramifications of the caste as a system indicate that it has neither been uniformly rigid and elaborate in different parts of India nor has it been so with regard to specific caste groups. A scale of 'elaboration' or 'rigidity-fluidity' dimension of caste suggests the possibility of change in the system, and that too not of the same magnitude. As we know that economic and political considerations have penetrated into the caste system from times immemorial, and therefore, at times this has made the ideology of 'pure' and 'impure' with regard to caste—'weak' and 'upside down' in certain respects. Even though 'individual' is not quite significant and visible in the caste system, but due to onslaught of certain economic and political factors, 'group' as the basis of caste ranking has received a setback, and 'individual' has made his presence felt. Such a situation explains the incorporation of class and power in the core of the caste system. One can also say that ritual status implies power. Crystallisation of social (caste), economic and political domains calls for a study of change and mobility in the caste system. Our concern here is to understand the extent and magnitude (both internal and external factors) of social mobility in the Indian society. We have noticed an increased presence of 'individual' in the patterns of migration, mobility, decision-making, etc.

While analysing the dynamics of social stratification, we would like to locate middle castes and classes in contemporary India to see how colonialism, education, social reforms, land reforms, green revolution, adult franchise, etc., have brought about social mobility (including downward mobility). Some questions may be posed here: Is there a middle class? Is there a new middle class? What is the nature of clash of interests among different castes and classes? What is the nature and extent of migration from rural to urban? Which are the areas of new spaces for the traditionally deprived people? Is a new social formation in the offing? In the light of these questions we intend to understand the role of 'globalisation' in transformation of India's social stratification. What is 'globalisation'? What is 'just globalisation'? How does it affect different social groups (castes and classes)? An attempt to know 'globalisation' in the context of peasants, workers, artisans, castes, and rural and urban people is also warranted.

II

"Social stratification means the differentiation of a given population into hierarchically superposed classes. It is manifested in the existence of upper and lower layers. Its basis and very existence consist in an unequal distribution of rights and privileges, duties and responsibilities, social values and privations, social power and influences among the members of a society. Concrete forms of social stratification are different and numerous" (Sorokin, 1959: 11). Sorokin's conceptualisation applies to the caste system to a great extent. While analysing members of a society economically, politically and occupationally stratified, Sorokin observes: "A real picture of social stratification in any society is very complex. In order to make its analysis easier, only the most fundamental traits must be taken. Many details must be omitted, and the situation simplified, without, however, disfiguring it" (ibid.: 12). One more statement from Sorokin's classical work—*Social and Cultural Mobility*—is quite relevant here. He writes: "Any organised social group is always a stratified social body. There has not been and does not exist any permanent social group which is 'flat' and in which all members are equal. Unstratified society, with a real equality of its members, is a myth which has never been realised in the history of mankind" (ibid.: 12–13).

How does a society get stratified? Who is the main unit/basis of social stratification—individual or group? Take the example of Karl Marx (1888: 12), who pronounces class (group) as the basis of high and low positions. Marx observes: "The history of all hitherto existing society is the history of class struggles. Freeman and slave, patrician and plebeian, lord and serf, guildmaster and journeyman, or in a word, oppressor and oppressed, stood in constant opposition to one another, carried on an uninterrupted, now hidden, now open fight, a fight that each time ended, either in a revolutionary re-constitution of society at large, or in the common ruin of the contending classes. Thus, group is the basis of formation of society and it has never been stable. Industrialisation, for example, has transformed the earlier structure into two classes, namely, bourgeoisie and proletariat. No fixed and frozen relations exist because the bourgeoisie constantly revolutionise the instruments of production, and with them whole relations of society. Though the proletariats are an instrument of production, and yet they alone are a revolutionary agent of social change. No significant middle class exists. The lower of the middle class—the small tradespeople, shopkeepers, and retired tradesmen generally the handicrafts men and peasants-all these sink gradually into the proletariat ..." (ibid., 1888: 12–32). The proletariat is special and essential product of the capitalist society because it stands face-to-face with the bourgeoisie, and the lower-middle classes do not survive in the fight against the bourgeoisie, and therefore, manufacturer, shopkeeper, artisan, peasant, etc., are not revolutionary but conservative.

A different view is proposed by Max Weber. He observes: "A class is any group of persons occupying the same 'class status'" (Weber, 1948: 429). A class could be: (a) a 'property class', (b) an 'acquisition class', and (c) a 'social class'. Individual is the axis of class. An aggregation of individuals based on common traits may constitute a particular class. Like Marx, Weber also recognises a 'positively privileged property class' and a 'negatively privileged class' ('outcastes/proletarians'). However, Weber recognises the 'middle classes' more significantly than Marx. Between the two—the upper and the lower classes—stand the 'middle' classes. They have all sorts of property or marketable abilities through training. Some of them may be 'acquisition' classes. Entrepreneurs fall in this category. Merchants, shop-owners, industrial and agricultural entrepreneurs, bankers and financiers, members of the 'liberal' professions, and workers with special skills commanding a monopolistic position may constitute the middle classes (ibid.: 424–29).

In French literature the English middle class corresponds with the bourgeoisie, whereas Marx considers the middle class as petty bourgeoisie. However, Marx and Engles did not make a systematic distinction between the 'old middle class' of small producers, artisans, independent professional people, farmers and peasants, and the 'new middle class' of clerical, supervisory and technical workers, teachers, government officials, etc. (Bottomore, 1983: 333). Two other considerations in the understanding of the middle classes are: (1) political orientation—conservative or radical, and (2) size or growth in numbers. In the wake of the recent global developments and also in the context of Indian society in particular, these two points may be worthy of discussion.

The middle class is a heterogeneous social layer. Income, property, natural or physical inequality, civil and political inequality are the main criteria for defining commonality of a group of people as a (middle) class. Education, standard of living, nature of occupation and wealth determine varying quality of social prestige and power. The growth of the middle class in England was initially characterised by differentiation of the industrial and commercial functions. Production and trade became distinct activities. Entrepreneurship and management vis-à-vis factory production were required. This heralded a new social order replacing the feudalism in England. Industrial workers emerged from the differentiation of industry and trade. Thus, a number of new groups and categories emerged from the expansion of trade and industry, education and professions (Misra, 1961: 1–7). Further, capitalism made the middle classes an integral part of a unitary social order (ibid.). The old trading middle class was called 'middle' because it was situated in-between the baronage and the peasant or artisan class (ibid.). The new middle class was not simply the capitalist and the worker; it had a wide range of occupational interests and was bound together by a common style of living and behaviour pattern. The new middle classes stood for certain liberal, democratic values which they expressed in their social and political conduct (ibid.). There was respect for the individual, intellectual freedom and social mobility, liberal individualism and political democracy. Thus, the new middle classes reflected a new standard of values (ibid.).

Before the British advent, the immobility of the caste organisation and the despotism of bureaucracy precluded development of a middle-class bourgeois. Even Buddhism, Jainism and Bhakti movements could not reduce the rigidity of the caste system to a noticeable extent (ibid.: 9). The caste system remained static because it was related to the law of property, land, economy, inheritance, etc. These were fixed status groups and intermediate categories and there were no middle classes. The British rule also saw an emergence of a middle class in India. Administration, education, business and occupation played a significant role in the rise of a new middle class. The British-born Indian middle class exhibited in great measure an element of behavioural uniformity and style of life, and similarity in their mode of thinking and social values. The middle classes comprised of the members of the educated professions, namely, government servants and lawyers, college teachers and doctors in general. The merchants and industrialists were a minority and limited to big cities (ibid.: 12–13). Excluding the top people like owners of industries and corporations and top political leaders, and the people at the bottom like small peasants, agricultural workers, all the people such as merchants, agents, proprietors, salaried executives, officers, civil servants, judges, professionals, peasant proprietors, rentiers, shopkeepers and hotelkeepers, rural entrepreneurs, full-time higher education students and senior level school teachers and officials of the local bodies were included in the middle classes during the British rule in India. A confluence of official hierarchies, professional hierarchies and caste hierarchy was quite evident at the end of the 19th century in most parts of the British India. Despite reactionary revivalism, liberal reformism was quite visible in the Indian society. What has happened to such a formation after India's independence? How do we analyse Indian society today?

III

We may discuss briefly also about the caste system and particularly about the empowered castes with a view to know the role of the Indian state, education and exogenous forces. For a long time caste has been perceived as an overarching ideological system of status determination. Two logical queries would be: In what way caste is a normative system? And, how is it a system of social relations? Louis Dumont (1970) considers more specifically caste as a special type of inequality as ideas and values are basic to know actual and observable behaviour of the people. As such, caste is certainly a means of identity. But, then, the question is: Can caste not be an interest group? We have discussed (Sharma, 1996: 130–46; 1994: 50–78; 2001: 45–74) that caste and class are not polar opposites and antithetical to each other. Caste and class are nearly inseparable as one can be transposed into other by way of appropriating caste status for class gains and the latter for social superiority and cultural enhancement. Bourdieu's concept of 'capital' (1991: 14–15) is in tune with our understanding of the caste-class nexus. The two refer to intertwined processes along with their internal differentiations. "The caste-class divide was never as rigid as reported in various writings, and hence Indian society was also not as rigidly structured as depicted in several accounts of the caste system" (Sharma, 1998: 1). The 'ideal' and the 'actual' statues were never the same. The inter-caste marriages produced 'mixed castes'. There were status incongruities in ancient India. 'Production' rather than kinship was given premium in shaping of the social formation in olden times. Thus, neither homo hierarchicus nor homo equalis was the absolute system of hierarchy and equality in India and Europe, respectively.

Contradictions within the caste system and influence of external forces of social change on it rule out the possibility of it being homo hierarchicus. A long history of discontinuities, breakdowns, contradictions and changes in the caste system negates its absolutist, unchanging and holistic nature as perceived by some scholars (Dumont, 1970; Srinivas, 1998).

Both inequality and equality are built into the ideology and practice of the caste system, and both have changed from time to time, providing scope for continuity, change and nexus of the two aspects, namely, 'social' and 'economic' in India's social formation. It is the caste system, which provides priest and contra-priest, inequality and equality, and as such a semblance of the 'unity of opposites'. Because of such a confluence caste has always acquired a new form and functioning in Indian history. It has not been a static (closed) system of social relations. Changes in the caste system have resulted into changes in class, structure and power relations. "The emergence of a new middle class, disproportionate to the forces of production and the size of the upper and the lower classes, has forged a new nexus between caste, class and power" (Sharma, 1998: 2). The principal agricultural castes have given a new direction to the nexus between, caste, class and politics. Economic and political power has become a focal theme today of the study of the caste system. Incongruities between caste, class and power clearly hint at the diminution of caste as an all-encompassing system and the emergence of a new nexus of caste with economy, polity, migration and religion as interlocking sub-systems. Agrarian relations, economic transactions and service relations have set in a process of role reversal in the caste system. Several studies have emphasised the role of migration, education, occupation, political power, style of life, ownership, control and use of land, inter-caste feuds, competition and bargaining for higher wages as the new criteria of status determination and the caste-class nexus. Agrarian relations and green revolution have affected caste, class and land relations by creating divides of gainers and losers.

Today, processes of pauperisation, proletarianisation and downward social mobility on the one hand, and upward mobility and embourgeoisiement on the other, are found simultaneously among different castes and sub-castes. In such a situation caste cannot be a precise equivalent or opposite of class and vice versa. Castes are 'discrete' (Gupta, 1992, 2000), and therefore, they are flexible and segmentary.

The changing nature of nexus between caste and class not only refers to the multifaceted form and substance of social stratification, but it also implies that there is considerable departure from the hierarchical model of consensus, resilience, and summation of roles and statuses in the context of caste. Various social segments and families have witnessed visible change in their social standings. Beteille (1966a, 1966b) has observed 'caste-free areas' of social activities. We have also observed (Sharma, 1973: 59–77) 'downward social mobility' and incompatibility of the pollution-purity principle as a result of the entrenchment of the middle and the lower castes in politics and modern jobs. The problems such as exploitation, domination, poverty, alienation, distributive injustice, suppression of human rights, etc., call upon a reconceptualisation of the caste stratification (Sharma, 2001). We can say that caste is transforming itself rapidly finding out a place for itself in new and secular domains of social, political and economic life. Caste gives coherence and meaning to actual social relations and as such it is both an actual structure of social relationships and an ideology (Harriss, 1982: 42–56). It is realised that today a dominant caste is also a dominant class. However, there is no uniform pattern of caste-class congruence. Assam and Kerala, for example, show resemblance between caste stratification and corresponding class positions. Bihar has a different pattern as it is characterised by the forwards (the twice-born), the upper backwards, the lower backwards, the minorities, the Scheduled Castes (SCs) and the Scheduled Tribes (STs). The West Bengal has considerable radical mobilisation due to an overwhelming presence of the lower caste people, who are extremely poor. We may like to infer here that the emergence of a well-off peasantry belonging to the intermediate castes, white-collar groups from amongst the upper castes and enhanced migration and mobility of these groups (country-town nexus), politicisation of caste identity, differentiation among the SCs and the STs, considerable presence of the class of capitalists, entrepreneurs, professionals, white-collar workers, a select group of elites from amongst the SCs and the STs, etc., are some of the recent actual developments. A continuous change in the caste-class nexus and levels of occupational and social mobility have contributed to the survival of caste as a means of mobilisation for economic and political goals.

IV

In a very forthright manner Nicholas B. Dirks (2001: 3–18) starts with a statement: "When thinking of India, it is hard not to think of caste." But there is a paradox. Dirks observes: "Caste defines the core of Indian tradition, and it is seen today as the major threat to Indian modernity" (ibid.: 3). However, according to Dirks, caste is not in fact some unchanged survival of ancient India, not some single system that reflects a core civilisational value, not a basic expression of Indian tradition (ibid.: 5). More important point in Dirks' analysis is that caste is a modern phenomenon, the product of an historical encounter between Indian and Western colonial rule. The British (Risley, 1969; Hutton, 1946) made "caste capable of expressing, organizing an above all 'systematizing' India's diverse forms of social identity, community, and organization" (Dirks, 2001; 5). Thus, colonialism made caste what it is today. Castes were transformed into middle classes as B.B. Misra observes in *The Indian Middle Classes* (1961). Dirks writes: "Caste itself was seen as a form of colonial civil society in India, which provided an ironic and inferior, anthropological analogue for the colonized world" (2001: 12). Caste served the interests of a private domain at the instance of the British. As such, caste was opposed to the basic premises of individualism, voluntarism and reinforcement of the modern state. Its functioning remained restricted to social and ritual spheres, rather than political domain and individual and social mobilisation. Thus, during colonialism, caste was a more pervasive, totalising and uniform than it had ever been before (Dirks, 2001: 13). There were other multiple identities other than caste during the British period. However, caste was always a political phenomenon by a way of classifications of people in terms of high and low, superior and inferior, and pure and impure ranks.

Caste has not disappeared despite the claim of having enhanced urbanisation and industrialisation. The constitutional stroke regarding its annihilation has also been falsified. Challenges to dominant caste(s) have been frustrated. Caste violence occurs frequently. Reservations have generated a lot of violence and animosities. Despite all this, "caste did not die, it did not fade away, and it could no longer be diagnosed as benign" (ibid.: 16). "At the same time, caste remains the single most powerful category for reminding the nation of the resilience of poverty, oppression, domination, exclusion, and the social life of privilege" (ibid.: 16). Caste provides the basis for new forms of social mobilisation and progressive politics. At the same time, "it has become the subject of national shame" (ibid.: 17). Today, as in the past, caste is imagined and then appropriated for social and political mobilisation; hence *Castes of Mind* as Dirks rightly names his book to explain caste as a political creation. At the empirical level, castes are segments and not organically interlinked units of a holistic system. Dipankar Gupta (2004: 77–78) observes: "The distinguishing characteristic of the caste order is the discrete character of its constituent units that resist being forced into a single hierarchical frame. As these castes are discrete and semaphore their separation on multiple fronts, caste competition is built in at various levels. It is only by accepting the reality of multiple hierarchies that we can conceptually make room for the existence of caste politics. If one were to go by the traditional understanding of a single hierarchy of purity/ pollution, with Brahmins at the top, then any evidence of caste conflict should have meant the dissolution of the caste order." A similar view was articulated by Edmund Leach (1960: 1–10) that as soon as castes began to compete with each other, they ceased to be castes. However, castes have not only been competing with each other, they have had intense fights and violence, and never ceased to be castes, nor they transformed themselves into antagonistic classes in the Marxian sense.

A caste is in mind, a means of identity of the people and so is class based on certain criteria/indices (Sharma, 2001: 45–74). Landowners, landless labourers, traders and moneylenders are not abstractions or conceptual constructions; they are existential structural entities of India's class structure. Both conflict and cooperation refer to life-situations of different classes. One can see interconnectedness of the mode of production and production relations in caste, kinship, family and marriage (Gough, 1980: 337–64). Class relations have been seen as a 'domain assumption' in the treatment of caste and kinship in India (Namboodiripad, 1979: 329–36; Ranadive, 1979: 337–48). Thus, to a large extent, caste and class represent the same structural reality. "Classes operate within the framework of castes" (Singh, 1968: 31). Since the hiatus between the upper and lower castes is the same as it is between the upper and the lower classes, caste conflicts tantamount to class conflicts. At times castes function as classes with a view to realise their economic (class) interests. Caste associations serve economic interests of their members.

V

What about the middle classes? The middle classes are not necessarily the middle castes. On the contrary, they may be from amongst the upper castes to a great extent, and only a minority of them may belong to the middle and the lower castes, minorities and the STs. As such, correspondence between caste and class remains quite unrealistic as well. Broadly speaking, there are three main classes—the bourgeoisie/capitalist class; the middle classes; and the working class. No doubt, all the three are internally differentiated and they cannot also be seen independent of each other. In the first category, we may include the property-owning, entrepreneurial, capitalist-employer. Secondly, in the recent times, capital and industry are controlled by professional salaried management. Thirdly, in the developing countries like India, due to the new state formation, middle classes have grown enormously. Finally, the material standards of workers have also improved considerably.

We have made a brief reference to the middle classes relating to the pre-independence period. After independence the middle classes have changed in terms of their size, role and functions mainly due to the nature and character of the Indian state. Ghanshyam Shah (1986: 149–83) reports that the middle class has grown in size disproportionately with economic growth in Gujarat. In the new middle classes the members are from amongst the upper and the middle castes on the one hand and the lower castes on the other. Since the middle classes are a product of both the capitalist development and the state, there would be a conflict situation between the entrenched middle classes and the lower classes aspiring for the status of the middle classes by having access to lucrative white-collar jobs.

Satish Deshpande (1997: 294–318) observes that in the post-independence years, the ideology of development helped to create and sustain a strongly synergistic relationship between the developmental state, a relatively small but significant middle class, and the nation. However, in due course of time, due to decline in the development ideology, a new middle class has emerged with different interests and desires. The new middle class can be characterised by transnationally dominant ideologies of globalisation and structural adjustment. This has resulted into the growth and differentiation of the Indian middle class. The developmental state of the Nehruvian era resulted in swelling the ranks of the middle classes. The era of 'globalisation' has marked a new phase in the growth and differentiation of the middle classes, and this calls for an examination of continuity and change in development, state and middle classes in India.

However, it is not an easy task to ascertain the exact nature and contents of 'middle class'. In everyday life, the term 'middle class' is referred in a very vague sense. Satish Deshpande (2003: 125–50) observes that it is more of a symbolic term than a factual description. Now, the question is: Can we conceptualise 'middle class' based on the capita consumption? What about the assets possessed by the people? Deshpande says that consumer as the basis of the middle class is too narrow to capture the critical multidimensional role of the middle class in post-colonial societies. A couple of observations by Deshpande may be useful in the conceptualisation of the middle class: (1) The middle class is the class of the people that articulates the hegemony of the ruling bloc by way of the language of legitimation and mediation between the ruling bloc and other classes. (2) The middle is most dependent on 'cultural capital' and on the mechanisms of its reproduction. (3) The middle class specialises in the production and dissemination of ideologies.

Despite the ideological base and moorings as the strongest point of the Indian middle class, the consumerist thirst of the present middle class cannot be overlooked, and it is a clear indicator of the Indian market. Pawan K. Varma (1998: 170–214) talks of three middle classes based on a survey by the National Council of Applied Economic Research (NCAER) in 1994. These are: (1) the consuming class (150 million people); (2) the climbers (275 million); and (3) the aspirants (275 million). Besides these middle classes, at the top are the very rich (6 million people). However, Varma does not endorse the consumerist view of the new middle class in India. The middle class in India has a 'history' and its specific characteristic features and relations with the higher and the lower classes. Hence, the middle class is a socio-economic and political phenomenon because mere economic standing does not make a class a middle class. As such, the middle class is a systemic construction and an action entity.

A study of elite formation in India (Navlakha, 1989) shows that select positions are usually taken by persons from select social strata. Such a group controls the positions of prestige, power and responsibility. Higher education is under the grip of upper castes, hence, it is 'status stabilizer' (Jayaram, 1977) or it results into social/cultural reproduction (Bourdieu, 1996: 50–51) rather than an increase in status rigidities. A couple of studies of lawyers, university teachers, technocrats, scientists and managers have brought about social-structural and organisational aspects of the upper-middle class professionals (Sharma, 1997: 124–29; Lal, 1988). The members of the middle classes have their origins in agriculture and industry (Rudra, 1989). Besides these, there is the class of intelligentsia, who have co-opted a number of members and the two classes having their social origins in agriculture and industry (ibid.). The intelligentsia include all white-collar workers, all office workers, teachers, writers, journalists, artists and skilled workers, professionals, journalists, politicians, trade union leaders, etc. The intelligentsia do not themselves produce any values in the material product sense of the value. Members of this middle class (intelligentsia) depend for their economic gains on the largesse of the other two ruling classes as well as the state. Middle classes are not direct rulers nor are they economic producers like the industrialists, workers and peasants. At the same time, there is a marked lack of homogeneity among different middle classes (Sharma, 1997: 129).

The foregoing account of the middle classes shows that the upper castes constitute the middle classes in Indian society. Widespread political consciousness and democratisation of politics and land reforms and massive irrigation scheme, education and migration have resulted into an attack on the age-old hold of the upper castes on high-status positions. India's independence has created various contradictions and conflicts of interests between the better off and the deprived sections of Indian society (Kamat, 1980: 1673; Das, 1984: 1616–19; Prasad, 1979: 1955–58 and 1980: 215–19). The entire gamut of social change and mobility centres around caste, class and state (power). Social change could be gauged in terms of gain and loss between groups of people, and by both persistence and emergence of tensions, contradictions and conflicts (Sharma, 1998: 159). For example, in Bihar, the middle castes have registered a stiff opposition to the upper castes and have further legitimised their meteoric rise in the class and power hierarchies leading to rapid decline of the persisting 'semi-feudalism'. Caste-based mobilisation by the middle castes in favour of the policy of reservation of jobs has further sharpened and intensified the class contradictions. Capitalist transformation in agriculture in Tamil Nadu, for example, has created a middle class, though caste and kinship have blocked the process of change to reach at the top level. The process of modernisation needs to be viewed in relation to caste, family and village community.

No doubt, 'new status groups' or 'new castes' (Beteille, 1969) have emerged due to role differentiation and occupational diversification, which can be characterised by both upward and downward social mobility (Sharma, 1973). Such a situation of differentiation and diversification has arisen due to interpenetration of caste into class and vice versa, and also due to change in the perception of caste, which can be characterised by 'micro-ideology and micro-utopia' (Kolenda, 1989: 1831–38) and by functioning of varna ideology merely as a social practice, rather than an effectual praxis (Franco, Chand and Sarvar, 1989: 2601–12). K.L. Sharma (1997: 161) observes: "Social mobility in the caste system is evident in the ever-increasing violations of the traditional criteria of status, namely, hereditary occupations, jajmani obligations, observance of certain rituals, and in the acceptance of modern secular occupations, education, migration and positions of power in formal political bodies. At times, competition between different castes accentuates into conflicts and violence." I.P. Desai (1984: 1106–16), in the wake of the problems arising out of the Mandal Commission (1978–80), recognises type of society, role of political power and social mobility movements as significant factors to understand social and educational backwardness, and does not consider these as an offshoot of the ascribed status of a community/collectivity. Desai observes that today contractual relationships and performance matter a lot in the occupational field. Caste plays a minor role in it. However, this view is contradicted by Ghanshyam Shah (1985: 132–36) by way of persistence of caste consciousness and ineffectiveness of the state in annihilation of the caste system. Immobility generates contradictions and tensions; and such a situation brings about mobility, hence equality. Today, we are talking of the Harijan and the tribal elites and the Kulaks among the upper backward castes.

The state in India has consciously encouraged participation of the backward sections of the society in the polity and economy. Equality and participation are positively correlated. From social participation of a cross-section of society comes out equality and genuine citizenship. 'Equality of outcome' is very difficult to achieve and to sustain over any length of time. Bryan S. Turner (1986: 120) observers: "The historical origins of equality are bound up with the preconditions for the development of rational capitalism—the occidental city, Roman law, system of monetary exchange, administration by officials and a this-worldly religious ethic. Equality requires equity in terms of the delivery of a service and the achievement of desirable standards of efficiency and reliability requires bureaucracy." Turner follows strictly the Weberian approach on rational development of capitalism as a sure means of equality. Without reaching a certain level of capitalist development, equality cannot be achieved in Indian society. However, Turner (ibid.: 123) is right in his observation when he says, "equality emerges out of the active and conscious struggle of social groups to achieve social participation through citizenship rights".

Earlier, I have observed (Sharma, 2001: 61) that inter-caste and intra-caste relations are no more the basis of caste hierarchy, division of labour, and asymmetrical power relations. Today, people identify themselves as very rich, rich, well-off, not-so-poor and poor. In a different sense, they perceive themselves as 'powerful' and 'weak' families or as 'superior' and 'inferior' people. And yet in another sense, people identify themselves as engaged in lucrative and prestigious jobs, and in middle and lower level occupations. Thus, economic status, esteem and power are clearly the underlying criteria in the current evaluative expressions. Today, people prefer to have equal etiquette and equal rights. Inter-caste marriages and communal violations are no more a taboo, and inter-caste relations have become rarest of the rare. Caste is increasingly becoming a matter of interpretation rather than a pre-given substantialisation. Caste refers to purposive rationality, and therefore, it provides a description, and an explanation of the pathologies of modern polity and economy. Occasional caste outbursts and ostracisations on the basis of the so-called violations of caste ethics may not be taken as an actual pattern of inter- and intra-caste relations. Inter-caste relations are no more the bedrock of the caste system. Family and individual have largely replaced caste in everyday life. Caste is becoming a desideratum, a state of mind, a plastic and malleable institution. There is no more caste hypersymbolisation to express caste differences and typifications.

Despite the process of delegitimisation of the 'essential' of caste, the sporadic appearance of caste-based decisions, articulation of religion and metaphysical interpretations of caste and its divinity pose a serious challenge to the secularised understanding of social reality. Historically speaking, politico-economic interpretations of caste indicate its significance as the system of class exploitation, social distance and rivalry, an instrument of power and social injustice. Clustering of castes in the form of categories for political mobilisation, employment and resources has also been there with a view to question the supremacy of the superior castes. In everyday life, caste has become quite feeble. Summation of statuses at the levels of individual and family implies weakening of the caste system and strengthening of the extra-caste considerations in Indian society.

Because of the incorporation of the economic and political considerations into the caste system, social mobility has become somewhat easy. Development in the post-independence era has brought about a substantial middle class in India and this class dominates the power structure of the society. Yogendra Singh (1993: 11–21) states that the Indian middle classes are a very articulate, active and powerful segment of our society. Expansion of market and trade, information networking and media exposure of the people, expansion of services and strengthening of the integrative impulses selectively are some of the economic, cultural and political consequences of the strong new middle class in India. At least four points may be noted as reported by Singh with regard to the role of the new middle classes: (1) structural cleavages in its composition; (2) a lack of harmony with the national ideology/social change; (3) dominance of the upper and middle castes among the middle classes; and (4) creation of cleavages between the upper-middle and the lower caste groups within the reserved categories.

Further, Singh states that the middle classes tend to have a mindset, which decries values of liberalism, social justice, and principles of sharing or sacrifice. The middle class is rapidly taking to consumerism and short-run utilisation values. Such a situation creates conflict of values and expectations and misdirected radicalism alongwith ethical and social opportunism. In Singh's view, Indian society is faced with a situation of double crisis—one of success and the other of failures. No doubt, there is an ascendancy of a new middle class, and it implies both social and economic change and resilience. The middle class strengthens market, trade and media and provides a huge base of the skilled manpower. But this is negated by the self-centred ideological moorings and narrow social base of the middle classes. This is the double crisis—crisis of success and crisis of failures.

VI

While analysing 'the future of equality', Rudolphs (1967: 111) observe: "Four processes are making Indians more alike and, in doing so, are laying the necessary but not sufficient conditions for national integration: ascriptive boundaries are expanding; the culture and status of the twice-born varnas are spreading to the Sudra castes; westernisation is affecting the ideas and occupations of broader sections of society; and secularisation is dismantling ritual barriers and disarming sacred sanctions." This is how 'the modernity of tradition' was observed by the Rudolphs in the late 1960s. However, we also know very well that legally group identity has been recognised in India by way of reservations. This is a case of controlled transformation of central social and cultural arrangements. The policy of the compensatory discrimination amounts to substantive equality added to the formal equality. But so long as 'group' (caste) remains the basis of such a policy, tradition-modernity nexus persists (Galanter, 1984: 547–67). Dipankar Gupta (2000: 225–64), while interrogating caste in terms of the pre-given construction, observes that instead of group "at the root of man is man himself". "Social forces must work through the human agent, the social actor, who is essentially, a reflexive cognito. This person contemplates and thinks, rationalises and maximises, such that no social force is left entirely in its pristine form once it has undergone such active human mediations" (ibid.: 263–64). Thus, we may infer the following points:

1. Group alone has never been the basis of social action in Indian society.
2. 'Social' dimension has always existed with economic and political considerations.
3. Social mobility with varying degrees and magnitudes has always been there in Indian society.
4. Internal contradictions and constraints on the one hand, and the external forces and factors on the other, have transformed the Indian society; hence, continuity and change have co-existed.

VII

Let us see now how 'globalisation' is impinging upon the Indian society in general and with regard to specific segments and sections in particular. However, before we map out the impact of globalisation, it is necessary to define this concept, which is still somewhat hazy and ad hoc. In the Indian context, the concepts of westernisation, modernisation, development, etc., are being sidelined by the concept of 'globalisation' since 1990s. In fact, with the increasing internationalisation of trade and investment in the developing countries by the developed world has put face-to-face the developed and the developing countries as superior and inferior entities in today's situation. The process of globalisation goes beyond transnationalisation or internationalisation of capital. It is a profound reorganisation of manufacturing, trade and services within a globally encompassing system. Globalisation thus refers to mega corporations and transnational corporations (TNCs) which operate worldwide (Martinussen, 1997: 119–22). Besides accomplishment of economy globally, globalisation refers to a globalising knowledge and global consciousness based on its historical and social contexts. To restrict the concept of globalisation to rapid harmonisation of the world in terms of the power and influence of the transnational corporations is only one side of this reality. The other side refers to destruction of diversity and marginalisation of democratic rights, culture, environment, etc., by way of external implosion. Thus, according to Robbie Robertson (2003: 3–13), "globalisation is more than just McWorld or Westernisation". Robertson further observes: "It is about human intercommunications that have assumed global proportions and transformed themselves" (ibid.: 3).

No doubt, globalisation is a modern strategy of power; it is to be seen also in terms of its historical and social depths. Robertson talks of 'three waves of globalisation', namely, the globalisation of the regional trade, industrialisation, and the new world order after 1945. The three waves cover a span of nearly five hundred years. In a way, this applies to the Indian situation as well. The first wave was the pre-British period dominated by the East India Company, the second may refer to the British rule, and the third naturally would be the post-independence period. All the three periods imply epochal structural changes characterised by internal dynamics and external influences. Trading groups and white-collar workers were the creation of the first two waves. The third wave partly transformed the earlier groups and partly created new groups in terms of India as a newly independent nation. Robertson puts more emphasis on 'human interconnectiveness' in the discussion about the three waves of globalisation and its historical and social dimensions. Another way to look at the concept of globalisation is freedom for investment, production, supply and sale without any constraints whatsoever. Such a conception, if actualised, may result into a ruthless dominance of the strong MNCs over the people of the developing countries.

Globalisation is a process that changes sites and levels of economic decision-making. Christian Comeliau (2002: 96–108), while analysing 'the contradictions of globalisation', observes that it (globalisation) brings new players onto the scene, and transform the relationship of forces among those present on it. Three points are important today in the globalisation of economy: concentration of power in a small number of 'multi-national' and 'transnational' corporations and their national branches; emergence of a small number of international public organisations at global and regional levels; and a significant change in the place and role of national public authorities. The new power relations with unequal power of decision-making are an obvious result of globalisation.

Pulapra Balakrishnan (2003: 3166–72) considers globalisation as policy, as process and as justice in an interconnected manner. In the context of India, keeping in view these general features of globalisation, Balakrishnan observes that the economic constraints that bind its economy are very likely internal ones rather than anything external. "The current bout of globalisation is unlikely to affect her fortunes dramatically either way" (ibid.: 3171). Poverty, health and education have continued to improve in the 1990s. The 1990s have not witnessed either 'unprecedented improvement' or 'widespread impoverishment'. Some segments of economy have integrated with the rest of the world and some cannot be affected adversely because most Indians have either very low incomes or very low skills to be affected by globalisation either way (ibid.). Since integration of the possession of low incomes and low skills with the world economy is not possible, adverse effects are simply not there. The report of the World Commission on the Social Dimension of Globalisation (2004) insists on conducting social dialogues within a democratic framework, at the local, national and international levels, to create a 'fair globalisation' that is inclusive. The Commission calls for 'fair globalisation' that will 'create opportunities for all'. Emphasis is on ethical, economic and social dimensions of globalisation, hence, a strong plea for human development.

A Marxist critique of globalisation is in Samir Amin's recent work (Harshe, 2002: 1407–12). Rajan Harshe, the reviewer of Amin's seminal work, looks at globalisation as an offshoot of capitalism and modernity. Marxism, capitalism and globalisation have been seen as inextricably interrelated developments. While tracing the history of the world capitalist system (1945–90), according to Harshe, Amin looks at globalisation as a fresh crisis and a challenge in the management of the world capitalist system. Three limitations may be noted in this process: (1) a lack of evolution of compatible institutions beyond nation-states to effect global transactions; (2) a failure to take the newly industrialising countries of Asia and Latin America (including India) along with the developed ('global') countries; and (3) absence of the process of competitive industrialisation. Further, with continuing strong 'ethnic complexities' and 'ontology of nation-state' and hegemonic capitalism of the USA, Western Europe and Japan, globalisation remains a new form of monopoly and dominance in the hands of the countries of the First World.

Recently, D.L. Sheth and others (*EPW*, 2004: 45–116), in a series of 11 articles, have discussed different aspects of globalisation. In a nutshell, globalisation has created 'new politics with old dilemmas'. Opposition to globalisation has resulted into micro-movements with a view to check onslaught on the interests of farmers, women, artisans and poor sections of Indian society. This has raised a new discourse on democracy, beyond the conventional institutions of elections and political parties. Participatory democracy is being reinvented through such a discourse of politics and micro-movements challenging globalisation as a new hegemonic development. Transnational activities are touching almost all aspects of India's social fabric, including religion, media, migration, economy, polity, women, labour, family, community, etc. India is confronted with the dilemma of joining the global race on the one hand, and to retain its national distinctive character, on the other. Besides this, the differential nature of gains and losses of the globalisation process for the nation as a whole and for specific socio-economic entities in particular cannot be overlooked. But 'localisation' or insulation of a nation from the global order is no way as it would obstruct modernisation of economy and migration and mobility of the people. How does localism benefit the poor? Or, how does globalisation harm the people at the bottom? It depends upon the strength of the indigenous economy in providing employment and security to the members of a given country, and the nature of globalisation may also affect the poor, but not necessarily, and may affect the middle classes alone.

To understand globalisation in the Indian context we may have to know clearly the concepts such as 'individual', 'development', 'freedom', 'opportunities', 'market', 'state', etc., as formulated by Amartya Sen (2000). Sen looks for the 'social' behind all human endeavours. The concept of 'social opportunity' proposed by Sen becomes relevant for us as it covers a wide range of societal dimensions having implications for Indian polity, economy and culture. Development is freedom, and freedom is social opportunity, and it is constrained by social arrangements. Thus, freedom is 'social' and unfreedom is inequality. The removal of unfreedom is constitutive of development. Effective social arrangements alone can ensure freedom leading to development. Sen talks of 'substantive freedoms'. Is globalisation weakening the social arrangements? What happens to the marginalised groups due to globalisation? Does globalisation result into reproduction of the old middle classes and continuation of the dominance of the upper and the upper-middle castes?

Bihar, Uttar Pradesh, Gujarat, Maharashtra, etc., have witnessed 'caste wars' which tantamount to 'class wars' between the landless and the landed people. 'Attacks' and 'counter-attacks' have become quite frequent in Bihar in particular. Susan Bayly (1999: 355–59) observes that 'caste war'/violence has tended to become a conflict between urban centres and the rural hinterlands as many students and factory workers are drawn in such a situation. She observes: "Such outbreaks are not then to be seen as a reversion to the 'feudal' or 'traditional' past. 'Modern' institutions, especially the courts, the universities and the mass media, have figured prominently in the so-called caste-feud phenomena" (ibid.: 355). The anti-Mandal agitation in the wake of 27 per cent reservation in jobs for the OBCs was geared by the urban middle class youth and students who normally looked for government jobs, which even today provide security and social status to the incumbents. Caste divides among students and staff have become a common feature in colleges and universities in India. Even hostels are dominated by students of specific castes/sub-castes. Recent decision of the Government of India to implement 27 per cent reservation for the OBCs in the central universities and institutions has once again evoked protests, particularly by students of medicine, JNU and Delhi University.

Since the 1970s, the English-speaking intelligentsia have watched the growth and diversification of the Indian middle classes with considerable alarm (ibid.: 360). This particular class of people was engaged in government jobs, professions and middle-level entrepreneurship. However, with the expansion of trade and industry and the commercialisation of agriculture, new aspirants for the jobs, cornered by the old middle class, have come up to claim their shares in professions and other white-collar jobs. Reservations have also added to the aspirations and claims of the formerly deprived groups. However, the gap remains unbridged between the upper and the middle castes or between the traditional middle classes and the newly aspiring groups of people for white-collar jobs because the old middle classes have been looking for new pastures and possibilities in the wake of globalisation. The newly aspiring groups at this juncture are not in a position to compete with the traditionally privileged groups. More or less this was the case a few decades ago when the lower castes tried to move up by way of sanskritisation and the upper castes opted to de-sanskritise their cultural pantheon and decided to take up new and secular jobs and practices. A similar situation prevails today. Globalisation calls for new adjustments and alterations in our society and culture. The intensity of the hiatus between the upper and the lower social segments would remain there despite very basic changes in economy and social milieu. This is how resilience of Indian society becomes a perpetual focal point.

Indian society is characterised by a semblance of tradition and modernity, continuity and change having differentiated effects on individual, family and group. Hence, no uniform pattern of change and its impact on different social units. The pre-British period had witnessed large-scale transformation as a result of the agrarian policy and administrative structuring. The British created a new class structure to serve its colonial interests and along with a reconceptualisation of caste and inter-caste relations. Constitutional provisions, Five-Year Plans, adult franchise, reservation policy and social movements have brought about a new consciousness and transformation of the pre-independence society and culture.

At any given epochal phase no complete overhauling of the structure of Indian society has occurred. Part continuity and part change have characterised the Indian society. Such resilience is peculiar to Indian society. The upper castes might have partly lost their traditional high status after independence, but at the same time, they remained as the main middle classes for quite some time. Since, for some time, new middle classes from amongst the middle and lower castes have been showing their presence challenging the continuing middle classes in their new reincarnation, the latter are busy in search of greener pastures in India and abroad. Initially, when a challenge was thrown to the upper castes living in the villages, by the politically upcoming middle and lower castes, the former moved out of their villages to settle down in towns and cities. Today, they are either looking for those avenues in India which are not accessible to the upcoming mobile groups and individuals, or they are moving out of India. In a note, Rajesh Kochhar (2004: 20) rightly observes: "Globalisation has prevented Indian upper castes from accepting a diminished role and status consistent with their actual numbers. Aspirations of an Indian middle class that reveals in emulating the west are costing India dear and glorifying trivia in an unprecedented fashion."

A sort of 'cultural lag' persists between the formerly privileged middle class and the new class of people aspiring for middle class status. Globalisation has created a new 'space', which is taken by the entrenched middle class being in an advantageous position. The 'space' vacated by this class is occupied by the aspiring class. The trajectory of the class structure demonstrates such a dynamics all over the world. However, one has to see the class of people who get adversely affected or who remain stagnant due to global/local factors of social change. The question is: What is 'just globalisation'? How does it help or does not help the poor, peasants, artisans, labourers, petty shopkeepers and women? Primordial structures in India have not obstructed the processes of social change and globalisation. Adaptive capability of Indian society is evident in its continuity and change even in face of both external and internal threats.

References

Balakrishnan, Pulapra, 2003, "Globalisation, Growth and Justice", *Economic and Political Weekly*, Vol. XXXVIII, No. 30.

Bayly, Susan, 1999, *Caste, Society and Politics in India from the Eighteenth Century to the Modern Age*, Cambridge: Cambridge University Press.

Beteille, Andre, 1966a, *Caste, Class and Power*, Bombay: Oxford University Press.

——, 1966b, "Class and Open Social Stratification in India", *European Journal of Sociology*, Vol. VII, *Castes: Old and New*, Bombay: Asia Publishing House.

——, 1969, "Closed and Open Social Stratification in India", *European Journal of Sociology*, Vol. VII, pp. 224–46.

Bottomore, Tom, 1983, *A Dictionary of Marxist Thought*, Oxford: Basil Blackwell.

Bourdieu, Pierre, 1991, *Language and Symbolic Power*, Cambridge: Polity Press.

——, 1996, *The State Nobility*, Cambridge: Polity Press.

Comeliau, Christian, 2002, *The Impasse of Modernity*, London: Zed Books.

Das, A.N., 1984, "Caste in Itself, Caste for Itself: Social Articulation in Bihar", *Economic and Political Weekly*, Vol. XIX, No. 37.

Desai, I.P., 1984, "Western Educated Elites and Social Change in India", *Economic and Political Weekly*, Vol. XIX, No. 15.

Deshpande, Satish, 1997, "From Development to Adjustments: Economic Ideologies, the Middle Class and 50 Years of Independence", *Review of Development and Change*, Vol. 2, No. 2, pp. 294–318.

——, 2003, *Contemporary India: A Sociological View*, New Delhi: Penguin.

Dirks, B. Nicholas, 2001, *Castes of Mind*, Princeton: Princeton University Press.

Dumont, Louis, 1970, *Homo Hierarchicus: The Caste System and Its Implications*, London: Weidenfeld and Nicholson.

Franco, F., Sherry Chand and V. Sarvar, 1989, "Ideology as Social Practice: The Functioning of Varna", *Economic and Political Weekly*, Vol. XXIV, No. 47.

Galanter, Marc, 1984, *Competing Equalities: Law and the Backward Classes in India*, Delhi: Oxford University Press.

Gough, E. Kathleen, 1980, "Modes of Production in Southern India", *Economic and Political Weekly*, Vol. XV, Nos. 5–7, Annual Number.

Gupta, Dipankar, 1992, "Continuous Hierarchies and Discrete Castes", in Dipankar Gupta (ed.), *Social Stratification*, Delhi: Oxford University Press.

——, 2000, *Interrogating Caste: Understanding Hierarchy and Difference in Indian Society*, New Delhi: Penguin Books.

——, 2004, "Caste Is Not Race: But, Let's Go to the UN Forum Anyway" and "Caste, Race, Politics", in Sukhadeo Thorat and Umakant (eds.), *Caste, Race and Discrimination*, Jaipur and New Delhi: Rawat Publications.

Harshe, Rajen, 2002, "Marxism, Capitalism, Globalisation", *Economic and Political Weekly*, Vol. XXXVII, No. 15. This is a review article on Samir Amin's Book, *Capitalism in the Age of Globalisation: The Management of Contemporary Society*, London: Zed Books.

Harriss, John, 1982, *Capitalism and Peasant Farming*, Delhi: Oxford University Press.

Hutton, J.H., 1946, *Caste in India*, Oxford: Oxford University Press.

Jayaram, N., 1977, "Higher Education as a Status-Stabliser: Students in Bangalore", *Contributions to Indian Sociology* (New Series), Vol. II(1).

Kamat, A.R., 1980, "Politico-economic Development in Maharashtra: A Review of the Post-independence Period", *Economic and Political Weekly*, Vol. XV, Nos. 39 and 40.

Kanan, K.P., 2004, "For a Fair Globalisation", *Economic and Political Weekly*, Vol. XXXIX, No. 38. A brief account of the report of the World Commission on Social Dimension of Globalisation is given in this note by Kanan.

Kochhar, Rajesh, 2004, "Denationalised Middle Class: Global Escape from Mandal", *Economic and Political Weekly*, Vol. XXXIX, No. 1.

Kolenda, P., 1989, "Micro-ideology and Micro-utopia in Khalapur: Changes in the Discourse on Caste over Thirty Years", *Economic and Political Weekly*, Vol. XXIV, No. 32.

Lal, S.K., (ed.) 1988, *Readings in the Sociology of Professions*, Delhi: Gian Publishing House.

Leach, Edmund R., 1960, "Introduction: What Should We Mean by Caste", in Edmund R. Leach (ed.), *Aspects of Caste in South India, Cylon and North-West Pakistan*, Cambridge: Cambridge University Press.

Marx, Karl, 1888, *Manifesto of the Communist Party*, Chicago: Charles H. Kess.

Martinussen, John, 1997, *Society, State and Market: A Guide to Competing Theories of Development*, London: Zed Books Ltd.

Misra, B.B., 1961, *The Indian Middle Classes: Their Growth in Modern Times*, Delhi: Oxford University Press.

Namboodiripad, E.M.S., 1979, "Caste Conflicts Versus Growing Unity of Popular Democratic Forces", *Economic and Political Weekly*, Vol. XIV, No. 7 and 8, Annual Number.

Navlakha, Suren, 1989, *Elite and Social Change: A Study of Elite Formation in India*, New Delhi: Sage Publications.

Prasad, Pradhan H., 1979, "Caste and Class in Bihar", *Economic and Political Weekly*, Vol. XIV, Nos. 7 and 8.

——, 1980, "Rising Middle Peasantry in North India", *Economic and Political Weekly*, Vol. XV, No. 4.

Ranadive, B.T., 1979, "Caste, Class and Property Relations", *Economic and Political Weekly*, Vol. XIV, Nos. 7 and 8, Annual Number.

Risley, H.H., 1969, *The Peoples of India* (2nd ed.), Delhi: Orient Books.

Robertson, Robbie, 2003, *The Three Waves of Globalization: A History of a Developing Global Consciousness*, London: Zed Books Ltd.

Rudolph, Lyold I. and Susanne Hoeber Rudolph, 1967, *The Modernity of Tradition: Political Development in India*, Chicago: The University of Chicago Press.

Rudra, Ashok, 1989, "Emergence of the Intelligentsia as a Ruling Class in India", *Economic and Political Weekly*, Vol. XXIV, No. 3.

Shah, Ghanshyam, 1985, "Caste, Class and Reservation", *Economic and Political Weekly*, Vol. XX, No. 3.

——, 1986, "Social Stratification among the Scheduled Tribes in the Bharuch and Panch Mahals Districts of Gujarat", in S.C. Malik (ed.), *Determinants of Social Status in India*, Shimla: Indian Institute of Advanced Study.

Sen, Amartya, 2000, *Development as Freedom*, New Delhi: Oxford University Press.

Sharma, K.L., 1973, "Downward Social Mobility: Some Observations", *Sociological Bulletin*, Vol. 22, No. 1.

——, 1977, *Essays on Social Stratification*, Jaipur: Rawat Publications.

——, 1989, *Caste, Feudalism and Peasantry: The Social Formation of Shekhawati*, New Delhi: Manohar.

——, 1994, *Social Stratification and Mobility*, Jaipur and New Delhi: Rawat Publications.

——, 1996, "Conceptualisation of Caste-Class Nexus as an Alternative to Caste-Class Dichotomy", in A.R. Momin (ed.), *The Legacy of G.S. Ghurye: A Centennial Festschrift*, Bombay: Popular Prakashan.

——, 1997, *Social Stratification in India: Issues and Themes*, New Delhi: Sage Publications.

——, 1998, *Caste, Feudalism and Peasantary: The Social Formation of Shekhawati*, New Delhi: Manohar.

——, 2001, *Reconceptualising Caste, Class and Tribe*, Jaipur and Delhi: Rawat Publications.

Sheth, D.L., 2004, "Globalisation and New Politics of Micro-Movements", *Economic and Political Weekly*, Vol. XXXIX, No. 1. Other special articles in this number are by Abhay Kumar Dubey, Ravi Sundram, Aditya Nigam, Shail Mayaram, Madhulika Banerjee, Ashis Nandy, Nivedita Menon, Supriya Roy Choudhary, Rahul Mukherji and Vivek Kumar.

Singh, Yogendra, 1968, "Caste and Class: Some Aspects of Continuity and Change", *Sociological Bulletin*, Vol. XVII, No. 2.

——, 1993, *Social Change in India: Crisis and Resilience*, New Delhi: Har Anand Publications.

Sorokin, Pitirim A., 1959, *Social and Cultural Mobility*, New York: The Free Press.

Srinivas, M.N., 1998, *Village, Caste, Gender and Method: Essays in Indian Social Anthropology*, New Delhi: Oxford University Press (Paperback).

Turner, Bryan S., 1986, *Equality*, New York: Tavistock Publications.

Varma, Pawan K., 1998, *The Great Indian Middle Class*, New Delhi: Penguin Books.

Weber, Max, 1948, *From Max Weber: Essays in Sociology*, Translated, Edited and with an Introduction by H.H. Gerth and C. Wright Mills, London: Routledge and Kegan Paul Ltd.

3

Caste and Peasantry

Some Questions and Clarifications

Caste and peasantry co-existed in the first half of the 20th century in the erstwhile princely states of Rajputana, named as Rajasthan, after independence. Nexus between caste and peasantry was distinctly present in the Shekhawati region of the former Jaipur State. Rajputs ruled in nineteen of twenty-two princely states, and of the three non-Rajput-ruled states, two were ruled by Jat rulers, and one had a Muslim ruler. Peasants were mainly from amongst the intermediate castes. Jats from amongst the peasant castes were the principal agricultural caste. Relations between Rajputs and Jats formed the nucleus of caste conflict, ruler-ruled dichotomy, and caste and peasant questions.

Shekhawati, which was taken over by the Shekhawat Rajputs in the 15th century, was a part of the Jaipur State. The Shekhawat jagirdars/thikanedars (grantees of the Jaipur State) enjoyed autonomy with *illaqua gair* status (non-interference territory) (Tod, 1990: 1378–80). Absence of land reforms, presence of forced labour and revenue extraction, ruler-subject relations, feudal paraphernalia and methods of suppression characterised the jagirdari system in Shekhawati. The *mai-bap* (patrimonial) image was created and perpetuated despite of the jagirdars (Sharma, 1982: 95–132).

Besides the jagirdari system, Shekhawati had khalsa and bhomichara systems of land tenure. Besides these three broad systems, there were also other 45 types of jagirs. The holders of jagirs were known as jagirdars, thikanedars, rajas and sardars. The kinsmen of jagirdars, namely, brothers, cousins and uncles, were called as *chhutbhaiyas* (small holders). The bhomias were grantees of jagirdars, who were assigned the task of revenue collection and management of land on agreed terms and conditions. The bhomias also belonged to the ruling caste/clan. A structure of aristocracies of Thakurs and Sardars could be seen in the thikanas and jagirs, and in the courts of the leading Rajput states. Prestige and glamour were the main concern shown by the jagirdars in the princely courts. A distinct style of life and unique cultural paraphernalia of the princes and their jagirdars used to be on tongue of the people (Tod, 1990). Admitting some exaggeration in James Tod's description of Rajputana, some grain of truth is evident in his statement that "there is a martial system peculiar to these Rajpoot states, so extensive in its operation as to embrace every object of study" (ibid.). … Further, Tod observes that the zamindars of Hindustan resembled with the fiefs of Europe. The Rajpoot system was a pure relation of feuds. The system of grants, deeds, charters and traditions reflected feudal character of Rajputana. 'Traditionary custom' was the only regulate of the rights and tenures of the feudal system. Each feudal state had many petty states. More than prosperity of a state or a petty state, the pride of ancestry, aristocratic ideas, respect, honour and privileges, and the gradations of ranks among the jagirdars in a given state and between the states, characterised the state of feudal society in Rajputana. Normally, no interference from outside the state was entertained. The system remained free from innovation (ibid.).

'Shekhawati' or 'Shekhawat Federation' had attained a consideration of power and authority like the parent state of Amber from which it had sprung up in the 15th century. There were no written laws, a permanent congress, and head of state. Shekhawati subsisted by a sense of common interest. No system of policy was found. To meet contingencies the barons of Shekhawati used to meet to decide about the course of action to be pursued (ibid. See also Arya, 1987: 158–65).

In admiration and justification of feudal system several books and booklets appeared before independence. However, recent studies have focussed on atrocities on the people and appropriation of resources by the jagirdars and bhomias in the Shekhawati region. Such a feudal system allowed a free play for *bigori/hasil* (land revenue), cesses and *begar* (forced labour) (Singh, 1981). Since the thikanas of Shekhawati claimed their right for levying taxes, they feared none from outside their regimes. Non-interference by the state of Jaipur and sympathetic attitude of the British towards the thikanedars and jagirdars made these local rulers unkind to the people in general and cruel to the peasantry in particular. In 1924, the peasants launched an agitation against the enhanced land revenue, cesses and taxes. Though this agitation was suppressed, but in 1935–36 a new agitation surfaced with intense mobilisation of the Jat peasantry. Religious fervour by organising a *mahavaina* with participation of 80 thousand Jat peasants was appropriated to send a message of mass mobilisation against the autocratic rule of jagirdars (Ram, 1987: 151–58; see also Raj, 1961).

Shekhawati was the biggest region in the state of Jaipur, and the latter was the largest state in Rajputana. The land tenure system comprised of the *jagir,* the *inam,* and the *khalsa,* and about three-fifths of the total area were given as grants in the form of *jagirs* or *inams* to the nobles, ministers, priests, courtiers, etc. The remaining two-fifths were under the *khalsa,* known as crown's land. Grant of jagirs created 'tributary feudalism', patrimonial enslavement, hierarchical bondage and hereditary power.

Besides these there systems of land grants, the pernicious nexus between feudalism and caste was quite disturbing. Except the beneficiaries of jagir grants, inam grants (such as priests, servants, favourites), and the those who looked after the khalsa lands, majority of the people suffered in one way or other. The amount of land revenue varied according to the caste or tribe of the farmer and the nature and capabilities of soil. On cultivation alone 32 different types of cesses were levied, on kharif 20, on rabi 8, and on ijara 4. Caste rank was a serious consideration not only with regard to cesses, but in awarding punishment for the same offence to the members of different castes too. The Jat-Kisans of Shekhawati, being a principal agricultural group, suffered more than any other group at the hands of their jagirdars. From 1934 onwards, the Jat-Kisans of Shekhawati began agitating for fixing of land revenue after proper assessment of cultivated land, abolition of *lagbag* and *begar,* and opening of schools and dispensaries in villages.

Nazarana (tribute) was offered by jagirdars to the maharaja, who belonged to their clan, and he treated them as his kinsmen. The jagirdars had their sub-grantees. The present districts of Sikar and Jhunjhunu were part of the Shekhawati Nizamat, which was the largest one in Rajputana. The jagirs of Sikar and Khetri in Shekhawati were the largest jagirs, even larger than some of the princely states of Rajputana. The chiefs of Shekhawati, particularly of Sikar, Khetri, Patan and Bissau, enjoyed freedom and autonomy and power and prestige, being class-one thikanas. Shekhawati thikanas never accepted *ijaredar* (contractual) status, though their autonomy remained generally a bone of contention between them and the state of Jaipur. Such a system of jagirs had serious repercussions on the peasants of Shekhawati (ibid. See also Sisson, 1969).

Grantees, sub-grantees, bhomias, occupancy tenants, tenants-at-will, sharecroppers and sub-cultivators were main stratificational entities in rural Rajputana. Besides these groups of people, priests, merchants, artisans, and professional classes also existed. But, the hierarchies of jagirdars, zamindars and bhomias and of the peasants were quite pronounced. Forty-five types of jagirs and 175 types of cesses and taxes, being in operation, made social relations quite elaborate and rigid. Differentiated feudalism created uneven and unequal categories of peasants, such as ryots, tenants-at-will, tenants of the khalsa, sharecroppers etc. (Sharma, 1989).

Caste played an important role in the hierarchy of landlords because all those who belonged to the caste and clan of the ruler and the jagirdars and held land-grants enjoyed superior status and honour than those grantees who belonged to other castes including Brahmins. Many lower castes such as Nai, Balai, Dhobi had inam-grants in lieu of their services to jagirdars, and their lands were cultivated by superior castes like Brahmins and Jats. Though, formally the ties between the lower caste landlords and the upper caste tenants were that of landlord-tenant, but in actual interactional terms these were different from that of the upper caste landlord, and the lower caste tenants. Thus, feudalism and caste had such an uneasy relationship. Though caste was not the sole determinant of social hierarchy, but it was also reducible to jagirdari system, and vice versa. Jats, being the principal and numerically preponderant agricultural caste, never received favours from Rajput jagirdars. Upper castes like Brahmins and Banias and the lower castes such as Naiks, Balais, Nais, etc., received grants and patronage from the Rajput rulers. Since Jats were at the top of the middle castes in the Shekhawati region, they look their exploitation, oppression and dehumanisation rather with a sense of retaliation and vengeance.

Caste-peasantry (Jat-Kisan) nexus in the Shekhawati region raises the following questions:

(i) Can we treat the peasantry as a class, a constructed stratum?
(ii) Is peasantry synonymous with caste/community?
(iii) Does differentiation of peasantry reflect caste stratification?
(iv) Is peasantry an isolated entity?

Basing on history and social formation of Shekhawati, one can safely state that peasants are a part of the wider society. Peasants are a 'part society'. Differentiation of peasants is dependent upon the hierarchy of the rulers. Accordingly, peasants are in varying degrees in relation to the outside world. Peasants form a stratum, with internal differentiation, in relation to other social entities. They do not suffer isolation neither within the system nor in the context of towns, markets and the state. Since peasants have their base in agriculture and allied economic activities, they form an intimate local group with strong clan and kinship ties. Fictive kinship ties and little traditions play a significant role in their social life.

Though the main social groups (castes) in Shekhawati are Brahmin, Rajput, Bania, Jat, Gujar, Ahir and Meena, several functionary castes, such as Khatri, Luhar, Sunar, Nai, Dhobi, Darjee, Teli, Lakhera, Rangrej, Teli and Thathera, have also played significant role during the pre-independence period. A large number of SCs and STs are there. Several Muslim groups like Kayamkhani, Sayyaid, Pathan, Sheikh, etc., also occupied an important place being rulers of Shekhawati prior to Rajputs. All these castes and groups are further divided into several sub-castes and sub-groups. However, more than such a hierarchy of castes and groups was their division into agricultural and non-agricultural castes—the former into the principal agricultural castes and other agricultural castes. The Jats were a principal agricultural caste before abolition of the jagirdari system, and they continue to be so to a large extent even today. In Shekhawati Jats were cultivators, and lived under severely oppressive rule and command of the Rajput jagirdars. Though Jats were at the top of the non-*dwij* castes, they were a dehumanised, oppressed and exploited lot. This made them a peasant force against Rajput jagirdars and bhomias. So much was the enimosity that Jats became a synonym of oppressed peasantry, and Rajputs a symbol of cruel rule. Health and education of common people were utterly neglected, and the arbitrary system of land revenue collection like Batai, Kunta, Ijara, etc., and innumerable lagbag impoverished the peasantry beyond redemption. Begar was a routine practice. In the neighbouring Marwar region situation was no better. Begar, bigori/hasil and lagbag were three main sources of *zulum* (atrocities) on the common man. I have observed elsewhere that the main reason of discontent among the peasants in Shekhawati was their dehumanised existence brought about by the jagirdars and bhomias. Social degradation, economic enslavement, political oppression, and terror and insecurity, created by the feudal lords, had reduced the people and particularly the peasantry to the level of nothingness. A class of parasites and sycophants evolved around the jagirdars, and they too contributed to the miserable plight of the people (Sharma, 1982, 1989).

To desegregate caste and class is not an easy exercise. Caste is not class, and class is not a replica of caste. The two are not reducible to each other, but are also used as interchangeable phenomena. For example, Jat Sabha was both a caste association as well as an organisation of peasants. Kshatriya Mahasabha was a caste alliance/organisation as well as an association of landlords (Bhooswami Sangh). This is true today about Vaishya Mahasabha as well because it functions as a trader's outfit. Jats were Kisans and Rajputs were their landlords. The two castes were also two antagonistic classes—one without control over the land they cultivated, and the other had autocratic rule over the peasants. The non-Rajput grantees and maufidars were though legally landlords, never maltreated the Jat-Kisans. Thus, Rajput landlords were above the landlords of other castes as well.

For the reasons stated earlier Jats alone demanded social equality with Rajputs, and they never did so with Brahmins and Banias. One demand of the Jats was permission to ride horses and elephants at weddings, like the Rajputs and other upper castes. Other agricultural and lower castes were not subjected to much inhuman treatment as the Jats. Some of the lower castes who enjoyed patronage of the jagirdars, at times ill-treated the Jat-Kisans on behest of their masters.

Contrary to our view, however, some believe that it is not correct to perceive the peasant movement in Shekhawati as the *jat* (caste) movement. Jats, being numerically preponderant, a principal agricultural caste, and also sufferers of atrocities by Rajput jagirdars, led the peasant movement. Precisely because of these reasons, the peasant movement in Shekhawati tantamounted to a caste movement. This view is contradicted when it is stated that it becomes easy to organise people on a caste basis, hence, the movement looks like a caste movement. This is how the situation boiled down to Thakur-Bhomias versus Jats in the region. I have stated that what in form was a movement of Kisans, in essence was overwhelmingly a movement of Jats, particularly of the articulate among them. So strong was the castiest complexion of the movement that peasants from other castes (Brahmin, Gujar, Ahir, Meena, etc.) were not taken seriously. Glorification of Jats as the ablest peasantry proved to be a deterrent factor for other castes and communities to join the movement.

The Jat leadership of the organisation spearheading the movement sent a message that the whole movement was a Jat affair, and it was a fight between Jats and Rajputs. Even those who had sympathy for the cause of the peasantry belonging to other castes were not inducted into the movement. The movement manifestly did not acquire the character of a struggle between the ruler and the ruled, the privileged and the oppressed and the strong and the weak, though this was the underlying motive force of the Jat-Kisan movement.

Though the demands made included 'occupancy tenancy', land settlement, proper assessment of land revenue and its payment in cash, but since these were voiced by Jats alone, these demands did not receive support from Brahmins, Mahajans and Kayasthas, who were at the top of feudal administration in Shekhawati. Demands for 'social honour' also received a setback because of the indifference and opposition of the twice-born castes. With a view to evoke consciousness among the Jat peasants, Jat saints toured Rajasthan and also organised fairs and festivals. In the 1920s the All-India Jat Mahasabha became active and organised its first conference of kisans in 1925. Following the all-India pattern, in 1930s, the Shekhawati Jat Mahasabha was formed to educate Jat peasants about their demands. With similar purposes, organisations such as Jat Shiksha Samiti, Jat Vidyarthi Parishad, Shekhwati Jat Panchayats and Sabhas were formed in early 1930s. In 1932, a conference of the All-India Jat Mahasabha was held at Jhunjhunu, and in January 1935, Jat-Prajapati Mahayajna was organised at Sikar. The purpose of all these organisations and activities was inculcation of awareness among the Jats of Shekhawati with a view to enable them to demand social equality with Rajputs. The Mahayajna in particular created a new identity and community-feeling among the Jats of this region. It proved to be a political mobilisation against Rajput jagirdars and bhomias. A procession on elephants was taken out violating the restriction to ride on elephants and horses by non-*dwij* castes. An organisation, named as Jat Krishak Sudharak, organised the Pushkar Mela in 1938. All such activities enthused the Jat peasants for stopping payment of taxes, cesses and forced labour. Literature glorifying the Jat community, 'Jat power' appeared during the late 1930s. *Jat Shakti Ka Itihas* (The History of Jat Power) by Thakur Desh

Raj is a popular book of this period. Sir Chhotu Ram and Thakur Desh Raj were the well-known Jat leaders of the day (Raj, 1961).

A memorandum signed by 200 Jat leaders was submitted to the Prime Minister of Jaipur State, in which it was demanded that Jats be accorded priority and encouragement in jobs in thikanas, social status and privileges equal to Rajputs, and all partisan orders, customs and practices against Jats must be abolished. Leading Jats were arrested after the submission of this memorandum. However, the protests continued. Jats imitated the nomenclature system of Rajputs by suffixing the title of 'Singh' (lion). Kisans of fifteen villages took a vow not to pay land revenue to the thikana. It was declared that those who violated this decision would face ostracisation and social boycott. In the meanwhile, a situation favourable to Jat-Kisans emerged on the basis of the C.U. Wills report on the Shekhawati thikanas in which the thikanedars and jagirdars of Shekhawati were declared as ijaredars of Jaipur and the latter as ijaredar of the British. This was taken as a challenge to their freedom and autonomy by the Rajput rulers, and it was welcomed by the Jat-Kisans. The Jat-Kisans invited the wrath of the Rajputs. Jats were arrested, Jat organisations were banned, schools run by the Jat organisations were demolished. Jat processions and demonstrations were ruthlessly crushed. In Khoori and Kudan villages police fired mercilessly on Jats. No leader of any other caste was arrested (Rubin, 1983: 20–36).

The incidents of 1935 at Khoori and Kudan villages in Sikar thikana revealed the intensity of Jat-Rajput conflict. On March 20, 1935, at the wedding of a Jat girl, the groom was denied the privilege of going to bride's place on horseback, as this privilege was available to the twice-born castes only. Jats protested the obstruction created by bhomias (Rajputs). Ignoring the complaint and protest of the Jats, the officials of the Sikar thikana arrested a relative of the Jat bridegroom. Two days later, a Jat was murdered in broad daylight by some bhomias.

On March 27, about a hundred people were wounded and two died in a brutal lathi-charge, ordered by a British official. In May 1935, in an incident of police firing, 12 Jats were killed. Again 300 Jats were ill-treated when they could not pay *hasil* (land revenue) due to drought in Shekhawati. Belongings of a Jat family were confiscated and his wife and children were forced to stand in the scorching heat for several hours. A prominent Jat leader was taken out in the streets and beaten up with shoes in full public view.

Several accounts of such atrocities are available indicating a notorious nexus between caste, peasantry and feudalism in Shekhawati's social formation. Despite the presence of Brahmins and Banias on the one hand, and the lower castes (artisans and functionaries) on the other, Jats and Rajputs were the key communities in the agrarian issues and conflicts. The former demanded concessions and reliefs from the jagirdars, and the latter were defensive of their actions and at times also counter-offensive to justify their hold over the people, particularly the aggressive Jat peasants.

A certain pattern of caste alliances is evident vis-à-vis Jat-Kisan movement and the Wills Report. Jats alone constituted the leadership and rank and file of the peasant movement. So was the overwhelming presence of Jats in the movement that it discouraged even the genuine sympathisers of the cause of peasants. Opposition to the movement was from Rajputs alone, and they were united because it challenged their legitimacy as rulers. The Rajput jagirdars also forged unity in the wake of the Wills Report which declared them as *ijaredars* (custodians) of the Crown's land (Wills, 1933). Since this verdict clearly went against the autonomy of the jagirdars and thikanedars of Shekhawati, Rajputs had no option but to suppress the kisan movement to reaffirm their autonomy and supremacy. Thus, the late thirties in Shekhawati, projected two camps—one of Jats and the other of Rajputs. Such was the intensity of their conflict, that all other castes/communities and interest groups became non-entities and marginalised, including Brahmins and Banias.

The two issues, namely, the Jat-Kisan movement against the Rajput jagirdars and the autonomy of the jagirdars vis-à-vis the Jaipur *durbar*, were though interrelated in some ways, they were not quite identical in their repercussions. The kisan movement kept out all other castes except Jats and Rajputs. The C.U. Wills Report united all the feudal groups against the *durbar*, and the sections of society other than Jat peasants, also sympathised with the jagirdars. A third issue, namely, interference by the Jaipur *durbar* in the affairs of the Rao Raja of Sikar thikana, not only united all the jagirdars and bhomias, the Banias and Kayasthas of Sikar extended whole-hearted support to the Rao Raja. Except Jats, all other sections of people came forward in favour of the Rao Raja. All these three issues bring out the deadly conflict between Jats and Rajputs in the idiom of caste/peasant-landlord conflict in class terms. The urban upper castes, particularly Brahmins, were generally aligned with Praja Mandals. The accounts of Bijolia movement in Mewar and of the kisan movement in Marwar too bring out the ramifications of feudalism in Rajasthan.

Jat-Kisan solidarity could be seen in the annual meeting of the All-India Jat Mahasabha held at Pushkar in 1925, in which thousands of Jats participated. The Jats of Shekhawati formed Jat Sabha in 1926 to voice their demands through this outfit. Books, booklets, magazines and newspapers were published to claim a place of honour for the Jats of Shekhawati. Jat Shiksha Mandal and Jat Boarding Houses were established. A function of Jat Mahasabha was organised in Jhunjhunu in 1932, and in 1934, the Jat-Prajapati Mahayagna was organised at Sikar. On this occasion the Jat-Kisan Panchayat was also formed. But, from 1934 to 1937, most of these initiatives were undone by the Rajput jagirdars and thikanedars out of vengeance fearing a threat to their dominance and power. The silence of the upper castes implied support to feudal elements. 'Interest enclaves' of the upper castes generally thought of extracting benefits from the jagirdars and thikanedars. The upper castes (other than Rajputs) provided leadership to the organisations such as the Rajputana-Madhya Bharat Sabha, All-India States People's Conference, Marwar Youth League, Rajasthan Sewa Sangh, Praja Mandals, etc. (Sharma, 1989).

Caste was used as a source of mobilisation in 1930s for common interests of its members. However, in everyday life, status and power were not congruent with the established hierarchy of castes. Caste was not a rigid system in practice because of certain ambiguities relating to actual status of the upper castes. For example, though Brahmins were ritually superior to Rajput rulers, they were inferior to the latter in political and economic terms. In fact, Brahmins, while acknowledging the superior political status of Rajput jagirdars, offered them blessings and sought reverence only in response. Though Banias were lower to Brahmins and Rajputs were accepted superior because of their rulership, they were generally considered inferior to Banias in cultural terms for being alcoholic, non-vegetarian and autocratic. Such anomalies and incongruities characterised the actual functioning of caste in Shekhawati. Since caste did not function as per its ranked order, some favourite lower caste functionaries enjoyed dominance and power in many jagirs and thikanas. Such a situation kept ritual hierarchy under check in Shekhawati. Rajput rulers quite often superseded and overruled decisions of caste councils and village panchayats. In fact, Rajputs were less of a caste, and more of a ruling clan and an aristocracy. Jats too were more of a peasantry. However, both Rajputs and Jats vocalised their standpoints as two communities—one against the other.

Actual distances between different castes were reduced because of the land grants given to some lower castes, such as Nai (barber), Dholi (dancer), Kumhar (potter), Khati (carpenter) etc., in lieu of their services. It was a fact that such land grantees could not be equated with Rajput Bhomias and kinsmen of the jagirdar. What comes out of such a situation is that feudalism made a dent in the normative caste hierarchy. The anti-feudal sentiment also weakened caste hierarchy. The exploited groups of people always looked for opportunities to debunk caste and feudalism.

Jat-Rajput hostilities acquired a proverbial stance in everyday life. After the abolition of the jagirdari system in 1954, the traditional hostilities transformed into electoral rivalries between the two communities. Jats have moved up economically by being beneficiaries of land reforms. Strengthening of their economic standing invoked potential in them for political mobilisation and electoral gains. Rajputs have witnessed downward social mobility, and Brahmins and Banias have moved out of the rural scene either by way of out-migration or by self-alienation realising their helplessness in the current situation.

A recent study of two villages in Shekhawati shows that a sea change has occurred since 1960s. In Khoor (a village in Sikar district), today, most of the Jats have *pucca* houses and *havelis*. Standards of living have improved; longevity has increased; expenditure on social occasions has gone up; and debt traps are unheard of. The families and individuals, who were under the clutches of the Jagirdar, expressed a sense of emancipation and fresh air (Sharma, 1996: 166–38). Thus, the parameters of social status and stratification are today landholding, education, white-collar jobs, entrepreneurship, etc. Most of the recent opportunities of status and employment have been grabbed by Jats due to political milieu favourable to them.

The village Singara of the Jhunjhunu district, like Khoor of Sikar, has witnessed rise of Jat peasants, by way of land ownership and government jobs. The people think that the jagirdari system was anti-people and anti-democratic. People have a sense of new epoch which grants them freedom in every possible way. Jats have emerged as a strong socio-political entity despite presence of other castes and communities, mainly because of the overall dominance of Jats in Jhunjhunu district. Rajputs as a political entity were not visible in both Khoor and Singara because they were small in number and more importantly the loss of political legitimacy proved a great setback to their dominance and social status.

My earlier study of six villages in Rajasthan and the recent case study of two villages clearly indicate abhorrence to Rajput rule in Shekhawati (Sharma, 1974). To see 'chivalric reputation' as the basis of Rajput rule and traditions of Rajput domination as a Kshatriya model of Sanskritisation in a way tend to reaffirm James Tod's eulogisation of feudalism in Shekhawati (Rudolph and Rudolph, 1984). Narain and Mathur (in Frankel and Rao, 1990: 1–58) observe that there was 'a remarkable continuity for nearly a thousand years' of society and polity, ecology and socio-cultural values. The stranglehold of Rajput rule is projected by Narain and Mathur as "a type of secularisation of politics and society unknown in other parts of India". No doubt, this affected adversely operation of ideal caste hierarchy in actual terms, but this kept Rajasthan backward in the fields of education, communications, press, economy, etc., more than other parts of India where such a 'primitive' rulership was absent.

Both Rudolphs (1984) and Narain and Mathur (1990) have undervalued the role played by the peasant movements and socio-political awakening in the princely states. The gap between the 'ideal' and the 'actual' character of caste hierarchy itself was a great source of social change in the jagirs. In fact, caste was never an impediment in social mobilisations.

Rajputs and Jats were always arch rivals, and they came out in open as sworn enemies after independence in everyday life as well as in elections. For quite sometime, Jat leadership obstructed the entry of the Rajputs in the ruling Congress party by declaring them as agents of feudal and reactionary forces. Even, the university campuses and colleges reflected Raiput-Jat divides and boundaries. Incidents of violence have also occurred on caste lines.

Jagirdari was an all-encompassing system, more than a simple mode of polity and administration. All castes looked at Jagirdars and Bhomias for patronage and protection. The more oppressed ones raised their voice against the Rajput rulers. Antagonism between Rajputs and Jats was so lethal that it has its echo even today. As a result of this, efforts to bring together Jats and Rajputs in Congress or BJP have generally not been successful. Rivalries between these two castes have taken a 'U' turn after independence because of the empowerment and embourgeoisement of the Jat peasants and withdrawal of status and downward social mobility of the Rajput jagirdars and bhomias. A historical sense of revenge among the Jats and a struggle to regain the lost status and power by way of education, modern occupations and political participation among Rajputs characterise the present situation. In general, Jats have decisively an upper hand in the Shekhawati region.

Repulsion to the traditional social order, which was overshadowed by feudalism, has been so strong after independence that at times even to find its fossils in everyday life becomes a difficult task. Today, caste functions as an agency of mobilisation promoting economic and political interests of its select members. Antagonism between Rajputs and Jats reflects the suppressed feelings of Jats who were tenants-at-will. Such an expression of the empowerment of Jats is in economic and political domains.

A remarkable discontinuity in distributive process and social relations has occurred after the abolition of the jagirdari system. Clearly, the gainers were the suppressed masses, particularly the Jat peasants, and losers were the landed people, namely, the Rajput jagirdars and bhomias. Such an obverse process of structural change has brought about a self-perpetuating process of social transformation. 'Semi-feudalism' as seen in eastern India is not at all found in Rajasthan—a birth place of archaic feudalism. Green Revolution has also not taken off because of natural limitations. Entrepreneurial syndrome as witnessed in Gujarat and Maharashtra has also eluded Rajasthan despite migration of Marwari traders to far off places in different parts of country for last three centuries.

References

Arya, Harphool Singh, 1987, *Shekhawati Ke Thinkanon Ka Itihas Aiwam Yogdan*, Jaipur: Panchsheel Prakashan.

Narain, Iqbal and P.C. Mathur, 1990, "The Thousand Year Raj: Regional Isolation and Rajput Hinduism in Rajasthan Before and After 1947," in Francine Frankel and M.S.A. Rao (eds.), *Dominance and State Power in Modern India: Decline of a Social Order*, Vol. II, Delhi: Oxford University Press.

Ram, Ghasi, 1987, Rajasthan Main Kisan Andolan Ka Udai Aur Vikas: Shekhawati Ke Vishesha Sandarbh Main—1893 se 1947 tak. Ph.D. thesis (mimeo), Department of Political Science, University of Rajasthan, Jaipur.

Raj, Desh, 1961, *Shekhawati Ke Jan-Jagran Aiwam Kisan Andolan Ke Char Dashak*, Jaipur: Rajasthan Printers.

Rubin, Barnett R., 1983, *Feudal Revolt and State-Building, The 1938 Sikar Agitation in Jaipur*, New Delhi: South Asian Publishers.

Rudolph, S.H. and L.I. Rudolph, 1984, *Essays on Rajputana: Reflections on History, Culture and Administration*, New Delhi: Concept Publishing Co.

Sharma, K.L., 1974, *The Changing Rural Stratification System*, New Delhi: Orient Longman.

——, 1982, "Land Tenure Systems, Social Structure and Change: Some Reflections on Land Reforms in Rajasthan", in S.K. Lal (ed.), *Sociological Perspectives of Land Reforms*, New Delhi: Agricole Publishing Academy.

——, 1989, *Caste, Feudalism and Peasantry: The Social Formation of Shekhawati*, New Delhi: Manohar.

——, 1996, "The Peasant Movement and the Cast-Class Power Nexus in Shekhawati", in P.C. Mathur (ed.), *Social Economic Dynamics of Rajasthan Politics*, Jaipur: Aalekh Publishers.

Singh, Heera, 1981, Decline of Feudalism: Marwar from 1870s to 1940s. Ph.D. thesis (mimeo), Department of Sociology, University of Delhi.

Sisson, Richard, 1969, "Peasant Movement and Political Mobilization: The Jats of Rajasthan", The Asian Survey, No. 9; and *The Congress Party in Rajasthan: Political Integration in an Indian State*, Berkeley: University of California Press.

Tod, James, 1990, *Annals and Antiquities of Rajasthan*, 3 Vols., Delhi: Low Price Publications. The first edition of Tod's seminal work on Rajasthan was published in 1829.

Wills, C.U., 1933, *The Report on Land Tenures and Special Powers of Certain Thikanedars of the Jaipur State*, Delhi: TMH Press.

4

Why There is Only Caste and Not Caste System in India Today?

The question about caste as a "system" has always remained in vogue as it has been projected mistakenly as a sort of absolute institution relating to prescription and proscription of practice and behaviour of people, particularly among Hindus in Indian society. Available authentic sources indicate that the caste system has always been resilient and dynamic as it has been affected by its inner logical inconsistencies and contradictions on the one hand, and it has also affected economy, polity, culture and religion on the other, and due to this dual process, it has never been a static and stagnant system.

In a comprehensive historical analysis of caste, Susan Bayly (2000: 4) rightly states that not a single static system of caste has dominated Indian life since ancient times, though important scriptural writings have extolled generalised caste ideals. Bayly also mentions that no so-called caste society was formed out of the castelike observances of the medieval realms.

Today, manifestations of caste are far more generalised than before. She observes that caste as we now recognise has been endangered, shaped and perpetuated by recent political and social developments. The elements of "traditional" castes as we know today, Bayly says, have their roots in the early 18th century.

The main objective of this paper is to understand and analyse continuity and change in the caste system as a social force, having varying forms, manifestations and activities. Caste has always engaged people, often directly, with varied functions and obligations. Based on a set of norms, which acquired a sort of meta-legal approval, people have been grouped as *jatis*, and arranged as higher and lower entities.

Bayly (ibid.: 1–24) mentions that the British rule significantly expanded and sharpened caste norms and conventions, recreated many manifestations of caste language and ideology as a source of power and authority. Nicholas B. Dirks (2003) also considers caste as a modern political phenomenon, a creation of the British colonialism. Both Bayly and Dirks consider that the powerful colonial state supported norms and conventions of the caste system. Before the British, there were more of castelike elements rather than a rigid and static caste system. It is due to the British that caste became an effective mechanism and resource for the people across the boundaries of religion, language, faith and economic status. In view of such an understanding of caste, most of the theories of the origin of caste, and also the recent explanation given by Louis Dumont (1972) regarding the principle of pure and impure as the all-embracing theory of caste, do not stand validated. Since caste has its reincarnation in British colonialism, it cannot be explained in terms of the orientalist explanation as well.

Caste is unique in one significant manner that it refers to alliances/linkages among different caste groups in a given village or a setting, hence *jajmani* system or systemic incorporation of different castes in the organic whole. However, different castes also enjoyed a certain degree of autonomy, and this provided them a segmentary character. Caste had thus both organic as well as segmentary character at the same time. Because of this complexity and external political influences, caste has always been a "contentious" phenomenon. Despite its unique nature, caste is like race in America, class in Britain and faction in Italy (Bayly, op. cit.:1) in terms of a system of social stratification.

Defining Caste as a System

Before we explain in somewhat detail the nature and functioning of the caste system in general, and also in some particular contexts, it may be desirable to mention that within each caste, in principle, all members are equal, but in reality, individuals and families have also been distinguished and differentiated based on their achieved status, despite equal ascribed ritual status, that is, birth in the same caste. Thus, alongwith ritual hierarchy of castes, intracaste and intercaste distinctions based on non-ritual criteria, were given due consideration and weightage. Clearly, this implies that caste incorporated class, and the congruence of these two further implied inclusion of power in the orbit of caste. Though birth in a given caste could not be mutilated, but, at the same time, it did not rule out a noticeable play of extra-caste considerations. Thus, caste was always more than a simple hierarchy based on the notion of "pure" and "impure" or a set of values and ideas (Dumont, op. cit.; Srinivas, 1952, 1962), which encompassed the entire matrix of socio-economic and political relations.

Even ethnosociologist Ronald B. Inden (1990: 213–62) is of the view that castes were as political assemblages or "subject-citizenries" within medieval kingdoms. Each region had its specific schemes and groupings, hence no uniform all-embracing scheme of caste gradations. Caste was a dynamic, diverse and multidimensional reality of Indian society. Bayly argues that there is nothing like an orientalist fiction or monolithic cultural code regarding origin and functioning of the caste system (op. cit.: 6). Caste has become a system of oppression, a scheme of social disabilities and hindrances like any other system of inequities.

Today, caste is a reality, though of a different kind. It is a means of political mobilisation, of discrete use for specific goals, and more for seeking reservations in educational institutions and government services. Earlier, caste was more of a base for socio-cultural relations enacted through *jajmani* system and rules of marriage and commensality. Education, migration and mobility, secular occupations, office and political power have threatened the "caste society" to a very large extent.

The propagation of caste system as an absolute and rigid system has done more harm to the Indian society than the caste system itself. Projection of caste as an ideology itself became an ideology of its propagators. This became, no doubt, even before the advent of British rule in India, however, the British granted an added impetus to both caste and feudalism for the reasons best known to them. Writings by James Tod (1990), Herbert Risley (1969), J.H. Hutton (1963) and many others are a clear evidence of the glorification of feudalism and caste as institutions of highest merit and for good of the Indian people. Such a doctored blasphemy helped the British in pacifying the agitating souls against their rule and also sealed revelation of full facts relating to demerits of the caste system.

The British created two histories: (1) which they desired to create and produce; and (2) which they did not like to be written and desired to remain it dormant or dead. For example, at times, the functionaries of lower castes withdrew their services rendered to higher castes when they were not paid their just dues, wages and rewards. A barber, being dissatisfied, declined to do his job of cutting hair, and other multiple services. So was done by a potter, who refused to supply earthen pots. A carpenter denied supply of ploughs and other wooden implements required in agriculture, when he was dissatisfied with his patrons. Under a hierarchical system, these were the systemic provisions for seeking "fair justice", if not "absolute justice". The concept of "justice" as explained by John Rawls (1999) is quite appropriate here. After a tug of war, which ensued because of injustice done to the lower caste functionaries, under public pressure and because of non-availability of alternatives to the services rendered to the patrons, often the higher caste patrons acceded to the legitimate demands of their service castes.

While distinguishing between *jati* and *varna*, R.S. Khare (1983: 85) writes that the concept of *jati* implies the experience of caste in everyday social life, whereas the concept of *varna* refers to the "ideal and symbolic archetypes". Thus, caste is quite specific in its functioning; and *varna* is a loose/vague entity, being the fourfold division of society. *Jati* identifies its members in a village or in a given specific set of villages. Because of such an identification, caste persists as caste, despite distinctions based on wealth, education and other achievements of its members. Markers of castes are distinct, and not reducible to material, racial, religious and educational differences. This is why upper and lower castes are not necessarily rich and poor classes, respectively. Caste difference is distinct, but it has never been the sole basis of differences in other domains. The following questions emanate from the foregoing discussion:

1. Is caste an all-pervading essence of Indian society?
2. How the scriptural prescriptions are found in everyday life of the people?
3. Is sanskritisation not a superficial process of change?
4. What has nearly vanished the pure-impure syndrome from Indian social life?
5. Why the caste-based occupations have almost disappeared?

Despite the pure-impure dichotomy and relational matrix, caste was more than the purity/impurity contention. In caste, power emanated not just from ritualised ranks, it also originated from several other factors, including the nature of work, economic standing, numerical strength and performance of individual members. No doubt, some of the indigenous concepts provided clues for functioning of the Indian society, away from the prescriptions of the scriptural texts, but more important was the actual functioning of the caste system itself. There were always disputes about the ordering of castes, sometimes even in a given village, there were ambiguous ranks of people. As we have stated earlier that the lower castes, on certain occasions, challenged the upper castes, regarding their rights and claims for the duties which they performed for them as functionaries under the *jajmani* system. Claims, disputes, bargaining, denial and reconciliation were always there in everyday life.

Caste and Non-castelike Phenomena

Another point is also pertinent here that ritual hierarchy was not absolute even in principle as it has been made out to be, mainly because of propagation of a certain imagery of the caste system by the British. For example, certain rituals could be performed/completed, which were in the purview of the lower caste functionaries, such as sweepers, shoemakers, barbers, potters, blacksmiths, etc., only when they agreed to render their services. These lower caste ritual performers were treated as "pious" on given occasions, such as birth, marriage, death, etc., and they were paid customarily like the Brahmin priests. Harold Gould (1967: 26–55) has addressed the lower caste ritual performers as "contra-priests". A message of "equality" in an inequalitarian system is quite implicit through the concept of contra-priests.

In this way, caste system was not absolutely rigid, but flexibility was considerably less than its rigidity. There were mechanisms and devices which prevented openness in the system. It became an insulated system of intercaste relations. Endogamy and exogamy became the cardinal norms of marriage. Violation of rules of marriage, and deviation from hereditary occupations, and understanding of commensality were taken as an offence, and invited punishment, including ostracization from the caste, heavy fines and hardships. Even today, stray instances of punishment are reported from some parts of India, but the way, in which such punishments are carried out, is quite different from what it used to be. The modalities are very different and so are the motives behind such incidences of the so-called violations, and so are the agencies which take upon themselves to punish the "offenders".

Today, intercaste relations, which were the bedrock of the caste system, do not persist. The hierarchy, which was an overarching phenomenon, has given a way to stratification. Caste has become one of the several other criteria in status determination. *Jati* (group) is being replaced by family (Beteille, 1998: 435–451; Sharma, 1974: 125–168) and individual. The two imply less rigidity, more flexibility, mobility and achievement. Family and individual are also not completely devoid of ascription. Caste is being devalued to a certain extent, and achievement is considered as a desired goal. Values and norms related to caste system have thus shown increasing tendency towards their decline. The system has become considerably weak, it is hardly in existence as it used to be in the beginning of the 20th century or even upto India's independence in 1947. However, caste persists, not as a system so much, but as a means of reckoning and identity-making (Sharma, 2001: 17–43). Caste as a system has been "questioned" and "interrogated" (Gupta, 2000). Then, what is caste? In our view, caste is more of a notion, being appropriated by a select few, eclectically and discretely. The so-called leaders and strongmen of a given caste appropriate it for their specific aims and gains. It is used/misused as a plaything to have a mileage in community, politics, and to extract monetary benefit, out of the incidences of the so-called violations of the rules of marriage.

Another domain of appropriation of caste is elections at all levels, from Panchayati Raj Institutions (Village Civic Bodies) to Lok Sabha (Lower House of Indian Parliament). Even elections of the Students' Unions are not free from the caste virus, and nor are the trade unions. In all these elections, candidates are nominated by political parties and groups based on caste considerations, particularly in terms of numerical strength of a caste in a given parliamentary/legislative constituency, and the musclemen and money power of the contesting candidates of particular castes. Jawaharlal Nehru, the first Prime Minister of India, often argued in his public utterances that caste was antithetical to democracy and merit. On the contrary, some scholars are of the view that caste is not against democracy and development (Kothari, 1970a; 1970b). It is argued that caste-based nomination has a representative character, because an elected person would care for the interests and welfare of those fellowmen who have voted for him/her.

Caste as a system needs to be seen in terms of the ideology of pure and impure, division of labour, connubiality, commensality, caste panchayat or *biradari*, intracaste and intercaste relations, etc. Caste as a phenomenon as well as a notion of reckoning can be observed in political mobilisation, atrocities, violence, exploitation, etc. In a nutshell, the journey is though several centuries old, transformation of its systemic character into a discrete phenomenon is particularly a 20th century incarnation, and that too, mainly after India's independence, in 1947. In view of these observations, this author (Sharma, 2001: op. cit.) has suggested a comprehensive study of caste with a view to understand: (1) caste-class nexus: its continuity and change, (2) changing character of intercaste and intracaste relations, and (3) nature of practice and levels of mobility in the caste system.

Caste and the State

Caste and the Indian State have coexisted, and the latter has tried to twist and mutilate caste in innumerable ways. This was done more so by the British rule (Bayly, op. cit.; Dirks, op. cit.). The 1891 Census used the headings for social groups, such as "agricultural and pastoral", "artisans and menials", "professionals", and even "vagrants". Rankings were made based on local evidence of "social precedence". Earlier, in the 1881 Census, illustrated profiles of over 400 "races" and "tribes" were presented. "Orientalism" was clearly reflected in these census reports and in the 119–volume series of Imperial Gazetteers. "Titles", "Races", Stereotypes", and expressions such as "Civilized/Uncivilized" were used in the context of caste. The Indian people were described as irrational, violent, childlike, morally underdeveloped, etc. The 1901 Census was the first one to evoke fierce controversies as it ranked all castes in terms of specific *varna* context. Determining caste rank in terms of ritual distance throughout the country was done with a political end in view. Besides this, H.H. Risley (op. cit.), the Census Commissioner for the 1901 Census, also described some other categories, such as "casteless tribes" and "landed, trading, military and priestly castes".

However, such a statist view of the caste was negated by some other surveys and studies. For example, Denzil Ibbetson (1916) vividly describes diversity and historicity in the making of caste. He is of the opinion that no generalised view of a uniform "caste society" could be found. The rural areas of Punjab had distinctively non-"castelike" features. Norms and values of caste were found in different ways in different regional settings. Caste was dynamic and fluid, and material and political factors shaped the differences of *jati* and *varna* in different regional settings. In Punjab, half of the population comprised of landowners, cultivators and pastoralists in the late 19th century. Power and land control were the main bases of status. Society was quite open, and differences were of a fluid nature.

We have argued that caste is largely a creation of British colonialism, an instrument of British domination in terms of its policy of divide and rule. Caste was ritualised and hierarchised by the British by transforming the non-castelike elements into rigid ritualised phenomena. This was particularly done by H.H. Risley through 1901 Census. He worked out an index of ritual distance between castes/sub-castes and placed them in a rank order, assigning higher and lower ranks. This process of politicisation/statisation of caste was further carried forward by J.H. Hutton in the census of 1931, of which he was the Commissioner. Hutton eulogised caste by exaggerating its positive aspects (functions), which he pronounced as beneficial for the individual member of a caste, for his family, community, wider society, and the entire state. The views voiced by Risley (op. cit.) and Hutton (op. cit.) gave credence to the caste as a system of hierarchy and social relations. The census of 1941 was not a comprehensive one due to the ill-effects of the Second World War (1939–1945).

The first post-independence census, conducted in 1951, did not include enumeration of caste, except counting of the Scheduled Castes (SCs) and the Scheduled Tribes (STs). From 1951 to 2001, six censuses have been conducted without enumeration of caste, though caste has remained at the centre of Indian politics. Caste-based reservations were given to the Other Backward Castes (OBCs) in 1993, based on the recommendations of the B.P. Mandal Commission (1978–1980), through a decision of the Supreme Court of India, in which "caste" was accepted as the basis of "backwardness" of some communities, including the SCs and the OBCs. During the Mandalisation process, through intense debates, opinions were expressed in favour and against caste as the basis of reservation. It took quite sometime in settling down the turmoil caused by the acceptance of the Mandal Commission recommendations by the V.P. Singh government for reservation of 27 per cent jobs for the OBCs.

The United Progressive Alliance (UPA) government also introduced reservations in the central educational institutes, including Indian Institutes of Technology (IITs), Indian Institutes of Management (IIMs), Indian Institute of Science (IIS), All India Institute of Medical Sciences (AIIMSs), and the prestigious universities, such as Jawaharlal Nehru University, Delhi University, Banaras Hindu University, etc. Protests to this move was quite severe as it was said to be throttling of merit against the so-called caste-based social justice plank in educational institutions. Thus, it is not that only the colonial state used caste as a political instrument, this has persisted during the post-independence period as well, almost in all walks of life, including elections, reservations and socio-cultural mobilisations.

The present UPA government seems to inclined to use caste as a political tool more or less on the lines of British colonialism, perhaps under the influence of the regional parties, such as Janata Dal United (JDU), Rashtriya Janata Dal (RJD) and Samajvadi Party (SP), headed by the three Yadavs, namely, Sharad Yadav, Lalu Prasad Yadav and Mulayam Singh Yadav, respectively. The UPA government's inclination to enumerate castes/sub-castes/sub-sub-castes in the 2011 Census once again reminds us of the 1901 and the 1931 caste-based censuses and the Mandal Commission and its aftermath in 1990–93. In the aftermath of the acceptance of the Mandal Commission recommendations, several young people, particularly from amongst the upper castes, who protested against it, were killed and injured in police and paramilitary actions. There were also strong supporters of the Mandal Commission. Across the country, one could see a clear social and political divide on the Mandal issue.

The inclusion of caste enumeration in the 2011 Census would certainly generate more or less the similar mixed reactions, and the actors in this game are also more or less of the same sort. Why the present government has suddenly decided to consider incorporation of "caste" in the 2011 Census? How it would be done? In what way, castes, sub-castes and sub-sub-castes in different regions, sub-regions, districts and villages would be recorded? How the similar castes with different names, and different castes with similar names across the regions would be identified and recorded? Can simple caste enumeration, without relating it to each and every individual and family, economic standing, nature of occupations, assets, education, and ritual criteria, etc., be useful for accelerating the process of social justice and development? Is it that caste is information in knowledge society? Can caste be an index of solidarity? We are raising these questions because some have opined these views in favour of enumeration of caste. The protagonists of these views argue that caste has power. Caste is a code of behaviour. It enforces a range of behaviour, including rules of marriage as in a *khanp* panchayat. Caste creates the grammar of interaction (Visvanathan, 2010). It is the grid of familiarity and of survival. It is an instrument of the division of labour in society. Such an admiration of caste is a contradiction in terms, when we find "caste wars", and exploitation of the poor of the lower castes by the upper caste landowning families. The inhuman and cruel diktats of *khanp* panchayats, particularly in Haryana and western Uttar Pradesh, are examples of the oppression of the weak by the self-appointed caste leaders. None of the victims of the *khanps* are top political leaders and the rich people, who have often violated the rules of marriage, namely, caste endogamy and clan exogamy.

In another newspaper article by (Kanchan Chandra, *The Times of India*, 25 May 2010), the incorporation of enumeration of caste in the 2011 Census is stated as "a way of reinventing identities", because "a caste census can widen options for self-definition instead of narrowing them". Chandra also raises some relevant questions: How to do it? How to know inequalities based on caste? But then we may ask: Why not count only the poor and then relate them to their caste/sub-caste? Does caste today determine inequalities? To what extent caste has changed since independence, despite "caste wars" and caste-based reservations? Are all members/or a substantial section of a caste or of different castes are "backward"/poor or forward and well-off? How to segregate the poor and the well-off within the given castes/sub-castes? The problem is today to relate economic and social inequalities with caste/sub-caste, and not that of caste with economic and social disparities. What we need is to see several socio-economic segments in a given caste or a cluster of castes. Caste as such does not remain absolute or monolithic. It needs to be seen as an internally differentiated entity. Greater is the extent of differentiation, lesser becomes the relevance of caste as a determining factor in socio-economic inequalities.

Caste-based census would raise several questions and problems relating to identities, social precedence, politics and development. Chandra (op. cit.) rightly observes: "The main question raised by the prospect of a caste-based Census is not whether to collect Census data based on caste but how to do it in a way that does not trap citizens in caste identities." Can caste-based data be used to address inequalities based on caste? Claims and counter-claims for higher/equal ranks would be made on the one hand, and claims for the ranks which could perhaps accrue more benefits, by way of reservations/quotas, on the other. As we know, the British first created a situation of divide, and then intervened after the 1901 Census, when people questioned their ranks, and then granted decrees in some cases. What would the present government do in case of similar confusions, ambiguities, claims and counter-claims? Without addressing such likely problems, arising out of the caste-based census, the 2011 Census would be of no use and could cause irreparable damage to the Indian society. People would be further trapped in the caste tangles. The loosening ends of caste would be rejuvenated and reinvented, if the situation comparable with the 1901 and the 1931 censuses occurs again after the 2011 Census. Chandra rightly asks: "How can a caste-based census in India avoid setting its own identity traps?" The "caste parties", like the BSP, the SP and the RJD have made several experiments of caste constructions/alliances in terms of "backward" and "forward" entities. They are now celebrating the incorporation of caste in the 2011 Census, because their gameplan for "caste-based politics" seems to get a new life.

Dipankar Gupta (2010) says that inclusion of enumeration of castes in the 2011 Census is "against citizens" of India, because "the Census is in service of the future and not to serve past prejudices of sectional interests". Citizenship needs to be valued more than caste and family, Gupta further says, "As citizens we do not need caste but we need development, growth, employment and clear air." Caste is divisive, caste is against caste. "Caste politicians" and "caste academia" are on the same side of the coin. After the 2011 Census, there would be endless quarrels and claims for ranks and classifications which would suit for benefits in regard to education, jobs and elections. It seems that the political leaders are competing with each other as patrons to seek support of the people in general, and of the rural people in particular. By supporting the inclusion of caste as an item in the census, they would project themselves as the saviours of the rural people as particular castes would be there in the lists of beneficiary castes.

Caste and Electoral Politics: The Case of Rajasthan

A recent example of a nexus between caste and politics can be cited from Rajasthan – a north-western state in India. Amazing and bewildering scenes and situations were innumerable in the latest elections held in 2009 for Rajasthan assembly. These tantamounted to a mockery of Indian democracy and the Indian State. In the history of elections, since independence, such a vulgar political scenario was witnessed for the first time. Let us cite some instances of the political vulgarisation, which were not only having devastating effects, but also had long-term and incurable imprints on Indian polity and society.

All the major political parties unhesitatingly admitted caste/casteism as the main criterion in nominating their candidates. In fact, the idea of winnability of a candidate had been mooted based on the supposed and fabricated numerical preponderance and support to a nominee in the constituency. Most of the aspirants for nomination presented the exaggerated numerical preponderance of their respective castes and communities. Neither the aspirants nor their political parties articulated and voiced the criteria for nomination such as commitment to ideology and programmes of development and change, and educational qualifications, professions, personal honesty and integrity, social work, etc.

Almost all castes and communities, including Brahmins, Rajputs, Vaishyas, Jains, Jats, Bairwas, Valmikis, Gujars, Meenas, Nais, Sindhis, Muslims, etc., had demanded their particular share in political representation through nomination. All these castes and communities expressed their resolve to mobilise support for the parties which would nominate their respective caste leaders. Issues of nationalism, democracy and secularism were not raised in the elections as it was the case in the general elections of 1952, 1957 and 1962. Issues relating to communalism, terrorism, unemployment, economic regression, corruption and socio-economic backwardness had also been relegated to the background.

Besides casteism, considerations of kinship and nepotism were also advocated openly in nomination of candidates by the major political parties. Daughters, sons, wives, nephews, nieces and relatives were promoted based on their "winnability". Obviously, they were said to be "capable" because of their ancestry and kinship ties with the political leadership of the state.

Such an electoral game has raised several questions about the Indian State and Society. The state is unable to check this electoral malice, and the society, particularly the masses, due to their perennial incompetence, cannot stop this malady. The masses need leadership, and the leaders, taking undue advantage of this fact, become oligarchic, and develop greed for power.

Since India has a low level of development and asymmetrical structure of economic and cultural resources, its social base (caste and community) tends to orient itself for undeserving political acts and opinions. A caste leader becomes an oligarch, he/she does not delegate authority to leaders and workers down the line in his/her political party. A sort of opinion is created in favour of a leader based on his/her power, influence and social circles. Such a superimposed aura is a gross misrecognition of the masses and their capabilities. Ideology, education, honesty and integrity, etc., were not at all there in the electoral speeches and discourses in the elections held in 2009 for the State Legislature in Rajasthan. The issue of "development" came up in a mutilated and ambivalent form, and therefore, it did not become the focal theme in these elections.

The questions which we may ask are: What is political representation? Who are represented? Can masses question political oligarchy and its material interests? Are the downtrodden united in their efforts to challenge the power elite? Answers to these questions lie in the fact that the nominees are the so-called caste/community patrons/protectors, kinsmen of top political bosses, favourites of the High Commands of political parties, etc.

Caste-based political nominations would not provide "accomplished politicians", who could create a high degree of euphemisation of debates and discourses on issues of development, democracy, secularism, social justice, human rights, etc. What we have today is extreme vulnerability of political power due to uncertainty of its retention. Politicians, therefore, try to retain their power, and transform it into social and cultural resources. Further, this resource is appropriated for reinforcing the political power. Thus, a political leader is today more of a "banker" rather than a social worker. Such a leader also gains a personal notoriety. A political party with such entrenched leaders remains with a well-filled treasury, and as such represents the established social/caste interests.

Caste and Rules of Marriage

The so-called purity of descent/caste or sub-caste is being reinvented by punishing the same clan marriages. A province in India, namely, Haryana, has attained notoriety in "honour killings" of young men and women on the pretext of violation of rules of marriage. The preparators of such a heinous crime have become self-appointed *thekedars* (protectors) of honour of their castes/communities. Their advertent or inadvertent ignorance of the rules of marriage, namely, caste endogamy and clan exogamy is clearly evident in such barbarous inhuman acts in the mischievously assumed notion of purity of descent or blood group. The killing of Virender Singh (see *The Times of India*, October 28, 2009) is thus one more instance of Haryana's cruel orthodoxy and cognitive blindness. For such a horrifying situation in Haryana, which is otherwise not so backward, at least in the field of agriculture, proves that economic development does not necessarily result into social development and awakening. Men of letters, social workers and politicians are mainly responsible for such a grave crime. Sometimes, the "violators" are inhumanly tortured to such an extent that they feel compelled to commit suicide. The people ought to know the meaning of "clan exogamy" and rules of avoidance, relating to marriage. Such a tendency is today a new form of caste-related orthodoxy in rural India.

Generally, hypergamous marriages are enacted in India, in which the status of the bridegroom is higher socially than that of the bride. Such a custom is known as *anuloma*. The opposite to this type is called hypogamous marriages or *pratiloma*. Besides the consideration of higher and lower status, clan exogamy is considered as a criterion in Hindu marriages. A clan or *gotra* is an exogamous unit assuming descendence from a common ancestor. A given caste would have several *gotras* as exogamous units. Each *gotra* has a name, and each individual supposedly belongs to a specific *gotra*. Some castes/sub-castes could have common *gotra* names also. Often, the *gotra* names are drawn from the Brahminical system and from the *rishis* (religious teachers), authors of sacred texts. Adherence to the rule of *gotra* exogamy is found among Brahmins more than the middle and lower castes.

J.H. Hutton in *Caste in India* (op. cit.) observes that the exogamous group within the endogamous caste or sub-caste is very far from being a stable institution of consistent pattern. In fact, marriage is often regulated by prohibited degrees of kinship. The actual number of prohibited degrees varies from caste to caste as it depends upon the number of *gotras* in a given caste. There are also single *gotra* castes/sub-castes and the rule of clan exogamy becomes irrelevant to such castes. Avoidance of the *gotras* of father, mother, grandmother, and maternal grandmother, etc. is also based on the assumed names of the gotras. What one can know is *lineage*, that is, the line of descendence, and nothing beyond lineage is empirically known to the people. It is almost impractical to know lineage history beyond five or six generations.

Exogamous restrictions are observed in regard to sib, totem, village, *gotra* or *spinda* relationships. These criteria clearly indicate obscurantism or unscientific thinking in mate selection. K.M. Kapadia (1986: 117–135), a well-known authority on marriage, observes that there is nothing in the *Sanskrit* texts to object to clan endogamy. Marriage into the third generation or preferential marriage within the affines was prevalent even in 11th century A.D. Marriage was allowed within the same *gotra* or between those who recited the same *pravara* (mantra). Kapadia says: "Manu did not likewise regard *sagotra* marriage as constituting a sin, serious or minor" (ibid.: 127). Thus, Manu's rule of exogamy was loose and elastic. Some commentators linked *gotra* and *pravara*, but its observance became a mere formality. It did not have substantial bearing on realities of life.

Based on such a mythological construction of the *gotra* and other related conceptions, caste panchayats, clan leaders and the bullies within the given castes in the villages have taken upon themselves to regulate rules of marriage. The law of the land has been suppressed by such ill-practised institutions and notorious individuals with a view to extract political and social mileage out of the present-day ambivalence and flux in the Indian society. Some people have made it a source of social and political power. Control over the community by hook and crook has become their creed. The *thekedars* of caste and community have established nexus with politicians and bureaucrats to enhance their reputation and dominance through such acts. Thus, caste is more of a political phenomenon in the countryside than a basis of inter-group relations.

This is an opaque culturology. Continuity of conventional cultural conceptualisations or their renewed versions are antithetical to true democracy. Caste has lost its base, namely, intercaste relations, interdependence and work ethics, but its penetration into politics or its discrete appropriation (or misuse) in social fields are clearly indicative of a disjunction and dissonance in India's social life.

As politics is becoming a "family business", so is becoming monopoly/control or regulation of the so-called rules of marriage. An absolutely unscientific idea of the mythological *sagotra* is being projected as a pious act, simply for self-aggrandisement. Common people cannot stop this decadent practice because the rule of might prevails in the village. The state and the civil society (including social workers) may check such happenings with a firm hand. Since most of the preparators remain unpunished, they look for the so-called violations to occur for making a fortune out of such happenings.

A very recent example of politics of caste and violation of clan exogamy is the view expressed by a young Congress member of Parliament, Naveen Jindal, from Haryana, who is a tycoon and a graduate of the University of Texas Business School (Gupta, 2010). Jindal supported the *khanp*'s diktat for prohibition on same *gotra* marriage. Legally, such a prohibition cannot be sustained. Scientifically, in ten generations, genetic roots would disappear. Culturally, *gotra* is an assumed or mythological name assigned since time immemorial to a so-called caste/sub-caste. How, then, the *sagotra* marriages can be prohibited? On the contrary, there are communities which have preferential first cousin marriages, and a lot of prestige and premium are attached to such marriages. Are politicians doing hobnobbing with such issues to get a political mileage? What is a *khanp*? Who constitute it? How does it function? *Khanp* is a sort of *panchayat* (court) of a caste or a sub-caste, whose members are the so-called elders in a given village or a set of villages (*chaukhala*). The traditional caste panchayat in rural India used to help its weak and poor families, particularly in meeting expenses on marriages and in agricultural activities, including ploughing and harvesting of crops. It used to punish/ostracize the violators of caste ethics, but at the same as a champion of brotherhood, it was always there to support its members to bridge the gap between the strong and the weak.

The idea of *biradari* (community) connotes *barabari* (equality). The *khanp* as a panchayat has assumed only *punitive* functions, ignoring the basic tenet of community/equality. The fear of genetic disorder is falsely propagated for some ulterior motives, including power, money and social status. The *khanp* diktat is an onslaught on freedom of individuals. It is anti-democracy and anti-social justice.

In *India Today* (May 24, 2010), Dipankar Gupta, a well-known sociologist, observes: "Sadly, some of our elected leaders who blinded us by their demonstrations of modernity, have turned out to be closet traditionalists, or just plain political cowards. Many of those who we thought were young, bright and energetic, have already thrown in the towel and given in to traditional casteists." Gupta makes this observation on Jindal's support to the *khanp* diktat on *sagotra* marriages. Is the *khanp* an example of functioning of the caste system? Where is the caste system as the bedrock of inter-group social relations? Khanp is not even a caste panchayat in a proper sense. Caste panchayat is a persisting and regular phenomenon. Khanp is ad hoc, constructed sporadically and episodically, hence it has no systemic character. Anyway, *khanp* claims to stand/represent as a body of a caste/sub-caste. Once again, we may reiterate that there is only "caste", without the caste system. And, we need to understand the "caste" as it exists in this form.

Social Mobility: Individual and Family

In my study of six villages in Rajasthan (Sharma, 1974: 125–168), I have analysed three levels of mobility in caste structure, that is, of a *family*, of a *group*, and of an *individual*. In no case, mobility of an entire group, that is, of a caste/sub-caste was evident. At none of the three levels mobility was there in equal measure. Mobility of members of a given family was attributed to the family, but it did not engage all the members in the act/process of mobility in an equal measure. When a noticeable number of families moved upward – socially, economically or politically – it was commonly referred as caste mobility. Such a misnomer of caste/group mobility persists even today, though no efforts, by a *jati*/group as such, are there in sight. No doubt, family facilitates mobility of its potentially capable members, concrete instances are that of mobility of individuals in any given context.

Social mobility has brought about intra-family, intracaste and intercaste status distinctions and cleavages, which are neither determined by ritualistic considerations, nor have they created a new ritual hierarchy. Classlike differences of a high magnitude could be seen today in a given caste due to multifarious mobility of its individual members and families. Resultant social distinctions from mobility have significantly weakened hereditary occupations, connubiality and commensality. Let us make it clear here that no uniform pattern of mobility is evident among different castes, families and individuals, and it is not in congruence with the traditional caste hierarchy or with the notion of pure and impure. Downward mobility of some families and groups from among the higher castes, and upward mobility of the previously disadvantaged families and *jatis*, are a stark reality of the present system of social stratification (Sharma, 1974, 1997).

Increasing emphasis on the study of structural aspects of caste exposes the pre-eminence of caste as a unique cultural phenomenon, and brings out *analytic* and *empiric* distinctions between caste, class and power. Beyond caste, lies caste-class nexus and its ramifications, negating "caste alone" approach to the study of Indian society. Earlier, regarding caste, I have observed: "Increasingly, caste is becoming a desideratum, a state of mind, a plastic and malleable institution. No more hypersymbolisation is manifest to express caste differences and typifications on a continuing basis" (Sharma, 2001: 7–8). Though, the "essential" of caste is largely delegitimised, yet some sporadic caste-based pronouncements and religious and metaphysical interpretations of caste and its divinity pose a challenge to secularism and democracy in Indian society.

Alongwith the role played by family and individual in weakening of the caste system, political and economic factors have contributed immensely in shaping the dynamics of Indian society. Historian Irfan Habib (1995: 161–179) strongly denounces Louis Dumont's theory of caste as *Homo Hierarchicus* (Dumont, op. cit.). Habib observes: "The caste system, in its classical form, could therefore function with as much ease in a natural economy as in a market-oriented one. In either case, it helped essentially to maintain not a fabric of imagined purity (if it did, this was incidental), but a system of class exploitation as rigorous as any other." In medieval India, caste system remained a means of a system of class exploitation, and the British colonised the caste system by their policy of "divide and rule", and by propagating the norms of social distance. The census of 1901 by Herbert Risley (op. cit.) and the census of 1931 by J.H. Hutton (op. cit.) are unambiguous examples of sheer politicisation of caste by the British.

Some Western scholars, namely, Louis Dumont (op. cit.), McKim Marriott (1989), Ronald B. Inden (1990) and Akos Ostor (1984) have advocated a renewed culturological approach to the study of caste in particular. Emphasis is on application of ethnosociology and use of indigenous concepts and categories, with a view to revive the understanding of caste as a cultural aspect of Indian society. Those who distance from such a rejuvenated culturology, their view is that caste needs to be studied in the context of its setting and surroundings. For example, Dipankar Gupta (2000: 224–264) pleads emphatically for an intersubjective sociology/anthropology against typification to study the caste system. He is of the view that castes need to be seen as discrete entities, being all abiding and durable identities. Gupta also looks for "individual" in caste, as we did look for "family" and "individual", and Andre Beteille did look for "family". According to Gupta, individuals interrogate their own social existence, reflect on it, and maximise their options. By locating "individual" in caste, Gupta reinforces our earlier hypothesis of "levels of mobility" in caste structure (Sharma, 1974: 125–138), and demythologise the rigid and closed supersymbolisations, typifications and binary oppositions as vehemently proposed by Louis Dumont. Received knowledge and socio-cultural recipes are being questioned increasingly by "individual".

Attempts towards Reconceptualisation of Caste

The main motive is to see how and to what extent ideas and values are basic for knowing actual and observable behaviour of people. To what extent Louis Dumont's thesis of special type of inequality based on caste system is in practice? We have mentioned earlier that the idea of pure and impure is central to Dumont's notion of caste hierarchy. But, in our view, caste is in class and in other systems of social stratification, hence taxonomic problem persists relating to the distinction of caste from other stratificatory systems. Elsewhere, I have stated: "Caste is increasingly becoming a matter of interpretation rather than substantialisation. Caste refers to a purposive rationality, and at the same time, it provides a description and explanation of the pathologies of modern polity and economy. It is no more an absolutised system as it was characterised by punitive acts like ostracisation and social neglect. Caste obstructs, which occur occasionally by a way of killings and torture of the violators of caste ethics, are incongruent with the dwindling of the caste system in recent times" (Sharma, 2001: 7).

Secondly, cliches, such as tradition and modernity, continuity and change, hierarchy and stratification, organic and segmentary structures, have led to unfounded dichotomies/antinomies of a resilient and harmonic society. A continued èmphasis on caste as a *homo hierarchicus*, culture-bound and change-resisting system (Dumont, op. cit.) has undermined the very semblance of continuity and change. However, the encompassing capability of caste system has been questioned by several scholars, including Ram Krishna Mukherjee (1957), Andre Beteille (1966: 224–46; 1969: 219–35), K.L. Sharma (1974) and Dipankar Gupta (2000: op. cit.). Beteille has focused on the emergence of "differentiated institutional structures of various kinds", and the role of "interests" along with ideas, in shaping of social stratification. Further, he observes that a new "caste-free occupational structure" and modern education have created a non-traditional basis of social relations, weakening intercaste and intracaste relations. Gupta is of the view that ultimately "individual" matters a lot in the caste system.

A reconceptualisation of caste system is clearly evident in the notions, such as "multiple status hierarchies", "attributional" criteria of caste ranking, "new castes", "levels of social mobility", "downward social mobility", "obverse structural process of social change", "structural criteria of dominance", "new status images", etc. (Sharma, 1974, 1977, 1980, 2010). These are expressions and articulations relating to change of the conventional constructions and orientations. Obviously, there is today a new discourse in vogue reflecting distantiation from caste as the basis of social relations and stratification by the alert and articulate sections of the upper, middle, and even the erstwhile depressed sections.

Thirdly, we also see a revival of a culturological framework (Marriott, 1989) to look once again at the Indian society through caste and religious categories. Such an approach considerably underrates the relevance of structural criteria in effecting change in the caste system. Historical and contextual contexts of change (Singh, 1994: 28–59) cannot be sidelined in understanding of the changing face of intercaste and intracaste relations and emergence of individual and family as more effective institutions and units of social stratification. When caste becomes weak, then family and individual emerge as stronger agencies of reproduction of equality and inequality. The two, separately as well as in conjunction, attack the traditional impediments to social mobility, and become significant units of status evaluation.

Thus, "caste for itself" and "caste as an everyday life phenomenon" are two different aspects, generally unrelated to each other. In the first case, caste is an episodic, metaphoric and goal-oriented phenomenon; and in the second sense, it is a discrete, personalised and family-specific behavioural/interactional phenomenon. Both the interpretations are not in tune with the "caste model" (Beteille, 1966: 224–246) of Indian society. Caste-free relations, new patterns of alliances and configurations across *biradaries*, levels of mobility, downward mobility, etc., are reflected in new status dynamics and power equations. However, discrete use of caste identity, as a resource in mundane personal spheres, and as a symbolic entity in not-so-essential social domains, remains a reality of our social life.

Caste as a Phenomenon and not as a System

Thus, in our view, caste is becoming more of a state of mind of an individual rather than continuing as an ideology, directing collective actions and practices. A pre-given ideology is being questioned for caste identity and mobilisation. In her comprehensive analysis, Bayly (op. cit.) argues that caste has been for many centuries a real and active part of Indian life, and not just a self-serving orientalist fiction. Contemporary political and social developments have shaped it. Bayly adopts a middle path as she is of the view that caste is not reducible to the realm of imagination or discourse. Caste or castelike identities have been there in changing and often threatening circumstances. The titles, symbols and lifestyles of caste have proved remarkably durable and adaptable. Thus, according to Bayly, caste is neither an orientalist fiction nor a shameful crime to be disguised or ignored in discussing India's history. She writes: "Caste is not and never has been a fixed fact of Indian life" (op. cit.: 25).

Caste has been made and remade over a long period of time. Fluidity of caste has existed and persisted because of India's remarkable cultural diversity and physical environment, and the diversity of its states (provinces) and political systems. A sequence of complex but intelligible changes in Indian life has brought about changes in India's religion, state power and material environment. Caste is not just a coded way of communication or expression of differences in power and wealth. It is also not giving way to purely class-based social differences. It needs to be understood against the background of India's political and social experiences, that is, patterns of state craft, religion and economic life (Bayly, op. cit.: 366–367).

Why caste has become for so many the core symbol of community in India? Nicholas B. Dirks (op. cit.) addresses this question quite differently compared to Susan Bayly's analysis. Dirks explains that caste is not a single system that reflects a core civilisational value, and not a basic expression of Indian tradition. According to Dirks, caste is a modern phenomenon, that, it is, specifically, the product of a historical encounter between India and Western colonial rule. Dirks writes: "It was under the British rule that 'caste' became a single term capable of expressing, organizing, and above all, 'systematizing' India's diverse forms of social identity, community, and organisation" (ibid.: 5). He further states: "In short, colonialism made caste what it is today" (ibid.). Caste has been continuously reinvented. Under colonialism, it was made out to be far more pervasive, far more totalizing and far more uniform, and was made a fundamentally religious order.

Dirks considers caste as a political phenomenon in the British as well the post-British periods. Today, it is denied and accepted at the same time. Caste groups are asking for creation of social conditions essential for their development and progress. However, in everyday life, caste has become nearly non-existent and passive. Recent incidences of the so-called violation of rules of marriage present a horrifying picture of caste in some parts of India. A couple of times, for example, in the state of Haryana and western Uttar Pradesh, some self-appointed "caste leaders" have punished the violators of the rules of marriage, that is, caste endogamy and clan exogamy. Obscurantism, orthodoxy, cognitive blindness, inhuman and cruel acts, emanating from the punitive actions against the so-called violators, reflect a totally blurred and opaque picture of the caste system.

Another manifestation of "caste" is observable in congregations of *biradaris* (Jati Samaj). Today, a couple of the so-called leaders of the upper castes have been engaged in mobilizing the support of their fellowmen for political gains, in the name of realisation of the demands, such as *reservation*, as it is available to the SCs, the STs, the OBCs, etc. The B.P. Mandal Commission's Report (1978–80) and its acceptance by the Government of India drastically changed the Indian political scene in 1991–92. After-effects of the *Mandalisation* of Indian politics can be seen even today after two decades in the caste-based mobilisations for reservation by the upper castes, and in the demand for inclusion by some castes in the categories of the OBCs/STs/SCs.

While concluding, we agree with Ishita Banerjee-Dube (2008: XV) as she observes: "Caste, elusive yet enduring, retains a critical importance as concept and practice in India today." Caste has really a diverse and chequered career in history of India. Caste has become an imprecise and vague phenomenon. Today, caste is an episodic expression and articulation rather than a systemic institution. It is not, therefore, seen in everyday life. Because of such a blurring nature of caste, manipulations for its appropriation have surfaced, and its social and cultural fabric has been relegated to the background. Caste as an ideology of pure and impure is redundant in the present-day India.

References

Banerjee-Dube, Ishita, 2008, "Introduction: questioning of caste", Ishita Banerjee-Dube (ed.), *Caste in History*, New Delhi: Oxford University Press, pp. XC-LXIV.

Bayly, Susan, 2000, *Caste, Society and Politics in India*, Cambridge: Cambridge University Press (First Indian Edition).

Beteille, Andre, 1966, *Caste, Class and Power*, Bombay: Oxford University Press.

——, 1966, "Closed and Open Social Stratification in India", *European Journal of Sociology*, Vol. VII, pp. 224–246.

——, 1969, "Ideas and Interests: Some Conceptual Problems in the Study of Social Stratification in India", *International Social Science Journal*, Vol 21, No. 7, pp. 17–31.

——, 1998, "The Reproduction of Inequality: Occupation, Caste and Family", in Patricia Uberoi (ed.), *Family, Kinship and Marriage in India*, Delhi: Oxford University Press, pp. 435–51.

Census of India 1891, Vol. I, General Report, by J.A. Baines, London, 1893.

Census of India 1901, Vol. I, Part I Report, by H.H. Risley and E.A. Gait, Calcutta, 1903. Risley published the volume, *The Peoples of India* (1909) based on the data of this census.

Census of India 1931, Vol. I, Part III, Ethnographic Section, by J.H. Hutton, Simla, 1935. Hutton published the book, *Caste in India* (1948) based on the data of this census.

Chandra, Kanchan, 2010, "A Way of Reinventing Identities: A Caste Census can Widen Options for Self-definition Instead of Narrowing Them", *The Times of India*, May 25, 2010.

Dirks, Nicholas B., 2003, *Castes of Mind: Colonialism and the Making of Modern India*, Delhi: Permanent Black.

Dumont, Louis, 1972, *Homo Hierarchicus: The Caste System and Its Implications*, London: Paladin, Granda Publishing Limited.

Gould, Harold A., 1967, "Priest and Contrapriest: A Structural Analysis of Jajmani Relationships in the Hindu Plains and the Nilgiri Hills", *Contributions to Indian Sociology*, New Series, No. 1, pp. 26–55.

Gupta, Dipankar, 2000, *Interrogating Caste: Understanding Hierarchy and Difference in Indian Society*, New Delhi: Penguin Books.

——, 2010, "Caste Against Citizens", *India Today*, May 24, 2010.

Habib, Irfan, 1995, *Essays in Indian History: Towards a Marxist Perception*, New Delhi: Tulika.

Hutton, J.H., 1963, *Caste in India: Its Nature, Functions and Origin,* Bombay: Oxford University Press.

Ibbetson, Denzil, 1916, *Punjab Castes,* quoted from Susan Bayly, op. cit., pp. 138–143.

Imperial Gazetteers of India, 119–Volumes, quoted from Susan Bayly, op. cit., p. 123.

Inden, Ronald B., 1990, *Imagining India*, Oxford: Basil Blackwell Ltd.

India Today, 2010, "The Caste Curse" (Cover Story Census), May 24, 2010, pp. 24–34.

Kapadia, K.M., 1986, *Marriage and Family in India* (Ninth Impression), Oxford: Oxford University Press.

Khare, R.S., 1983, *Normative Culture and Kinship: Essays on Hindu Categories, Processes and Perspectives*, New Delhi: Oxford University Press.

Kothari, Rajni, 1970a, *Politics in India*, New Delhi: Orient Longman Ltd.

——, 1970b, *Caste in Indian Politics* (ed.), New Delhi: Orient Longman Ltd.

Mandal, B.P., 1978–80, *The Backward Classes Commission*, New Delhi: Government of India.

Marriott, McKim, 1989, *India Through Hindu Categories* (ed.), New Delhi: Sage Publications.

Mukherjee, R.K., 1957, *The Dynamics of a Rural Society*, Berlin: Academie Verlag.

Ostor, Akos, 1984, *Culture and Power: Legend, Ritual, Bazaar and Religion in a Bengali Society*, New Delhi: Sage Publications.

Rawls, John, 1999, *A Theory of Justice* (revised ed.), Oxford: Oxford University Press.

Risley, H.H., 1969, *The Peoples of India* (2nd ed.), Delhi: Orient Books. It was first published in 1909 from London.

Sharma, K.L., 1974, *The Changing Rural Stratification System*, New Delhi: Orient Longman.

——, 1977, "New Introduction", *Review of Caste in India*, Jaipur, Rawat Publications, pp. I-XXIX.

——, 1980, *Essays on Social Stratification*, Jaipur: Rawat Publications.

——, 1997, *Social Stratification in India: Issues and Themes*, New Delhi: Sage Publications.

——, 2001, *Reconceptualising Caste, Class and Power*, Jaipur and New Delhi: Rawat Publications.

——, 2010, *Perspectives on Social Stratification*, Jaipur and New Delhi: Rawat Publications.

Singh, Yogendra, 1994, *Modernisation of Indian Tradition* (reprinted), Jaipur and New Delhi: Rawat Publications.

Srinivas, M.N., 1952, *Religion and Society among the Coorgs of South India*, Oxford: Clarendon Press.

——, 1962, *Caste in Modern India and Other Essays*, Delhi: Oxford University Press.

The Times of India, October 28, 2009.

Times of India, 2010, Editorial: "Tackling Caste, Time to Swing the Pendulum towards Universalist Policies" and "A Dangerous Step Backwards: Giving into the Khanp Panchayats could Legalise Caste Divisions", by Mary E. John, May 28, 2010.

Tod, James, 1990, *Annals and Antiquities of Rajasthan* (3 vols.) (reprinted), Delhi: Low Price Publications. The first edition of Tod's seminal work on Rajasthan was published in 1829.

Visvanathan, Shiv, 2010 "Caste is Information in Knowledge Society", *The Times of India*, May 16, 2010.

5

Gender and Social Stratification in Contemporary India

The advocates of women's studies in India and elsewhere have been engaged in making a demand for opening of centres and departments within the university and institutional systems and outside as well with a view to set up women's regimes and power structures. Though such a demand has been met out by opening up of centres and cells for women's studies by the University Grants Commission (UGC) in India, but not much has been achieved so far in explication of the women's question. Even after three decades of women's studies in India, clarity still awaits on issues relating to research, analysis and diagnosis of women's woes. No clear explanation/justification for autonomy of women's studies or for alliance with social sciences has been put forth. The Indian women's studies have not moved beyond the grants and projects provided by the UGC, and Indian Council of Social Science Research (ICSSR), and celebration of women's year and decade. Though, well-known magazine *Economic & Political Weekly* and *Journal of Gender Studies* have rendered valuable service,[1] however, on the whole, "politics of women's studies" has overshadowed the real issues relating to gender and social stratification.

I

One important condition of the protagonists of the exclusivity of women's studies is that the academia have treated them as trivial and outside the mainstream social sciences. The protagonists believe that the studies of caste, kinship, marriage, family, etc., have subsumed women in men and patriarchy. Their perception is that the opposition to the feminist scholarship or feminism by the mainstream disciplines is the main hindrance in the promotion of women's studies. The established disciplines fear a decline in their hegemonic control due to power sharing by the feminist colleagues (John, 2001: 237–58). However, 'feminist politics' has perhaps caused more harm to the women's studies than its so-called opposition by or exclusion from the mainstream sociology/social sciences (Gupta, 1995: 617–20).

The main gender issues have remained hazy. Some issues need to be discussed succinctly and with greater emphasis. The making of a discipline is a long-drawn curved process. 'Naming' alone does not make a discipline.[2] The following questions cannot escape our attention:

- Have women been subsumed in men?
- How the present social sciences are primarily oriented to patriarchal understanding?
- What is maleness?
- Can research and analysis be seen in terms of men-women dichotomy?

The available studies on women are biased in favour of urban middle class women. Women are highly differentiated, socially, culturally and contextually vis-à-vis Indian society. The shaping of the women's question reflects essentially the ethos of 'western feminism', namely, the problems of the urban educated women. Populist political nuances also occupy a centre stage in the women's question. These features have drifted away the women's studies from its core concerns. Real and substantive concerns of a cross-section of Indian women have thus remained elusive and opaque.

Narrowing down of the women's studies to the problems of women of India's urban middle classes and suspicion about trustworthiness of women's studies by masculine scholarship have been rather detrimental to its advancement in right direction. Men-women divide in academia has sharpened due to suspicion and exclusion of male scholars from the domain of women's studies. But, then, the questions are: Who should study the gender-neutral or common tasks, men or women or both? Is masculine scholarship an answer to the feminist one?

The main presuppositions of the male bias, patriarchal instincts and impulses in women's studies amount to accusations which would also apply to all those who are engaged in the studies of specific social categories, such as minorities, ethnic groups, the scheduled castes (SCs), the scheduled tribes (STs), the other backward classes (OBCs), etc. If so, then the question is: How one can ensure objectivity in human sciences? It is not a question of only men or women engaged in research.[3] Can we say that the SCs, the STs, the OBCs, minorities, religious and linguistic groups be studied by the men/women scholars belonging to these categories, respectively?

II

The main points are: Why women are continually seen as 'objects'? What makes society to see them as such ? Why reproduction, sexuality and socialisation of children are considered as obligations and duties of women? What are the visible and invisible aspects in everyday life of a woman which make her subordinate to a man? What is the real and imagined nature of man-woman relations? Why reforms, legislations and movements have not produced desired results?[4]

Answers to these and many other questions lie in proper understanding of the institutionalisation of the so-called functionality of the gendering in the social fabric. Child marriage, *sati*, etc., persist because of the weak Indian State. Why men decide what women do? It is precisely because of the fact that a woman derives her status from a man, and therefore she does not have her own status. Her identity is that of her father, her husband and of her family. An unmarried girl is not registered as a voter in many parts of Rajasthan. A girl is sent to a school for the sake of family status and *anuloma* (hypergamy) marriage alliance. This is why, a woman is not a person. She is treated as an 'object' in many ways.

Status inequality is reinforced between man and woman through institutions of patriarchy, marriage, dowry, property and inheritance, subordination and gendered division of labour. Patriarchy runs through all walks of life, and it has not got lessened in the wake of development in contemporary India. The new forms of subordination and gender asymmetry have superseded the old, leaving patriarchal control undisturbed in India (Mazumdar and Sharma, 1990: 185–97). The idealisation of women, though glamourises their status and honour, but, in fact, forbids their equality with men. The notions of an ideal woman, a girl, a daughter, a mother, a daughter-in-law, etc., are appropriated to bind women to certain roles and obligations. In practice, these idealised expectations become inviolable bindings, which adversely affect women's health, education and personality.

III

Non-inclusion of gender as a basis of social stratification and of the stratification theory (Mann, 1986: 40–56; Mann, 1994: 177–94) has resulted into its neglect as a status determinant. Five main areas of stratification, namely, individual, family, division of labour, social classes and nation-building, have also been influenced by gender. Each of these areas have mediated between gender and stratification. Mann's strong advocacy for incorporation of gender as a dimension of social stratification is based on the thesis that stratification is gendered and gender is stratified. The Indian feminists have not explicated fully Mann's thesis of 'gendering' of social stratification as they have been overtaken by a populist path of feminism.[5]

Several studies (e.g., Dube, Leacock and Ardener, 1986; Palriwala and Risseeuw, 1996; Cornell, 1994: 20–40; Kabeer, 1995) have highlighted the insignificance and passivity of women and primacy of men in understanding of human behaviour and thought, structures and processes of human societies. It has been pointed out that how have women been made invisible to provide them controlled access to education, employment, property, decision-making, etc. But we do not have yet valid knowledge of the genesis of women's subordination, and of the situations, contexts and institutional mechanisms of their low position in Indian society. What is the male reason? Why there is no female reason? What really makes the 'male' superior to 'female'? How has masculinity been created, re-created and reinforced endlessly? What makes feminity to remain weak and subordinate in actual life?

Answers to these questions are in history, culture, economy, polity and social formation of Indian society. Male/female reason could be seen in the parellels of dynamics of gender and society. In general, social change would determine visibility/invisibility of women and male/female reason or norms and practices of masculinity and feminity (Sharma, 1997: 133–56).

A well-orchestrated explanation is given by Kabeer (1994). According to her, gender forms a basis in all forms of social inequality. Gender hierarchies have implications for the production of knowledge and the allocation of resources. Hence, 'deconstruction' of conventional concepts and dismantling of the structures and the processes of actual production of all forms is the only way to mitigate 'gendering' of biology. Kabeer states: "Biology is gendered as well as sexed" (ibid.: 37). Male and female are translated as man and woman based on mutually exclusive traits of masculinity and feminity, hence, translation of biological categories into social roles. Kabeer's strong plea for deconstruction of exclusivity of man and woman provides, at least, heuristically, a space for the gender factor in the stratification theory. However, the general trend in women's studies is for exclusive studies of women, clearly indicating an anti-man bias.

Since all women are not equally unequal, gendering of thought and action is also hierarchical. Women are stratified in relation to men and other women. Observance of *purdah*, for example, in the presence of mother-in-law and other elderly women, is a common practice in the countryside. Similarly, a young woman does not uncover her face before her husband if some children are around. A young husband is expected to keep distance from his wife during day time in the presence of family members. Man-woman relations would make an inexhaustible inventory, and such an exercise can provide a correct understanding of 'gendering' of social relations.

A girl is sent to school/college for the sake of family-status and good marriage. Her achievements are attributed to her parents, and after marriage to her in-laws and husband. Thus, even 'achieved status' is considered as 'derived'. Such a practice indicates a mindset, which is continually nurtured through socialisation. Gendering thus implies absence of independence for women, man-woman segregation and male domination. Projection of such a value system and its practice is made as a highly positive basis of social status in India's countryside. Contradictions of such a system have persisted without hindrance. Compartmentalisation and segregation exist with dependency. Achievement is turned into an ascribed or derived act.

A policy-centred action depends upon the realisation of antagonisms, which are projected as 'functional' and time-tested useful practices. "Negation, repression and opposition characterise women" (Kumar, 1994: 211–31). Nita Kumar suggests four ways to deal with the women's question. These are: (a) to make women the object of human 'gaze', (b) to see women as actors and subjects, (c) to focus on the patriarchal, ideological, discursive structures within which women exist and which seemingly control them, and (d) to look at the hidden, subversive ways in which women exercise agency and actions. Thus, women are treated as 'subjects', and as such they cannot equal with men without knowledge and power which make men superior to them. The question is: How to go about such a praxis of knowledge and power for women? The reforms, legislations and movements have not been strong enough to effect equalitarian man-woman relations.

IV

Gendered stratification encompasses entire gamut of women in Indian society, including rural, urban, educated, illiterate, housewife, employed, married, divorced, widow, unmarried, poor, rich, and of different castes and communities. Issues relating to such ramified strata of women are also diversified. Visibility, violence, oppression, dowry, ill-health, malnutrition, etc., have varying magnitude for different sections of women.

Not much is hidden (invisible) in the case of a lower caste/class woman, dowry is not a problem in her case, but ill-health, malnutrition and perhaps violence are serious problems for her.

Also equally important is the differential valuation of the roles and tasks performed by men and women. A valuable task performed by a woman is valued as insignificant, and on the contrary, a trivial male role is accorded a high premium. Differential valuation of male-female tasks is a common phenomenon among all castes and communities, though with varying degrees. Gendering varies with different tasks and roles, and also among different castes and communities. Economic activities are not sharply gendered, for example, among the lower castes, because both men and women are engaged in the same economic pursuits. Differential pursuits by men and women would entail more gendering, particularly among the middle and upper castes/classes, because of their engagement in a wide range of economic activities.

Nothing belongs to a woman in her family. Everything belongs to a family, its head, and adult male members. In this way, patriarchy is a value and a practice at the same time. Inculcation of the value that a woman would be looked after by her family and male members is quite strong. Self-respect, individuality and social consciousness are thus suppressed through such a socialisation process. A woman is pronounced as a responsibility of a man. This is how a woman becomes invisible as an independent person. The very idea of equality of a woman with a man is thus kept frozen and suppressed.

In her remarkable study of gender and land rights in South Asia, Bina Agarwal (1994) argues that employment, education and healthcare for women imply a top-down manner to analyse their problems projecting 'statisation' and patronage and not right of women in property. A lack of women's effective property (land) rights is the main cause of their economic, social and political subordination. By having land/property rights women can have more equal gender relations. Agarwal's main contention is a resource theory rather than the reform theory. Not just ownership, control of land is crucial for a woman, because land defines social status and political power in the village, and it structures relationships both within and outside the household.[6]

Development is thus not gender-neutral. Land reforms have not given actually land rights to women. And for women land rights could be the most effective instrument of empowerment. By now we know that the reservation of one-third seats for women in local bodies (*panchayats* and municipal bodies) has not brought about the expected empowerment of women. *Pati-Sarpanch* (husband head of the village *panchayat*) has emerged as a new phenomenon in the form of reincarnation of patriarchy and dominance.[7] The questions are thus as follows: What facilitates women's equality with men? What is the way to actualise the facilitators of gender equality and empowerment of women?

The government policies and legislations, for example, relating to marriage, divorce dowry, rape etc., do not have requisite potential for systemic change in gender relations. Social reforms too touch upon a tip of iceberg of the problems such as *sati*, child marriage, etc. Similarly, the role of the UN agencies, Planning Commission of India, and National Commission for Women in ensuring gender justice and equality is negligible. Feminist movements and the NGOs have been concerned with their narrow ideological and strategic goals to cater select sections of women.

V

Gender inequality is not an episodic, ephemeral or a situational phenomenon. Its ramifications correspond with social and cultural differences in Indian society. Gendering is perennially a socio-cultural reality of all sections of society, though in varying proportions and degrees. This is so because the ideals are differently gendered for men and women and for members of different castes and communities. Gendering pervades over all aspects of social life, including food, clothes, allocation of work, decision-making, community representation, intra-familial relations, etiquette, etc. Even sitting arrangements are gendered.

Gendering can be seen in political arena as well. The Bill which introduced in Indian Parliament to make a provision of reservation of one-third seats for women in Lok Sabha and State Legislatures, was generally opposed by most male members. The major political parties like the BJP and the Congress, in effect, extended only a token support. Vehement opposition was made by the parties dominated by strong peasant castes. One member, who happened to be a Cabinet Minister in the Vajpayee government, while opposing the Bill, sarcastically observed that only the 'Bal Kati' (women with boy-cut hair style) urban women would be benefited by such a provision because the women of the OBCs would not be able to defeat them in elections.[8]

Let me make here a few observations from everyday life. The saying—*"dhol-ganwar, pashu, shudra, nari, ye sab tadan ke adhikari"*—is still very much in the male mindset. The saying reads: All idiots, animals, untouchables and women deserve reprimand. A girl is generally perceived as *bhar* (burden) and *paraya dhan* (property of others), because she has to leave her parental home after marriage. Marriage for a girl is inevitable, and it has to be *anuloma* (hypergamy). Dowry needs to be arranged. Even, the present-day adverse male-female ratio in India ought to go in favour of marriageable girls because they are less in number. But, the number-based principle of demand and supply does not apply to young girls because they are much less educated and qualified than the marriageable boys, hence, boys become scarce and more marketable.

A boy (son) stays with his parental family even after his marriage. He is expected to look after his old parents and siblings. This is why he is given all the attention to become a well-qualified earning member for the family. He is, therefore, considered the right claimant of family's land and property, and not the daughter. Education of girls is thus adversely affected because of such a mindset.

Enrolment of girls in schools and colleges has gone up in recent years. But it has not changed much the male mindset. A school in a village in Rajasthan has 40 per cent girl students out of about 1,000 total students.[9] And, a large number of female students come from middle and lower castes. There are not many girl students from among Brahmins and Jains because they have migrated to towns and cities within and outside the state. The middle and lower castes' parents are encouraged to send their daughters to the school because they are today better off socially, economically and politically than at the time of independence. Some of them share political power in the village. However, gender-neutrality is still a dream. Sitting arrangements are gendered. Parents and teachers consider such arrangements desirable because girls should keep 'reasonable' distance from the boys.

Now, the question is: Education for what? Obviously it is not for knowledge. It is not essentially for employment. Certainly it is for the sake of family's reputation and for a good marriage alliance. Thus, as such, gender equality is not an obvious intent of female education. The fact is that it reinforces the ideal and practice of hypergamy.

It would not be correct to infer from the above description that education is a futile path of gender equality and empowerment. Today, school-going girls know something about our history, culture and role of eminent women in shaping of Indian society. Names like Indira Gandhi and Kiran Bedi are on fingertips of most women like the names of well-known female cinema personalities. Our contention is that it is risky to propose a one-to-one correspondence between education and gender equality. We know that even educated and employed women are tortured and coerced to surrender their pay packets to the in-laws and husbands. Torture, desertion/divorce and killings for dowry are quite often reported in a metropolis like Delhi. Stigma of desertion/divorce makes remarriage difficult even for educated women. Living alone for a woman is a nightmare.

Thus, once again, we come to the question: How to ensure equality of women with men? A synchronisation of understanding, policy and action and consideration of all the possible ramifications of the women's question, seems to be the only plausible answer to this question. When nothing can move and work without women, why are they then treated much less than men? We have to hammer on this question every moment in our all everyday life activities.

Notes

1. The University Grants Commission has opened up centres and cells for women's studies in some universities. A cell is a smaller unit compared to a centre . However, both have been provided skeleton faculty, staff and resources. The ICSSR has declared women's studies as one of its priority areas for research. Most of the feminist scholars in academia have been working drawing support from the UGC and the ICSSR. *Economic and Political Weekly* has brought out special issues on women's studies during last several years, and the *Journal of Gender Studies* too has published studies and analyses on the women's question.
2. The apparent vehemence with which the cause of women's studies is being advocated amounts to the cult of 'genderology'. And this has angered the mainstream sociology and other social sciences. 'Naming' as such, without substantiation, may not do much good to the gender studies.

3. So far women studies have remained more or less an exclusive domain for women scholars. Even serious concerns of male scholars have been commented upon as 'patriarchal' and past-oriented views. The beginning of women's studies is thus somewhat based on suspicion and distrust. If women alone conduct women's studies, will that make them 'objective'?
4. Legislations, feminist movements, particularly after India's Independence, and the recent feminist movements against *sati*, dowry, discrimination, oppression, etc., have not provided significant visible and desirable results. Even political leaders and bureaucrats have violated norms and regulations relating to child marriage, dowry, *sati*, rape, etc. Legislations are somewhat soft and full of loopholes and lacunae.
5. Some of the women scholars from academia are more actively engaged in extra-academic feminist activities and programmes within and outside the university system than duly assigned teaching and research. 'Activism' has overtaken in many cases the genuine and objective understanding and analysis of the gender question. The very idea of the sequencing of theory and research, policy and action is under threat. Precedence of 'action' over research in academia creates a new culture of discourse. A serious debate on this trend is now unavoidable.
6. Most of the women's studies suffer from the bias of the problems of the urban middle class women. In fact, women scholars largely come from this stratum of Indian society. Bina Agarwal's studies of land (property) rights of rural women are certainly an exception. Some studies of female agricultural labour and rural and tribal women in *Economic and Political Weekly* have also highlighted on the women's question from the viewpoint of their oppression, subjugation and exploitation. A large number of studies have focused on the problems of education, unemployment, discrimination, dowry, rape, etc., in urban centres.
7. The 73rd Constitutional Amendment ensures one-third representation of women in village panchayats and municipal committees. Since most of the rural women who are elected as

Panch and Sarpanch happen to be illiterate, and have no exposure to power politics, their husbands substitute them even in formal meetings of the panchayat. The elected women remain just a rubber stamp. The actual power remains with husbands. This phenomenon is popularly known as Pati Sarpanch. Is this provision a resource for empowering of women? So far it is not.

8. Sharad Yadav, a Cabinet Minister in the Vajpayee government made such a denigrating observation. It was reacted upon by the women parliamentarians as an onslaught on their honour and dignity. Yadav and many others opposed the Bill on the plea that it would do a great injustice to the rural and the backward classes women, because the urban educated women of the elite families would get away with the proposed one-third seats for women.
9. This is a school in my native village in Rajasthan (India), which I visit once or twice a year. No doubt, the enrolment of girls has gone up beyond the expected level of the school management, but this has occurred mainly due to an overall betterment of the rural people, particularly the peasants and the former untouchables. Some of the girls aspire to become school teachers, etc., but their parents consider education of girls beneficial for good marriage alliance because today it is being insisted upon as an asset by the eligible boys and their families

References

Agarwal, Bina, 1994, *A Field of One's Own: Gender and Land Rights in South Asia*, Cambridge: Cambridge University Press and New Delhi: Foundation Books.

Cornell, R.W., 1994 "Gender Regimes and the Gender Order", in *The Polity Reader in Gender Studies*, Cambridge: Polity Press.

Dube, Leela, Eleanor Leacock and Shirley Ardener (eds.), 1986, *Visibility and Power: Essays on Women in Society and Development*, Delhi: Oxford University Press.

Gupta, Dipankar, 1995, "Feminification of Theory", *Economic and Political Weekly*, 30, 12: 617–20.

John, Mary E., 2001, "The Encounter of Sociology and Women's Studies: Questions From the Borders", *Contributions to Indian Sociology*, 35, 2: 237–58.

Kabeer, Naila, 1994, *Reversed Realities: Gender Hierarchies in Development Thought*, New Delhi: Kali for Women.

Kumar, Nita (ed.), 1994, *Women as Subjects: South Asian Histories*, New Delhi: Stree.

Mann, Michael, 1986, "A Crisis in Stratification Theory? Persons, Households/Families, Lineages, Gender, Classes and Nations", in Rosemary Crompton and Michael Mann (eds.), *Gender and Stratification*, Cambridge: Polity Press.

Mann, Michael, 1994, "Persons, Households, Families, Lineages, Gender, Classes and Nations," in *The Polity Reader in Gender Studies*.

Mazumdar, Vina and Kumud Sharma, 1990, "Sexual Division of Labour and the Subordination of Women: A Reappraisal from India", in Tinker Irene (ed.), *Persistent Inequalities: Women and World Development*, New York: Oxford University Press.

Palriwala, Rajni and Carla Risseeuw, 1996, "Introduction: Shifting Circles of Support", in Rajni Palriwala and Carla Risseeuw (eds.), *Shifting Circles of Supports: Contextualising Kinship and Gender in South Asia and Sub-Saharan Africa*, New Delhi: Sage Publications.

Sharma, K.L., 1997, *Social Stratification in India: Issues and Themes*, New Delhi: Sage Publications.

6

The Tamil Diaspora, Ethnicisation and State in Contemporary Sri Lanka

The Tamil diaspora in Sri Lanka is an act of the state and society on the one hand, and a consequence of the creation of social divides and ethnicisation on the other. Migration of Tamil labour in Ceylon's coffee, tea and rubber plantations was an indispensable step for the state and society at a particular point of time in Sri Lankan history. However, the same essential act for its economy over a period of time became an anachronism and a contentious issue because of the all out divides between the Sinhalese and the Tamil settlers. Neither the Sinhalese are a monolith nor are the Tamils. The Sinhalese are differentiated on the basis of ethnicity, caste, religion, language, region and economic standing. The Tamils are divided in terms of their relations to the Sri Lankan state and society, namely, the Sri Lankan Tamils, who have enjoyed citizenship like the

Sinhalese, and the Indian Tamils, who have remained deprived of the basic right of citizenship despite several pacts and agreements between Sri Lanka and India.

The root cause of the ongoing ethnic conflict in Sri Lanka is unequal access to resources and opportunities between the English-educated low-country Sinhalese and the Sri Lankan Indians. Such a process of differential access was initiated and nurtured by the British. The Sri Lankan Tamils were patronised by the British rulers in professions, public services, business and in positions of power and prestige. The British school system and the missionary schools were geared in such a way that mainly the low-country influential Sinhalese families and the Tamils of the Jaffna region could extract benefit of the new educational system to have ultimately an early access to public administration and government machinery with well-paid and secure jobs. Undoubtedly, the Buddhist educational institutions were ranked low (even today, they are ranked inferior) as they imparted education in Sinhala bhasha (language) and added emphasis on Buddhism. Obviously, the Sinhala-educated young could not have an easy access to white-collar jobs.

The currents of 'Ceylonisation' (later on Sinhalisation), revivalism of Sinhala, Buddhism and the ayurveda system of medicine and nationalisation of foreign-owned companies in the late 1960s and 1970s had its roots in this state-supported system of divides. The divides had become so obvious and critical for the society as a whole that even the ideological divide between the United National Party (UNP) as a liberal political party and the Sri Lanka Freedom Party (SLFP) as a left-oriented nationalist party became superficial and redundant, when the UNP too began the game of one-upmanship for the Sinhalese cause, which was initially advocated by S.W.R.D. Bandaranaike as the leader of the SLFP. The point is that Sinhalisation is not simply a cultural revivalism. The evoking of primordialism or traditionalism in the form of a new space to religion, education, language and ayurveda amounts to an assertion of the new power wielders in place of the Sri Lankan Tamils and the English-educated low-country Sinhalese and Christians (see Sharma, 1988, Ch. 1)). The author discusses at length in this book the issues relating to social stratification, ethnicity, religion, language, politics, ideology, conflict and change.

II

Let us have a look at the social structure of Sri Lanka. Nearly 70 per cent people are Sinhalese; they speak Sinhala, and are largely Buddhist, and they are concentrated in the wet zone of the pearl-shaped island country. A large number of the low-country Sinhalese now live in towns of the up-country. Generally, the low-country Sinhalese are tactful, mobile and beneficiary of the foreign investment. Besides the majority Sinhalese people, there are eight minority groups, which together constitute nearly 30 per cent of Sri Lanka's population. The Sri Lankan Tamils, who are the most dominant from amongst the minority groups, and who have been waging a war against the Sinhalese hegemony from the 1960s onwards, are just 11 per cent of the total population. They are mainly concentrated in the northern and eastern areas. Besides Jaffna, the Sri Lankan Tamils are also found in Colombo and Kandy. The other equally large group is of the Indian Tamils. They are recent migrants and most of them are workers in estates and plantations. The Indian Tamils were denied right to citizenship in 1948 when Sri Lanka achieved her independence. The Moors and the Burghers form about 7 per cent of the total population. Burghers are largely Christians, whereas Moors are Muslims. The other groups include Eurasians, Malays, Veddas and Europeans. In a nutshell, these social groups form the ethnic structure of Sri Lanka.

It may be mentioned here that of the total Sinhalese population, about 60 per cent are Goyigamas—a community of farmers. The service groups, below the Goyigamas, are of carpenters, smiths, potters, barbers, tailors, drummers, washermen and scavengers. The other important groups are of Durawa, Salagama, Karwa, Radalala and Halagama. These are known as 'castes', but castes in Sri Lanka do not make a rigid/flexible hierarchy uniformly in the manner one finds it in Indian society. In terms of religion, Buddhism, Hinduism, Christianity and Islam constitute the main communities of believers (see Pakeman, 1964: 13–25; Wriggins, 1960: 20–26; Wijesekara, 1965: xx-xxi for vivid accounts of Sri Lankan social structure).

It may look somewhat simplistic and naive to believe that before 1948 the Sri Lankan Tamils and the English-educated Christians and the select low-country Sinhalese were ahead of the Sinhala-educated Sinhalese, Indian Tamils, minority groups, etc. The fact is that the British patronised the former, particularly the Sri Lankan Tamils and the English-educated Christians, in their own interest. After independence, particularly from 1956 onwards, the Sinhala-educated youth, Buddhists and Sinhalese have received support to begin with from the Sri Lanka Freedom Party (SLFP), and also later on from the indifferent and reluctant United National Party (UNP) due to its political/vote bank compulsion. Such was the resurgence of Buddhism, Sinhala language and ayurveda that liberal face of the UNP turned into an indigenous bandwagon with a view to compete with the SLFP in electoral politics. Such an about-turn by the UNP disheartened the formerly privileged Sri Lankan Tamils and Christians. The Tamils, being the largest minority group, took it upon themselves to launch a protest against revivalism. It was feared that Sri Lanka would become a Sinhalese nation having no space for Tamils. The Tamil pride was also hurt because of alienation and marginalisation of Tamils in politics, professions and administration. Prior to 1948, their entrenchment was so deep in Sri Lankan polity that they even ridiculed their Sinhalese colleagues by calling them 'modus' (idiots). The SLFP took the first available opportunity to snatch power from the UNP, which had inherited it from the British in 1948. Popular support to the SLFP's policy and actions of 'Ceylonisation' was readily extended by the deprived

Sinhalese, particularly by the rural people (Myrdal, 1968: 57–69).

The genesis of the ethnic conflict is thus not in the clash of Sinhala and Tamil cultures or between tradition and modernity (see Gunawardana, 1992: 37–59; Dharmadasa, 1995: 135–70; also see Dharmadasa, 1992) While Gunawardana argues that the Sinhala identity has its origin in the 12th century, and it is not 2,000 years old as claimed by some other historians, Dharmadasa criticises the Gunawardana thesis and presents a polemical discourse of culture and history of the Sinhala society. Its root cause is deprivation of the Tamils by the Sinhalese with the support of the state and its institutional apparatuses (Sharma, 1988: 19–20). The formation of various Tamil political parties and groups and the demand for creation of a Tamil nation need to be seen and understood from this perspective. Who are involved in various Tamil outfits from amongst Tamils in Sri Lanka is also an important point to be discussed. Thus, the trajectory of discourse on ethnic conflict has not simply been on a cultural path. Ethnicity is not a culturally specific conception of the people. Quite often, ethnicity is structurally transformed to make it a tool for organising people in a particular mode or to moderate/accelerate interests of conflicting segments of a given population (Yinger, 1997; see also Jenkins, 1997).

Ethnicity may also be viewed in terms of the emphasis which is laid upon its meaning, practice or agency in a given situation. Region is a physical or geographic entity, but at times, it is turned into a cultural or social phenomenon. Based on regions, people talk of cultural areas, cultural boundaries, units, communities, affinities, etc. No ethnic/cultural regions (areas) can be absolute/uniform in its structure, size, etc., because of its internal divides and divisions. Hence, ethnicity is a cultural meta context (ibid.). The Indian Tamils and the Sri Lankan Tamils do not constitute a homogenous ethnic entity. Different mechanisms and rationals, to distinguish between 'I' and 'Other', have been deployed in projection of ethnicisation.

Ethnicity is not a natural hierarchy. Race and caste are natural hierarchies because they are pre-determined and destined for those who belong to a caste/race (Smaje, 2000). According to Smaje, race and caste are natural phenomena because they are pre-determined and immutable, whereas ethnicity can be made and unmade because generally it is formed on regional and linguistic affinities, which are changeable, though some what slowly and not so easily. Ethnicity is a modicum of expression of social relationship, and it is not an immutable or static medium.

The sharpening of divides between Tamils and Sinhalese, based on language, religion, political participation and some other existential ground conditions, led to emergence of ethnicisation as a cultural process, having underlying deprivations, aspirations and very survival of the educated, the formerly privileged Tamils in Sri Lanka after 1956, when the SLFP came to power in the place of the UNP. Thus, in the Sri Lankan situation, ethnicity may be referred to as a phenomenon concerning 'people', to politics of group identification, solidarity and advantage.

The question of 'collective' interests and collective actions can be addressed only by a precise meaning of the 'collective'. The way the ethnic strife and 'cleansing' have occurred provides a somewhat superficial idea of the 'collective'. Both the ethnic entities have suffered heavy losses of life and property. Thus, minority/majority syndrome, past/present antinomies, materialistic and individualistic goal orientation have characterised the process of 'ethnicisation' in Sri Lanka. In such a situation, it would be imperative to know the sources of strength of the two ethnic groups involved in a conflict, which has perpetuated for more than two decades.

In 1948, those who inherited political power from the British were Ceylonese, an aristocracy, economically well-off, of high caste and family background and English-educated

(Singer, 1964: 11–12; see also Sharma, 1988: 35–37). The UNP mandarins were the first rulers and remained in power upto 1956. The year 1956 marks a beginning of both ideological and structural change in Sri Lanka. The SLFP dislodged the UNP from power, and began its rule by 'Ceylonisation' of foreign-owned companies, adoption of Sinhala as the 'only' and national language, and Buddhism as the state religion. The new policy proclamations and actions were notified as steps for the welfare and upliftment of the common man. The leadership of the SLFP was, however, no less aristocratic than the UNP power elite. Though the SLFP sang the song of radicalism quite successfully, its leaders came from high caste and top families of Sri Lanka. Not only they were economically very well-off, they had high-level English education too (Myrdal, 1968: 350–51). The SLFP made, in a dramatic style, language, education and religion as sensitive issues by reviving them as the main election plank. For ten years, from 1956 to 1965, the SLFP-ruled Sri Lanka by voicing its commitment to radicalism and real socialism, despite withdrawal of favour by the USA (Sharma, 1988: 77–80). The problems of foreign exchange and shortage of food grains created by America paved a way for comeback of the UNP in 1965 elections. The UNP did not face any problem from the USA hence had tranquillity upto 1971. From 1980 onwards, Sri Lanka has witnessed the worst form of ethnic conflict till date (except truce for a brief period).

It may also be pointed out that the 'rootlessness' of ideological and political forces in Sri Lanka is due to commonality of the social background of the liberal and the radical strands. Hence, apparent differences in election manifestos, ideological rhetorics and proclamations do not indicate different paths of structural changes in Sri Lanka. Gunnar Myrdal has noted that the standard of living, exports and literacy rate have declined in Sri Lanka after independence. Despite the leftist character of the 'modernisation ideals' in Sri Lanka, there is neither leftward transformation nor a socialist revolution. The 'modernisation ideals' remain an ideology of the politically articulate elite in Sri Lanka like any other country, particularly India (Myrdal, 1968: 57–69).

III

Social formation of Sri Lanka was not clearly characterised in the pre-British period by rigidity of caste or by crystallisation of class distinctions or even by distinct ethnic boundaries. Arasaratnan's view is that royal absolutism and Buddhism did not permit privileged status groups to become harsh and oppressive divisions in Sri Lankan society. Flexible social arrangements (including castes) were in existence due to political, religious or ideological factors. Endogamy is not rigid, but functional groups form an essential part of Sri Lanka's agrarian economy. The notion of 'good people' has existed, marking a boundary between the 'low people' (service groups) and the high caste Goyigamas (Arasaratnam, 1964: 61).

Today's Sri Lanka has inherited remnants of monarchy and feudalism through styles of life and political culture. The privileged families bear feudal and aristocratic background. All the feudal chiefs and their favourites were the 'good people' by birth. They or their descendants are the leaders of the UNP, the SLFP and some left parties. The Senanayake and the Bandaranayake families (with negligible exception) have ruled Sri Lanka since 1948 till date. More than group/collectivity (caste), family and individual have been given premium in Sri Lanka. Nur Yalman observes: "The caste divisions themselves as well as the gradations within the caste are preserved not because of any law but because of the self-interest of the individuals. The caste barriers are not 'categorical imperatives' sanctioned by direct communal force, but are the cumulative result of individual divisions" (in E.R. Leach, ed., 1960: 94–95). Status considerations rooted in wealth and family background within the caste and also across the caste have shaped social relations in Sri Lanka.

The absence of Brahmin (priest) and the presence of Buddhism integrated castes with occupational (specialist) groups along with the feudal system of land tenure and political control. No ritual was attached to caste system. The service and artisan castes were organised in state departments, hence political ordering of caste. Sri Lanka also lacked castes of Kshatriya status. The Goyigamas were the supermost caste, and were differentiated into aristocratic and non-aristocratic layers (see, for example, on caste in Sri Lanka, Ryan, 1953; Pieris, 1956). Numerically, Brahmins and Kshatriyas are in small numbers compared to the middle-level peasant castes in India. But, in Sri Lanka, Goyigamas, the highest in rank order, were also numerically most preponderant, hence, an inverted pyramid. Though Buddhism disregards the ideology of caste, but recruits members on the basis of caste. Many of the temples possess feudal landholdings even today, and caste links are an essential part of the structure of temple rituals. But, the Buddhist public worship at all temples disregard of the caste status of monks. The layman does not recognise caste in the priesthood, but the priests themselves are organised by caste. Such a paradoxical situation of caste and no caste, rank order and its absence, characterised the Ceylonese society before 1948 and particularly before the advent of the British rule (Tambiah, 1968: 89–90).

The British rule brought about strategic changes in Sri Lankan economy and polity. Religious organisations were banned. The power of the minorities and the native officials was increased. The Sri Lankan Tamils received a pat on their back by the British over and above the high ranking Goyigamas. In 1815, the Kandy regime was abolished, and in 1833 the Rajakariya (*jajmani* system) was also banned. The paddy and forest economy was converted into coffee economy, hence the non-agricultural castes like the Karawas (merchants) were most benefited. The new economy of plantation and coffee threw incentive for migration. The Indian Tamils migrated to the island country at this point of time (Sharma, 1988: 19–20).

IV

English education received an all-out emphasis under the British rule and in growing commercial economy. The low-country Sinhalese, along with the Sri Lankan Tamils, recognised the advantages of learning English, and the new middle class, which emerged in the wake of such a situation, was formed out of these two communities. The English-knowing people were thus generally the upper layer of the Goyigamas. At this juncture, to seek favours from the British Raj, some castes like the Karawas, converted to Christianity. It is guessed that in Colombo about 90 per cent of the richest families are of the Karawas, precisely due to their legacy of enterprising capability and political patronage (ibid.).

The liberal policy of concessions adopted by the British moulded Sri Lanka's socio-economic structure in such a way that the people made no complaints and campaigns against the Raj. Neither they asked for freedom nor for richer food and better amenities. In the absence of political awakening, the British had absolute control over plantation economy of Ceylon. This was also achieved with the help of a group of people having liberal conservative orientation, who were sympathetic to the British rulers. Through the policy of English education, the British had created such a layer of people from amongst the Goyigamas and the Ceylonese Tamils. The latter being a minority received more patronage than the Sinhalese for obvious reason of seeking their support in the island country, and this was readily available to the Raj, because the Tamils were still foreigners, or they were made to think so by the Raj. Such was the connivance between the British and the Ceylonese leadership that in 1931 adult franchise was rejected, and in the same year welfare measures for lower class groups were also opposed. The description of the political scene by Myrdal, at the time of Sri Lanka's independence in 1948, does not at all speak of ethnic divides and bickerings, communal or otherwise. Myrdal (1968: 145) writes:

> Political independence came to Ceylone in a totally different manner than it did to Burma. In case of Ceylon there was no Japanese occupation, no revolutionary ferment, and no sudden break with the past. The colony did not even experience the sort of liberation struggle the Indian National Congress organized. There was no civil disobedience or non-cooperation and no imprisonment of national leaders. Ceylon emerged from colonial rule through a process of peaceful negotiation, but ... this was not an altogether unmixed blessing.

Some other observations by Myrdal are no less significant. According to him, Ceylon enjoyed much higher levels of living than India due to its strong plantation economy. Malnutrition was far less. The level of literacy was very high. Inequalities were much less than in India. Women were less subjugated. Caste was a functional arrangement than a rigid and ideologically determined actual hierarchy. There was a longer history of westernisation with more economic and professional opportunities for its people than India (ibid.). Why then ethnic conflict? What was that suppressed volcano of sentiments that suddenly busted into ethnic violence from 1983 onwards? What has happened between 1956 and 1983 that made the island country the worst violence torn formation (Sharma, 1988: 27–32)?

The Ceylon Tamils were far less numerically than the English-educated Sinhalese, top Sinhalese bureaucratic and power elite. The indigenously educated Sinhalese also occupied top slot along with their English-educated Sinhalese. Down the line most businessmen, landowners, traders, middlemen, moneylenders, rural intelligentsia, school teachers, notaries, ayurvedic physicians, monks, peasants, etc., all were Sinhalese, Muslims and Christians. Only the plantation labourers were mainly from amongst the Indian Tamils, and they were in no way strong enough even to extract the right of citizenship from the Sri Lankan state.

The Ceylonese Tamils no doubt were a formidable rival of the upper class of the Sinhalese in professions, politics, administration and education, but they were just a small fragment, that is, 11 per cent of the total population of Sri Lanka, who had enjoyed equal rights like the Sinhalese, Muslims and Christians. But this is also a fact that the Ceylon Tamils had more than double of the average income of the Indian Tamils. The Indian Tamils had highest ratio of people with no schooling. The Ceylonese Tamils were more urban and better placed occupationally and economically than the Indian Tamils. But, the Kandyan Sinhalese and the low-country Sinhalese were far ahead of the Ceylon Tamils in regard to income, and the small minorities like the Moors and Malays were even far ahead of the low-country Sinhalese. The Christians were at the top in bureaucracy and plantations, but not much hue and cry was made against them. Why Ceylon Tamils were taken as a serious threat to the emerging Sinhalese power elite? Why Ceylon Tamils have not been treated at par with the rest of Sri Lankan people?

V

Sri Lanka is a 'poly-ethnic society' and its multi-ethnicity refers to a situation of inter-ethnic cleavages and conflicts, between the Sinhalese and the Tamil. Some questions, as formulated by Urmila Phadnis (1990) relating to Sri Lanka's ethnic problem, cannot be set aside. These are:

1. Why is it that ethnic demands and competition entail some groups and not others in multi-ethnic societies?

2. What are the conditions under which ethnicity of a particular nature progressively becomes demanding, competitive and conflictual?
3. Under what situation does an ethnic community assert its status as a 'nation', and what are the requirements for its success?
4. What changes occur in various components of ethnic groups and in its boundary delineation in the processes of group-community nationality formation?
5. Under what conditions does ethnicity impede or/and facilitate the process of state building and state-centric nation-building? And how (ibid.).

Phadnis (ibid.), further points out that demographic setting of ethnic groups, levels of economic development, patterns of power sharing and the various points of inter-ethnic group competition, conflict and conflictual existence and their socio-economic bases should be analysed since 1948.

The ethnic conflict has surfaced from the feeling of the dominant Sinhalese community that Sri Lanka is a country of Sinhalese; it is a Sinhala country. Hence, Sinhalisation (or Ceylonisation) in the fields of education, language, religion, industry and politics was initiated in 1956 with a view to de-entrench the Ceylon Tamils from positions of power and authority. It was propagated that Sinhalese people should get priority over other ethnic groups in securing jobs and in availing other opportunities and facilities. As a result of such a pronouncement, the most adversely affected were Ceylon Tamils, because no other group was as much entrenched in Tamil polity and society as this particular group. The Ceylon Tamils are mainly concentrated in the northern and eastern Sri Lanka. They migrated to the island country between 400 and 1200 AD. In course of time the highly educated and mobile Ceylon Tamils also moved away to big cities like Colombo and Kandy with the ambition of reaching at the top of Ceylonese society.

The ongoing ethnic conflict is not due to the Indian Tamils, who were nearly 9,90,000 in 1953, about 90 per cent of the plantation labour force. They continue to live in estate enclaves and hutments. Their appalling and pathetic condition would forbid them to make demands from the Sri Lankan government. The fact is that before 1948, they were not allowed to leave Sri Lanka without permission of the government. The Ceylon Tamils, because of their deep roots in Sri Lankan society and polity, have become an eyeshore for the Sinhalese mandarins. Their entrenchment in prestigious jobs and positions and representation in politico-legal bodies scared the Sinhalese elite immediately after independence in 1948. Instead of accommodation, politics of hatred and opposition has reigned supreme since the second general elections in 1956. In the late fifties the Tamil United Liberation Front (TULF) was a strong political party as it effectively articulated interests of the Ceylon Tamils and voiced the grievances of the Indian Tamils as well. The new middle class, represented by Buddhist monks, ayurvedic physicians and Sinhalese school teachers, resented initially against the western-educated Sinhalese elites and later on protested against the domineering presence of the Ceylon Tamils in the independent Sri Lanka. The Ceylon Tamils were certainly ahead of the Sinhalese in general in many walks of life (Sharma, 1988: 29–30).

Intense rivalry has existed between the low-country Sinhalese and the Ceylon Tamils because both of them being in the same economic condition share the same scarce resources and opportunities. The Kandyan Sinhalese are below to both of them, and the Indian Tamils are at the bottom of class hierarchy. The Moors and the Malays are economically above all the groups, but being small in numbers and restricted to trade and commerce, they have not been perceived as a socio-political threat by the dominant Sinhalese (ibid.: 29–34). According to a survey by the Central Bank of Ceylon (1994: Table 15; 1973: 84–85), levels of education and extent of unemployment among the Sinhalese and the Ceylon Tamils are nearly of the same proportions. Presence of the Ceylon Tamils in the Ceylon Administrative Service, clerical services, professions (engineers, doctors, lecturers), armed forces and labour forces has been constantly declining since 1956. Increasing curbs and discouragement by the government and rising aspirations of the Sinhalese, for having all access to the lucrative jobs and positions, also culminated into ethnic conflict and mutual distrust and hatred.

The Ceylon Tamils have retained their ethnic identity intact by way of adherence to their language, religion and cultural practices, and such a distinctive Tamil identity has created suspicion and distrust among the Sinhalese elites. Such a situation does not prevail in case of Moors and Burghers. The Moors, a Muslim community, speak both Sinhala and Tamil, and have adjusted with their surroundings as they are engaged in trade, business and shopkeeping. Their distance from polity and administration has kept them in good looks of the Sinhalese. The Burghers are a mixed group, offsprings of Portuguese, Dutch, British and Ceylonese marriages. Christianity, English language and British style of life and customs though make them distinct from the Sinhalese people, but they are also not so distinct as they speak Sinhala. They are a small group, and have been quite dormant. A good number of them left Sri Lanka quietly as they could not adjust in the emergent situation after independence.

Thus, the Ceylon Tamils alone became a bone of contention because they were having white-collar jobs and uncreative positions, which the Sinhalese instinctively thought that in the independent Ceylon should be held by them rather than by a group of alien ethnicity. The government, instead of creating new jobs and positions for the Sinhalese youth, adopted a policy of de-entrenchment of the Sri Lankan Tamils by revival of Sinhala *bhasha*, Buddhism, ayurveda, etc. Confrontation, rather than accommodation, became the key *mantra* of the SLFP, and in course of time, also of the UNP. The message sent out by these two major political parties was that Ceylon was a country for Sinhalese people alone, hence, the non-Sinhalese, particularly the Ceylon Tamils, had no place in Sri Lankan polity, society and economy (Sharma, 1988: 42).

VI

Let us glance how religion and language have been politicised in the post-1948 Sri Lanka. It would not be an exaggeration to say that no political development has been free from religious strings in contemporary Sri Lanka. Today, the Sinhalese find their cultural identity through Buddhism and Sinhala language. The message sent out to the non-Buddhist and the non-Sinhala speaking people is that Sri Lanka is for the Sinhalese only, and it is the home of the Sinhalese Buddhists. The fear created by the zealots of Buddhism and the 'Sinhala only' was that the Ceylon Tamils and the Christians ultimately would become a threat to the existence of the Sinhalese people and to the stability of their social and religious structures by taking away lion's share from Sri Lanka's national resources. However, it is also opined that revivalism was not directly aimed at the sliding down of the Ceylon Tamils. Arasaratnam (1964: 23–24) writes:

> During colonial rule, Buddhist influence on state and society naturally suffered a setback. Christianity was the favoured religion and attracted to it the loyalties of some Sinhalese and Tamils. Favourable government policies, private missionary assistance from the West, and most particularly their control of educational institutions enabled the minority Christian communities to rise to a dominant position in society. In the absence of state support, Buddhism declined and at the time of independence showed the ill-effects of this unequal competition.

Even if the above view is taken on its face value as an objective analysis, the developments in Sri Lanka since 1956 do not substantiate such a perception. The Constitution of the Democratic Socialist Republic of Sri Lanka (1978) states: "The Republic of Sri Lanka shall give to Buddhism the foremost place and accordingly it shall be the duty of the state to protect and foster the Buddha Sasana ..." (as quoted in Sharma, 1988: 43). Prior to this, in 1959, two Buddhist universities were opened, which were closed down in 1962 after the University Grants Commission of Sri Lanka made a negative recommendation. A separate institution for monks was also established. The notions of Sinhaladipa (island of the Sinhalese) and Dhammadipa (island of Buddhism) have been propagated, which, in turn, have impinged upon the secular character of the Sri Lankan state of the pre-1978 period. Today, the city of Colombo is a home for influential Buddhist monasteries and *perivenas* (educational institutions for monks). The Buddhist Theosophical Society, Maha Bodhi Society, Young Men's Buddhist Association, etc., have their headquarters in Colombo. Colombo looks like Anuradhapuram (a Buddhist town) of yesteryears. Such developments have sharpened 'contradictions' and 'dialectical tensions'. It has become impossible to have co-existence of the Sangha (Buddhism) and the Devale (Hindu temple) (see Bechert, quoted from De Silva and Malagoda, in De Silva, ed., 1977; 382; see also Tambiah, 1967).

The presence of the Tamils in government employment declined sharply between 1953 and 1963 (Central Bank of Ceylon, 1954, 1973). This was the period of the demand for intense Sinhalisation of the Sri Lankan state and society. The Buddha Jayanti celebration as a national agenda was demanded. Introduction of Buddhism in school syllabi, nationalisation of English schools, statutory provision for the head of the state, the prime minister, the chiefs of the armed forces and heads of all important departments of the state were some of the vociferous demands made in the 1950s and 1960s. Admission to the universities and the public services was proposed in proportion to the island's ethnic and religious complexion (Sharma, 1988: 44–45).

VII

Besides Buddhism, Sinhala language was projected as a sort of 'official cult' between 1956 and 1965. By extreme advocacy of Sinhala *bhasha*, an attempt was made to do away with the privileges of the entrenched middle and upper classes and the English-educated elite with a view to substitute them by the Sinhala-educated intelligentsia. The Sinhalese literati, Ayurveda physicians, Sinhalese school teachers and Buddhist priests suddenly became the blue-eyed boys under the SLFP dispensation. The 'Sinhala Only Act' of 1956 marked a concrete beginning of the language acrimony, and it became subject of social disharmony like ethnicity and religion.

Prior to the promulgation of the Official Language Act of 1956, more than 90 per cent of the Sinhalese did not understand English. Hence, most of the coveted jobs went to those who were educated in the best English-medium schools. The new Act even angered this small number of the English-educated Sinhalese, because it went against them too like the Ceylonese Tamils (ibid.: 48). "The Ceylon Tamils saw in the prospect of Sinhala becoming the national language a threat to their culture, their identity and their economic status. It made them a fighting party. They were forced to demand the recognition of Tamil as a national language too, whereas previously they had been content to have English serve this purpose" (Myrdal, 1968: 350). S.W.R.D. Bhandaranaike, sensing the mounting indignation of the educated Sinhalese, set out himself to capitalise as a champion of the underprivileged and the defender of a besieged culture (ibid.), hence emotionalisation of the language issue. Thus, more than retrieval of culture, language issue became an existential concern of the Ceylon Tamils in particular.

Linguistic divides were made so sharp that every act of the government harmed the ethnic co-existence in Sri Lanka. In 1953, 80 per cent Ceylonese spoke only one language, a little less than 60 per cent spoke only Sinhala, and a little more than

20 per cent spoke only Tamil. Only 10 per cent Hindus spoke both Sinhala and Tamil (see Department of Census and Statistics, 1960, Table 17: 604). Language and ethnic composition corresponds to a great extent. About 70 per cent are Sinhalese, 20 per cent are Tamils, and 7 per cent are Moors (Muslims). And further, corresponding to this are about 67 per cent Buddhists, 18 per cent Hindus, 7 per cent Muslims and 8 per cent Christians. Only 16 per cent people are bilingual and 3 per cent are trilingual. The 59 per cent who speak only Sinhala are Sinhalese and Buddhists, and those 21 per cent who speak only Tamil are Hindus. Those who speak more than one language are generally Muslims and Christians (ibid. Also quoted in Sharma, 1988: 51–52). In such a situation of linguistic exclusiveness, attempt to impose one language would invite communal tensions and conflicts. The British might have done a lot of harm by pursuing their policy of 'divide and rule' regarding relations between Sinhalese and Tamils, and they might have even harmed Sinhalese culture, Buddhism and language, but the 'Sinhala Only Act' has not done any good, so far as retrieval of the pre-British glory of the island country is concerned.

S.W.R.D. Bhandaranike was English-educated, aristocratic, an Anglican Christian, owner of large and prosperous coconut plantations, and a prominent member of the UNP until he formed his new party in 1951 (Myrdal, 1968: 351). His wife, Sirimavo Bhandaranaike, who succeeded him after his assassination by a Bhikku, had inherited her husband's aristocracy and readymade political platform. She carried forward the contradictions of her husband. In 1965, she spoke in defence of the resurgence of Sinhalese culture as follows:

> Centuries of colonial rule had cut us adrift from our heritage. For sometimes after our formal independence, we unfortunately still remained wedded to alien values and guided by alien practices. Western culture, western habits, western education, still occupied the primary place, and our indigenous

> way of life was relegated to a lower status. The top-hat and the imperial honour became the symbols of our cultural subjugation, although politically we were free. From this state we have advanced far. (quoted from Kearney, 1967: 49)

The provisions of the Official Language Act (No. 33) of 1956, and the Constitution of Sri Lanka as adopted in 1978 (Chapter IV), put together, aimed at total Sinhalisation of Sri Lankan polity and society. The harshness of the 1978 Constitution forced several Tamilian officers to resign their jobs and positions (Coomarswamy, 1984; 99; also see Wilson, 1988; Roberts, ed., 1979). Mrs. Bhandaranaike was quite happy on account of her efforts towards Sinhalisation. She once spoke: "We have removed the disabilities placed on the majority of our people by the foreign ruler. The language and the religion of the majority ... have been developed and their rightful place ensured. While respecting the rights of minorities, the Government, mindful of its obligations to the majority of the people, has restored their lost rights"(quoted from Kearney, 1967: 123). All such statements and assertions communicate revengeful attitude against the Ceylon Tamils in particular. An atmosphere of distrust and hatred became inevitable consequence of such speech acts and legislative measures. The Swabhasha movement united all the Sinhalese outfits like the Mahajana Eksath Peramuna (MEP), the SLFP, the Lanka Sama Samaja Party (LSSP), the Bhasha Peramuna, etc. The 'Sinhala nationalism' has thus wide-ranging repercussions on the Sri Lankan polity and society.

VIII

The power elites of today in Sri Lanka are much different from the ones who were in 1948. At the time of transfer of power in 1948, the elite were broadly Ceylonese, largely Christian, mostly high-caste, highly urbanised, western-educated, engaged in western-type occupations and of the highest economic and social class. Such a ruling elite had a strong sense of identification with British values, attitudes and perspectives (Singer, 1964: 11–12). Marshall R. Singer (ibid.) observes that by the early sixties the political elite in Ceylon was quite different from the elite of 1948. They were overwhelming Sinhalese, heavily Buddhist, somewhat lower caste, largely rural, generally less educated but more *swabhasha*-educated, more engaged in traditional occupations, and very largely drawn from the middle economic and social classes. Further, Singer (ibid.) observes that the new elites have a deep sense of identification with their traditional culture and values, a very local perspective, and a strong sense of ethnic nationalism, that is, Sinhalese or Tamil as opposed to Ceylonese. Obviously, the new political leadership is immanently a consequence of the *swabhasha* movement and Buddhist nationalism.

Sri Lanka has been sandwiched in-between liberal ideology and radical nationalism as it has witnessed nearly alternative governments one after another headed by the UNP and the SLFP. The left parties, such as the LSSP, the CP, etc., and the liberal ones like the Federal Party (FP) and the Tamil Congress also trapped the Sri Lankan polity. Since 1983, the situation has been quite different, because both the ruling outfits, namely, the UNP and the SLFP, have been countering the LTTE as an inimical force demanding Tamil Eelam. However, before the LTTE-led separatist movement, Sri Lanka faced a grave crisis created by the extreme left group known as the Janatha Vimukhi Peramuna (JVP-People's Liberation Front). Normally, the left parties had sided with the SLFP upto 1970. But then, why JVP? Fred Halliday (in Blackburn, ed., 1975: 173; for more details, also see Sharma, 1988, Ch. VI) observes:

> Such a blatant record of apostasy and complicity with imperialism was bound to have serious consequences on the workings of traditional mystifications in Ceylon. In their economic despair, the masses had turned to the established left and to the SLFP, but the extreme seriousness of the crisis prevented either Sirimavo Bandaranaike's lachrymose

> hypocrisy or the fake Left of Perera and Keuneman from retaining control, or of meeting the real challenge that came from a force that had broken with the paralytic structures of Ceylonese parliamentarism Aryanism and was in direct contact with the exploited.

The JVP claimed to work for the ignored Ceylonese peasantry in the non-plantation sector. The JVP organised an armed insurrection on 5 April 1971 by attacking police stations and capturing of rifles and ammunition from the captured police stations and forces (Halliday, ibid.: 173). 'Reformism' was completely rejected by the JVP as a means of the upliftment of the downtrodden. The Tamil plantation proletariat was also included in the vanguard of 1971 insurrection along with the non-plantation peasantry. The JVP thought of an armed insurrection for realisation of the 'Sinhalese road' to revolution, hence attacks on police stations. Details of the JVP and its Marxist-Leninist orientation and stance on Maoism and Guevarism or Castroism may not be warranted here, it is necessary to glance at its after-effects on ethnic conflict which has engulfed Sri Lanka since 1983. Imposition of emergency became a frequent phenomenon, and instability has characterised Sri Lankan polity a lot since 1970s. Ideological confusions, wrangles and illusions, unemployment of the school-educated Sinhalese youth, misadministration, increasing dependence on foreign aid, favouritism and nepotism were some of the obvious consequences of the insurrection. Constitutional changes had added frequency. The SLFP and its left allies lost elections in 1977, and the UNP came to power with a thumping majority (ibid.: 84–186).

After the JVP insurrection, the Tamils were further frightened by the advocacy of a Sinhalese path of revolution. They formed a new party known as the Tamil United Left Front (TULF) in 1972, and in the elections of 1977, the TULP made the Tamil 'eelam' (a separate state) as an issue to solve their problems. The TULF was the second largest and the main opposition party in 1977, because all other parties, including the SLFP and the ULF, were routed in an unprecedented manner (Kearney and Janile, 1975: 40).

Let us repeat here once again that the root cause of the ongoing ethnic conflict is not cultural, but it is political. The Tamils feel that they are being uprooted from Sri Lanka, where they have lived for more than twelve centuries, and were in commanding position for nearly two centuries during the British rule. The Sinhalese think that no more Tamils can be allowed to enjoy superior status and privileges in their Sinhalese dominated country. Kearney (1967: 137) observes that modern communalism in Ceylon is pre-eminently a political phenomenon. But his explanation is based on the assumption of politicisation of culture and ethnicity by the Ceylon Tamils. Our view is that deprivation and de-entrenchment are the main causes of ethnic conflict. The Tamils thought of formation of a Tamil nation for themselves on the basis of their language and cultural identity as a distinct community compared to the Sinhalese. Since Tamils have lived in the north-east Sri Lanka, they have claimed this part of the island country as their homeland. The new middle class in Sri Lanka has questioned the continued dominance of the alien Tamils in the country of the Sinhalese.

The suspicion among the Tamil leaders regarding Sinhalese backlash had existed even before 1956 and also prior to 1948. The leadership of the Federal Party and the Tamil Congress, which later on converged into the TULF, thought of an honourable space for Tamils in Ceylon rather than choosing a path of confrontation and conflict. A policy of the repatriation of the Indian Tamils was also worked out which was never implemented faithfully. On the contrary, certain steps taken by the SLFP government in the mid-1960s, with a view to alienate and deemploy the Ceylon Tamils, aggravated suspicion amongst the Tamils. Ethnic situation was not so bad till 1983 as indications of give and take between Sinhalese and Tamils were evident. In May 1983, ethnic violence took a new turn. The Tamils made a categorical demand for 'eelam', and the state suppressed this demand with an iron hand. Killings and counter-killings, bomb blasts, arson and loot, etc., became a routine activity. Some Tamils left Sri Lanka fearing action, some police officers resigned their jobs apprehending action against their supposed non-action (Sharma, 1988: Ch. VI). Imposition of emergency was logical offshoot. Months of May, June and July witnessed bloodshed, massacres, rape, loot and arson. In about ten days alone, 300 persons were killed and 75,000 were rendered homeless (see *The Times of India*, 4 and 5 August, 1983, for the statement of the then President of Sri Lanka, J.R. Jayewardene in the Sri Lankan Parliament). Recurrence of violence has remained incessant, for some time from 2002 onwards till 2005. This happened after the LTTE's declaration to find out an acceptable solution of the Tamil problem. However, the recent violent incident indicates recurrence of the pre-2002 situation.

Who is to be blamed for ethnic turmoil, which has lasted in its barbaric form for the last more than two decades? Are Sinhalese and Tamils behaving as antagonistic classes? Can we demarcate between ethnicity and class based on the Sri Lankan situation? A clear answer to all such questions is that ethnic conflict in Sri Lanka has deep political and economic dimensions. It is a conflict between the aspiring new Sinhalese middle class and the traditionally entrenched class of Ceylon Tamils. The extent and magnitude of mutual suspicion between the two communities have reached such a level that assurances from either side for solving the crisis (including devolution of power, autonomy, etc.) have not been taken on their face value by both the groups.

Newton Gunasinghe (in Alavi and Harriss, eds., 1989: 247–55) refers to constellations of perception to the domain of the ethnic issue in particular and as indices to the texture of the social fabric in Sri Lanka. These are: (1) the 'nation besieged', (2) "its individuals, not ethnicity that matters", and (3) "recognition of nationalities and devolution of power", and (4) the 'eelam' perspectives. According to the first perspective, Sri Lanka is the country of the Sinhala, the descendant of the North Indian 'Aryans', who are original settlers of the island country, and the country has lived under the influence of Buddhism. If the Sinhala fabric and Buddhism are in danger, an iron hand policy needs to be adopted. Such a mythologisation of the Sinhalese culture and society has obstructed an amicable solution of the ethnic crisis. As per the second perspective, Sri Lanka is a multi-ethnic and multi-religious country. Devolution of power based on region and ethnic composition is the only workable solution. The third perspective calls for restoration of harmony and cooperation among various ethnic, religious and linguistic groups as it had prevailed in the past. Finally, according to the 'eelam' perspective, the Tamils have been discriminated by the Sinhala majority, hence devolution of power. These are not exclusive perceptions, though their votaries are not the same. The new middle class advocates the first perspective, whereas the second receives support from the top entrepreneurs and westernised business executives. The radical and left-oriented intelligentsia have articulated the third view, and the Tamil political parties and groups advocate the 'eelam' perspective.

IX

The main issue is to accommodate the interests of the new Sinhala middle class, the westernised elites, the peasantry and the proletariat and the Tamils keeping in view their past and present situations in Sri Lanka. No polemical discourses on ethnicity (Jenkins, 1997), superiority of Sinhala culture over the cultures of the rest of the communities can lead to an integrated and all-inclusive solution of the ethnic crisis. It is not a question of the Sinhalese cause or that of the Tamil eelam, or of the new constructions of ethnic identities by tracing deep-seated cultural wealth and sources of strength of language, religion and mythology. Solution lies in the understanding of the immediate past and the present juncture of the existence of various groups in relation to each other. Hence, no reinventions or re-mythologisations of the past, either by the Sinhalese or by the Tamils, can establish superiority of one over the other.

The fact that the Ceylon Tamils enjoyed superior status during the British period cannot be denied and delegitimised by a stroke of the 'Sinhala Only Act'. At the same time, the rising wave of aspirations of the Sinhalese youth and the new middle cannot be overlooked. A legitimate space to the newly educated rural people in free Sri Lanka must be conceded. A reconciliation of the two in some measure/proportion is the only way. Territorial segregation, when translated into cultural domains/boundaries, becomes a dangerous game for the entire country. Sri Lanka has suffered from this transformation of territory into culture, language and religion. Inter-territorial and inter-ethnic linkages were acknowledged as essential threading for keeping integrity and oneness in the past. The state has failed to realise this prerequisite of its national integration.

References

Arasaratnam, S., 1964, *Ceylon*, Englewood Cliffs, N.J.: Prentice Hall.

Bechert, Heinz, 1976, quoted from K.M. deSilva and K. Malagoda, in K.M. deSilva (ed.), *Sri Lanka: A Survey*, London: C. Hurst & Co.

Central Bank of Ceylon, 1954, Survey of Ceylon's Consumer Finances, Colombo.

——, 1973, Survey of Sri Lanka Consumer Finances, Colombo.

Coomarswamy, Radhika, 1984, *Sri Lanka: The Crisis of the Anglo-American Constitutional Traditions in a Developing Society*, New Delhi: Vikas Publishing House.

Department of Census and Statistics, 1960, *Census of Ceylon*, 195, Vol. III, Part 1, Colombo: Government Press.

Dharmadasa, K.N.O., 1992, *Language, Religion and Ethnic Aggressiveness: The Growth of Sinhalese Nationalism in Sri Lanka*, Ann Arbor: University of Michigan Press.

——, 1995, "The Roots of Sinhala Identity in Sri Lanka," *Ethnic Studies Report*, Vol. XIV(2).

Gunasinghe, Newton, 1989, "Ethnic Conflict", in Hamza Alavi and John Harriss (eds.), *Sri Lanka: Perceptions and Solutions in Sociology of Developing Societies of South Asia*, London: Macmillan.

Gunawardana, R.A.L.H., 1992, "The People of the Lion", *Ethnic Studies Report*, Vol. X(1).

Halliday, Fred, 1975, "The Ceylonese Insurrection", in Robin Blackburn (ed.), *Explosion in a Subcontinent*, New Delhi: Penguin Books.

Jenkins, Richard, 1997, *Rethinking Ethnicity: Arguments and Explorations*, New Delhi: Sage Publications.

Kearney, Robert N. and Jiggins Janice, 1975, "The Ceylon Insurrection of 1971," *Journal of Commonwealth and Comparative Politics*, Vol. 13, No. 1.

Kearney, Robert N., 1967, *Communalism and Language in Politics in Ceylon*, Durham: Duke University Press.

Myrdal, Gunnar, 1968, *Asian Drama*, Vol. 1, New Delhi: Penguin Books.

Pakeman, S.A., 1964, *Ceylon*, New York: Praeger.

Phadnis, Urmila, 1990, *Ethnicity and Nation-Building in South Asia: A Case Study of Sri Lanka*, New Delhi: Sage Publications.

Pieris, Ralph, 1956, *Sinhalese Social Organization*, Colombo: University of Colombo Press.

Roberts, Michael (ed.), 1979, *Collective Identities: Nationalism and Protest in Modern Sri Lanka*, Colombo: Marga Institute.

Ryan, Bryce, 1953, *Caste in Modern Ceylon*, New Brunswick, N.J.C.: Rutgers University Press.

Sharma, K.L., 1988, *Society and Polity in Modern Sri Lanka*, New Delhi: South Asian Publishers Pvt. Ltd.

Singer, Marshall R., 1964, *The Emerging Elite*, Cambridge, Mass: Massachusetts Institute of Technology.

Smaje, Chris, 2000, *Natural Hierarchies: The Historical Sociology of Race and Caste*, Oxford: Blackwell Publishers.

Tambiah, S.J., 1967, "The Politics of Language in India and Ceylon", *Modern Asian Studies*, Vol. 1, No. 3.

——, 1968, *Sinhala Laws and Customs*, Colombo: Lake House.

Wijesekara, N.D., 1965, *The People of Ceylon*, Colombo: Gunasena.

Wilson, A. Jeyaratnam, 1988, *The Break-up of Sri Lanka: The Sinhalese—Tamil Conflict*, London: C. Hurst Co. and Orient Longman Ltd.

Wriggins, W. Howard, 1960, *Ceylon: Dilemmas of a New Nation*, Princeton: Princeton University Press.

Yalman, Nur, 1960, "The Flexibility of Caste Principle in a Kandyan Community", in E.R. Leach (ed.), *Aspects of Caste in South India, Ceylon and North-West Pakistan*, Cambridge: Cambridge University Press.

Yinger, J. Milton, 1997, *Ethnicity* (Indian edition), Jaipur and New Delhi: Rawat Publications.

7

Interlinking Culture and Development

A Case of Chanderi in Madhya Pradesh

Both the viewpoints that culture is antithetical to development and that culture contributes to economic development (capitalism) are prevalent even today after more than one century old conceptualisations by Karl Marx and Max Weber, respectively. The first viewpoint has led to excessive materialism reducing culture as a superstructural phenomenon, while the second viewpoint upholds culture as a pragmatic construction imbibing a value system, friendly to capitalism, that is, trade and commerce. A third viewpoint counters these formulations by explicating transposition of culture as a variegated phenomenon, that is, economic capital can be transformed into social and political capital and vice versa. Language as a symbolic capital is transposable into other forms of capital. Excessive materialism has resulted into bringing back in culture and culture studies. Today, culture is seen in conjunction with economy and polity, space and status, private and public life. Based on my study of a small town in Central India, some aspects of culture, such as image and reality of culture, culture and community, culture and livelihood, culture as space, etc., would be discussed in this chapter.

I

The question is: What is culture? Culture may refer to the entire symbolic world and this may incorporate institutions, artifacts and modes of action. As such, culture is an empirical and substantive guide for meeting out requirements of everyday life. Culture motivates/discourages pursuits of life in a particular manner. 'Culture' for the sake of 'culture' is different from culture as a motivating factor for gratification of existential needs. We look at culture here more as a system of values with its embodiment in social, political and economic institutions. In this sense only, we can relate culture with development. Expression of culture in structural arrangements of a society brings out its relevance as a practice. While reconciling the Marxist and the non-Marxist uses of culture, Bottomore (1985: 109–12) observes that "the concept of culture is at the heart of the conception of consciousness as conscious existence, in which consciousness is seen both as bound up with an existing state of affairs and as a condition which makes it possible to change the state of affairs." What Lukacs (1920 [1970]) says seems to be quite relevant for our study of cultural mosaic and development in a small town in Madhya Pradesh. Lukacs defines culture in opposition to civilisation as "the ensemble of valuable products and abilities which are dispensable in relation to the immediate maintenance of life ..." (quoted from Bottomore, 1985). The precondition of culture should be in man as an end in himself. A socialist conception of culture was contrasted from a bourgeoisie formulation of culture, and this was to counter the process of the commodification of culture as the collapse of 'higher culture' into 'material culture' (Bottomore, 1985).

The role of culture is central in the reproduction of social structures, characterised by unequal power relations in everyday life, and all this is accepted as legitimate and real by members of a society. Bourdieu argues, in his seminal work *Distinction*, that systems of domination find expression in virtually all areas of social practice and symbolic exchange, including preferences in dress, sports, food, music, literature, art and taste, etc. Culture contributes to the process of social production (Bourdieu, 1995: 1–25). Bourdieu's formulation of symbolic power is closely intertwined with economic and political power like that of Max Weber's (1946) classification of 'class, status and party' as distinct phenomena, though intertwined but not reducible to each other.

Bourdieu combines subjectivism and objectivism in his analysis of structures of domination and power. He writes: "the representation which individuals and groups inevitably project through their practices and properties is an integral part of social reality. A class is defined as much by its being—perceived and by its being, by its consumption which need not be conspicuous to be symbolic—as much as by its position in the relation of production"(1996: 483). According to Bourdieu (1995: 4), symbolic aspects of social life are inseparably intertwined with the material conditions of existence without one being reducible to the other. Different forms of capital are unequally distributed among social classes and class fractions.

Culture's centrality to development or underdevelopment is the main issue in the one thousand years old town of Chanderi in the Guna district of Madhya Pradesh (India). Culture is interconnected with economic, political and social change in Chanderi. A town with a population of nearly 25,000 inhabitants has witnessed ups and downs, both political and economic, in its considerably long history beginning from 1200 AD. Political glory, economic well-being and social prestige adorned the town in the medieval period. The beginning of the 19th century marked its downfall reducing it to the status of nothingness and irrelevance. War, displacement, poverty, environmental degradation and decline of arts and crafts have occurred during the British period (Sharma, 1999: 29–33).

Before we analyse our data on Chanderi, let us state explicitly that culture, power and development as a nexus refer to practices and processes basic to all social structures. Power and stratification are central to culture, and the meanings and the ways of their construction are also a matter of contestation and resistance as much as they are referred as matters of social cohesion and unity. Development has the elements of representation, power and discourse, and these determine the rank order of the entire world or that of regions, with a given country or its citizens. Development is thus constitutive of those inequalities which it claims to address (Schech and Haggis, 2000: 10–29).

II

Many of the questions we have listed here have come up from our study of Chanderi because of its unique history, culture and locale. Its current image of a small and beautiful town and as a glorious town of the medieval times, being the headquarters of a *sarkar* (government) in the Malwa Sultanate, constitutes the basis of development of Chanderi. The dynamics of Chanderi range from the headquarters of a *sarkar* to a *tappa* (sub)-tehsil till recently. Chanderi's past glory, antiquity, cultural heritage, the present social composition (Hindus, Muslims and Jains), *sari* (a women's outer wear) manufacturing and trade make Chanderi a unique town, not a representative of the small towns of India (Sharma, 1999: 15–21).

Chanderi lives in antiquity but it looks for 'modernity'. 'Tradition' in Chanderi is visible in its culture, architecture, economy and social composition. Invasions on Chanderi and battles fought there on its soil, supralocal administrative and trade links—all speak of Chanderi's past. Culture, economy and power were intertwined in the past. A document named as *Chakarana deh* describes the situation in Chanderi in 1918–19, relating to the modus operandi of land revenue collection and duties and obligations of the local administration and different castes and communities. It also refers to obligations and duties of the kamins and rewards and wages in lieu of the services rendered to the patrons, and about the mechanisms of resolution of differences and disputes. Such an organic system of culture, economy and power is no more in existence, but it refers to prevalence of multiculturalism comprising of Muslims and Jains who are outside the Hindu fold (caste), but were included in the 'Chakrana deh' system.

What is the nature of multiculturalism today in Chanderi? How does it reflect inequalities or equalities in Chanderi? In what way multiculturalism in Chanderi represents nexus of culture, economy and power? Multiculturalism can be viewed in two ways: (1) as a way of life, an essential component of social existence, a mediating mechanism between individual and society and between groups of people having differentiated social origins and existential conditions, and (2) culture as a superorganic phenomenon, or as a reflection of economic reality, or as 'politics of mind', that is, an instrument of appropriation of people and their social life (see Milner and Browite, 2003: 142–44). In the first case, family, neighbourhood, community, village, town, country or even whole world become loci of multiculturalism. As such, culture tends to be a boundaried phenomenon. Within specific structures, we have observed uniqueness of culture in Chanderi, namely, in family, *mohalla* (neighbourhood) and *gali*, (lane) caste and community, and in the entire town. But culture is not a stop, it is a beginning, a relative entity, concerning the self and the other. Boundaried solidarities and inter-boundary divides can be gazed in Chanderi in terms of representations and classifications, and through the hierarchisation based on these devides, social recognitions and spaces are claimed with a view to appropriate honour, status and power. It amounts to reducing/derobing the others from their socio-cultural and political possessions (ibid.). Multiculturalism in Chanderi implies differentiated meanings, stratification and evaluation of social positions. Different social groups, namely, Brahmins, Jains, Muslims and Kolis have differentiated cultural and social possessions (that is, status and honour), hence culture amounts to power, or in other words, words become worlds (Bourdieu, 1991: 145–51). Chanderi is a town, full of visions and images about people, places, history, monuments, dynasties, and all of them shape and reshape, and create and recreate harmony and disorder.

Chanderi is one of the ancient towns of the Gwalior region of Madhya Pradesh, having a known history of nearly one thousand years. From its district headquarters at Guna town, it is situated at a distance of 115 km, and 38 km away from Lalitpur, a town of the neighbouring state of Uttar Pradesh, situated on the main north-south rail line, and also known for activities relating to trade and commerce. Upto 1982, Chanderi was a sub-tehsil in the Moongawali tehsil of the Guna district, and prior to independence, it was a part of the Isagarh district of the Gwalior State. During the reign of Moughal emperor Akbar, Chanderi was the headquarters of a *sarkar* (government) in the Malwa Sultanate (see Sharma, 1999; and Fussman et al., 2003).

III

Chanderi is not a usual small town of today because of its curved political and administrative history, cultural mosaic, social composition (Hindus, Muslims and Jains), and reliance on handloom industry (sari manufacturing and trade). Chanderi inhabits nearly forty castes and communities, and four of them are most perceptible, based on their numerical strength and socio-political and economic space in the town.

Numerically, in the order of their respective strength, these are: Muslims, Jains, Brahmins and Kolis (a scheduled caste of weavers). Muslims and Jains are outside the caste fold, though, as per the *Chakarana deh* they were part of the organic ties prevalent in Chanderi, nearly a century ago. These four groups, if put together, constitute about 90 per cent of Chanderi's population. Ansari Muslims and Kolis together comprise of the weavers of the town, and they are nearly 50 per cent of its population. Most of the traditional trading castes and communities, such as Jains and Maheshwaris, are engaged in trade and commerce, specially relating to sari. Ansaris and Kolis do not constitute a 'community' as weavers, because they lack occupational bonding and common defence of their interests and welfare. Communitarian segregation makes the two groups 'segmentary' and 'rigid', despite their occupational homogeneity. Muslims do not have commensal ties with Hindus and Jains, except formal greetings extended on festivals and social occasions. Though Muslims constitute nearly one-third of Chanderi's population, and they are economically superior than Kolis and some other castes, their social status and political standing are much lower than that of Jains and Brahmins. Traditionally, Brahmins are superior to all other castes and communities, but in practice, they are inferior to Jains, because of the latter's superior economic standing and political activism.

Such is the scene of multiculturalism in Chanderi. It is segmentary, boundaried and exclusivist. At the same time, some common features, namely, Chanderi's political and administrative status in the medieval period, monuments concerning Muslims, Hindus and Jains, ponds and stepwells, surroundings, sari manufacturing as an economic activity and artistic endeavour, literary and poetic ambience, and above all 'image' of the town, create a sense of oneness and solidarity amongst its people vis-à-vis other towns and outside people. One can see the enchantment of the people with its monumental cultural heritage in their way of life and chanting of praise for the town as a whole, and about its uniqueness and laudable description in the *Ain-e-Akbari*. Oneness and homogeneity on the one hand, and segmentation and rigidity on the other, 'co-exist' in Chanderi, generally, in a discrete way, and also as perceived realities of life.

Weavers do not have a common platform to promote their interests, because multiculturalism hinders coming together of Ansaris and Kolis as a class of weavers. However, at the same time, they do not come in each other's way. This is why, there is no trade union, or an NGO, protecting and promoting the interests of weavers as an economic entity. Socio-cultural divide discourages a unified base for a common economic or political cause. Such a state of socio-cultural affairs is endeared by the sari traders (master weavers) of Chanderi, because no one questions their excessive control on weavers and maximisation of profit. The main political parties, namely, the Bhartiya Janata Party (BJP) and the Congress have kept silence on this issue, because expression of their concern for weavers could annoy the dominant community of traders (Jains, Maheshwaris and Muslims).

Socio-cultural divides are evident in the bifurcation of Chanderi in the form of *andar shahar* (inner town) and *bahar shahar* (outer town). Largely, this spatial differentiation is also reflected in Chanderi's socio-cultural and economic stratification as well. The upper stratum of Muslims, namely, the Sheikhs and Pathans, reside in the inner town. Most of the Brahmins, Jains and Maheshwaris live in this part of the town. In fact, these groups of people constitute the upper, the upper-middle and the middle classes of Chanderi. The *andar shahar* is meticulously designed architecturally, and its *sadar bazaar* (main market) is bubbling with trade and commerce dominated by Jains, Brahmins, Maheshwaris and Pathans. On the contrary, the *bahar shahar* inhabits lower-middle and lower class people, mainly Ansari (Monuin) and Koli weavers, basketmakers, *bidi* (local cigarette) workers and manual labourers. Galis and mohallas have petty grocery shops owned by lower caste and class people.

Chanderi was a magnificent town because it possessed a stone fort, 14,000 stone houses, 384 markets, 360 spacious caravanserais, and 12,000 mosques (see Fazl, 1949: 207, 212–14). Such a cultural panorama is reflected even today in the ruins of the fort, buildings, town planning, monuments, shrines, stepwells, mosques, bazaars, mohallas, sari manufacturing, etc. Sari manufacturing and the insignia of Badal Mahal (a well-known medieval palace) on the Chanderi sari symbolise synthesis of culture and economy. Manufacturing of sari is more than a sheer means of livelihood. A magnificent picture/image of Chanderi is seen by the weavers in their products. Such a projection of the image of the town has made the craft of weaving a unique and specialised activity. Weavers from outside 'Chanderi', even after their long stay and work experience, have not been able to learn the craft of weaving equal to the native weavers. The name Chanderi evokes magnificence, beauty, artistic ability, a sense of past glory and pride and eagerness to perpetuate the same today through the sari manufacturing, belief systems, rituals and reverence for shrines and monuments.

Several rulers patronised the craft of weaving, but the Moughal emperor Aurangzeb had a hostile and indifferent attitude. The Maratha rulers and the princes of Gwalior, Baroda, Indore and some others extended unbounded patronage to the Chanderi turbans, *iugdas* (long women's wear) and scarfs. On ceremonial occasions and festivals, the Chanderi clothes were made obligatory for both men and women. After the British takeover, Chanderi was reduced to the status of a sub-tehsil and as such its past grandeur disappeared in no time. Chanderi also suffered from severe droughts and epidemics. Decline in political clout was accompanied by economic recession and scarcity. From the 1920s onwards, the government of the Gwalior State acted upon a plan for Chanderi's architectural revival and for reinvention of the handloom industry. After independence, the state government has launched a process of reorganisation of the town and rekindling of the miserable state of sari production. Thus, a renewed nexus between culture, economy and polity has been there during the past five decades.

IV

Today, Chanderi is a well-known special centre for sari manufacturing. Nearly 60 per cent of its population, including most of the Momins, Kolis, Jains and Maheshwaris, depend on this single economic activity. Chanderi is not a market for agricultural produce. Tourism has started picking up, particularly after its renewal and reurbanisation. Recently, the UNIDO and the state government, with the help of the local influentials, have established a Silk Club for master weavers and initiated a cluster approach for the weavers. Hopefully, this would put a check on the recession in the handloom industry which it has witnessed after the withdrawal of patronage and protection by the state government. Based on the P.K. Lahiri Committee's recommendations, the provincial government had revived the nearly dead industry by way of subsidies and loans, revival of the cooperative sector and other measures such as supply of raw materials and designs, purchase of the finished products and stipend and training for young men and women. The similar efforts are being made by the UNIDO and the state government.

However, Chanderi is not an industrial town having modern opportunities and communication networks (with an exception of some STD booths). There is hardly a visible degree of openness and anonymity. Political consciousness is also low. Intransigent groups and individuals are seemingly not found.

The people are more inward-looking and insulated. Their emic sensibility is quite strong. They are past-oriented as they remain unfettered by the current structural changes. Acculturation has been quite low due to vicissitudes of the past. Even the young men and women live with the nostalgia of their history and culture of the pre-British period. Such a pedigree characterised by archetypical particularism and unique socio-cultural roots has implications for development and politics in the present situation (Sharma, 1999: 18 and 91).

Such a state of mind of the people in Chanderi refers to the shared assumptions of an entire society. A sort of culture has been built into the life of the people, and they sustain it by practising certain beliefs and rituals. A deep devotion, fervour and pride to the past orientation has demotivated the people with regard to migration, mobility and better opportunities in and outside Chanderi. A sense of complacency is writ large on most faces in the town. Liberation or emancipation from the past can be possible by posing reason against culture (Gellner, 1994: 13–23). One needs to doubt one's own past and present. But this does not happen often in Chanderi. While practising custom and tradition, people make their living possible, in fact, by finding out reason in culture. Thus, Chanderi symbolises a synthesis of culture and reason, the two are not antithetical or poles apart. The question is: Why culture has not been properly subjected to its mundane relevance or instrumental efficacy?

In view of such a deep-seated and unique culturalism in Chanderi, we find many of the classifications of Indian towns and cities unfit for considering Chanderi as an 'entrepot market' or 'a regional entrepot', or a 'suburban village', or a 'service qasba' (Bayly, in Ballhatchet and Harrison, eds., 1980: 21–24; see also Bayly, 1992). Chanderi is also not a zamindari town or a 'factory town' or a 'transient mufassal town' (see for, example, Islam, 1980; see also Fox, 1969). Apparently, Chanderi looks like a large-sized or an overgrown village based on its socio-cultural moorings, but the fact is that everyone in Chanderi thinks of it as a town, a *nagar*, rather a *nagari* (a small beautiful town). Looking at Chanderi's present condition of the damaged walls, fortification, towers, gates, havelis, bazaars, temples, mosques, caves, etc., one gets the impression of Chanderi as a grand medieval town. But, at the same time, modernity is also reflected in its government offices, schools, college, transport and communication networks, new markets, etc. The co-existence of old and new, tradition and modernity, emic and etic perceptions and structures relate culture and development in Chanderi in an explicit manner (Sharma, 1999: 89–92).

A true urban consciousness prevails in Chanderi. More than the present infrastructure, the vestiges of the past, namely, ruined sites, inscriptions, the description about Chanderi in the *Ain-e-Akbari*, etc., have shaped urban consciousness in Chanderi. However, the modus operandi of its socio-cultural and economic transactions share village idioms. Though Chanderi is a town and its people are also conscious of its urbanity, they have hardly significant supralocal connections with the outside world. The fact is that the outside people have reached to Chanderi and not vice versa. The limited supralocal ties involve the trading families and of some white-collar workers. The master weavers of Chanderi have trade links with Delhi, Mumbai, Bhopal, Jaipur, Indore, Gwalior, Kolkata, etc., but such a connectivity does not percolate down to the weavers and other sections of society. The situation elsewhere is quite different. For example, The supralocal organisations of the Kaikkoolar weavers in Tamil Nadu are engaged in commercial trade, and as such they are quite different from that of the Chanderi weavers. The Kaikkoolar weavers have been a source of wealth, and an independent power to reckon with. They maintained their own armies in the past to protect their commercial interests and also to plunder the agrarian sector. Further, they competed with dominant agriculturists for status, a distinct status identity, showing a high degree of caste solidarity, and also appropriated the identity in politics (Mines, 1984: x).

V

The weavers of Chanderi are weak, poor, subservient and dependent people, compared to the Kaikkoolars. The Ansari and the Koli weavers are insulated and they are a local entity. The Kaikkoolars are a regional/sub-regional social entity in South India, hence their status identity has wider implications. The Chanderi weavers have hardly influenced socio-cultural life of the town. They manufacture for outsiders without connectivity with their customers/users. The master weavers dominate over the weavers, hence no solidarity either on the basis of common economic interests or on caste affinity. The question is: Why the weavers of Chanderi have not confronted the master weavers and the indifferent government, who have not done anything substantially to alleviate their pathetic plight?

The argument that culture obstructs development comes true to a considerable extent in the context of master weavers-weavers relations in Chanderi. The Chanderi weavers are a category, and not a group of people, like various castes and communities. And, they are so heuristically, and not socially and culturally. Since the weavers comprise of Ansaris (Muslims) and Kolis (a scheduled caste), social and cultural divide prevents them from coming together to strive at a common status identity as weavers. The two remain as Muslims and Kolis, rather than as weavers. The advantage of such a socio-cultural divide or of the absence of class solidarity goes to the Jain and Maheshwari master weavers, who are quite conscious of this intra-cultural differentiation of the weavers. The fact is that the master weavers are united both as a category of traders and as a community/caste of Banias (Jains and Maheshwaris). Such a commonality of purpose is possible among the traders because of their socio-cultural homogeneity and a heightened sense of intra-community and intra-class harmony and unity.

The two markets, namely, the Sadar Bazaar and the Main Road Bazaar, constitute the main shopping malls of Chanderi. Most of the Jains and Maheshwaris and some other groups, such as Brahmins and Pathans, conduct their trade transactions in these two bazaars. The poor from amongst these upper sections of society and the lower castes and communities from amongst the Hindus and the Muslims have small grocery shops and other different trade activities in the mohallas and galis of Chanderi.

Culture and development are intertwined somewhat negatively in Chanderi as it is abundantly evident from its social composition, space segregation and related social distances. The layout of its mohallas and galis clearly shows its caste and community centred space formation. The division of the town in terms of the inner and the outer city reflects the social division of the people as the upper caste/community and class people on the one hand and the lower caste/community and class on the other. Such a divide commensurates social, economic and political differences between the people inhabiting the two parts of Chanderi. Another dimension of social space segregation is the fact that out of 86 mohallas, 48 are inhabited by single castes, 14 have mainly Muslims along with some Hindu castes, and the remaining 24 have Hindu castes without Muslims. Of these, several mohallas are named after particular castes and communities, some also bear historically important landmarks. Thus, social space is ingrained in the town as a whole, and it is reflected in the actions and behaviour of individuals, families and groups of people. Space segregation, space distance and space negation are both objective and subjective constructions in Chanderi (Sharma, 2002; see also Lynch, 1977).

More than the caste-based pluralism, the community-centred multiculturalism characterises the social fabric of Chanderi. Muslims, Jains and Hindus (mainly Brahmins and Kolis) matter in Chanderi, numerically as well as economically and politically. Since the Muslims and Jains have a phenomenal presence (nearly 50% of Chanderi's population), the other groups, namely, Brahmins, Kolis, Chamars, Dhimars, etc., have remained dormant, and therefore, caste hierarchy has also not acquired a rigid and elaborate posture and functioning. In other words, multiculturalism has overtaken the caste hierarchy in Chanderi. Multiculturalism runs counter to caste hierarchy, and it promotes economic and political interests of the non-Hindu communities. Muslims and Jains are quite discrete with regard to their socio-cultural and economic and political ties with caste-Hindus. At times, they behave as exclusive social entities, and in some situations express their close proximity with Brahmins, Kolis and some other castes, keeping in view their economic and political interests.

However, this does not imply that caste does not remain central to people's perceptions of space segregation. At least, apparently, multiculturalism and pluralism have a balanced presence, by way of respective strength and standing of Hindus, Muslims and Jains. In general, such a situation discourages and demotivates people to achieve higher status by way of quality education, migration and mobility, but it has also some positive gains. In Chanderi, caste rivalries and communal divides have not been heard of in public spheres and spaces.

Non-antagonism has become an essential element of social life. Although people recognise classes, distinctions and differences based on assets and property, political power and influence, and caste and community, yet they live with all these inequalities with a sense of reconciliation and a reality 'taken for granted', without attempting crystallisation of the underlying contradictions of the class structure. Only once, a committee headed by P.K. Lahiri (1979), the then Commissioner of the Gwalior Division, highlighted on the exploitation and alienation of the weavers by the master weavers. Some points of the Lahiri Committee demythologised the gospel of harmony and cooperation between the weavers and the master weavers. However, implementation of the recommendations of the Lahiri Committee brought only momentary relief by way of one-time subsidies and loans to the weavers. A short-lived encouragement to the cooperatives and one-time financial support to the weavers could not shake up the deeply entrenched hold of the master weavers on the weavers. No direct restrictions and checks were slapped on the master weavers. After the weakening of the cooperative sector in Chanderi during the past ten years, the hold of the master weavers on the weaving and weavers has again become as strong as it was before the implementation of the recommendations of the Lahiri Committee. Multiculturalism, reinforcing inequality of its main actors, namely, Jains, Muslims and Kolis or of the master weavers and the weavers (Ansaris and Kolis), has resurfaced with old face and functioning. Withdrawal of the state support has weakened class antagonism and sharpening of the clash of interests (Sharma, 1999: 93–95).

Underlying such an apparent multiculturalism is the real face of Chanderi's social structure and its inequalities. Multiculturalism in Chanderi refers to its space-status nexus vis-à-vis space segregation. The geographical space distribution has been transformed and appropriated into the socio-cultural space allocation. The fact is that Chanderi is a socio-spatially divided formation, stratified in terms of recognisable castes/communities, families and individuals. Mohallas, galis and bazaars are arenas of such stratified entities. Appropriation of space is seen in social distances in everyday life. For example, the Sadar Bazaar is nearly an exclusive fiefdom of the upper castes, namely, Jains and

Brahmins. The Main Road Bazaar has new entrepreneurs who have recently taken up trade and commerce and they are very different from traditional Jains and Maheshwaris who have a near-monopoly over the sari trade.

VI

The clearly demarcated spatial segments (mohallas) in Chanderi commensurate with graded social divisions among its inhabitants. The wards, formally carved out divisions for municipal administration, do not reflect social divisions, like the mohallas and the *galis*. The spatial divisions are not viewed by the people as territorial units, but are recognised and accepted as cultural sites and living marks of abodes and identities. In Chanderi, geographical demarcations (mohallas and galis) thus amount to socio-cultural markers, insulations, and inclusions, though in varying degrees. Every mohalla comprises of one major caste/sub-caste/community, and by virtue of its long inhabitation and numerical strength, it becomes quite domineering in relation to some families of other castes and communities which have come to live there. Generally, the migrant families have their houses on the margins of the *mohallas* and *galis*. Their spatial marginality goes along with their social and cultural status in the mohallas in which they live. Even, the new localities (spaces) such as Fatehabad, Rajghat dam and Bunkar colonies have become status-specific settlements. Fatehabad houses government servants; Rajghat dam colony comprises of engineers and high-ranking officials of the project; and the Bunkar colony has weavers (Ansaris and Kolis).

Thus, allocation of space among different castes and communities is a well-recognised consideration of status determination. More than the type and the size of a house, the mohalla, in which one lives, is the basis of a family's status identity. Certainly, the perception of space segregation is largely formed by the underlying structural reality of caste, class and ancestry, and at the same time, such an identity reinforces the persisting social differentiation. People in Chanderi have a mindset to see themselves as space-segregated entities, and this has come to stay through a process of internalisation of their respective social enclaves (mohallas). But such a world view has not been a hinderance in acceptance of modernity, a new space structure, and new patterns of status and honour. Some families have bought lands on roadsides in the outskirts of the town. Some have come out of the Sadar Bazaar to open up new shops elsewhere.

It is clear that space segregation, as a basis of status identity, is acceptable to the people so long as it does not come in the way of decent living and livelihood. So far, in most cases, space, status (culture) and economy have been in harmony, and in perfect congruence. Within the mohallas, people have enacted changes in their specific abodes and domains of life, while retaining the basic character of their caste/community living. This is how one finds in Chanderi a co-existence of tradition and modernity, old and new forms and practices. The space which one occupies has a meaning and gives a message to a given person for presenting himself/herself in relation to others. Thus, cultural enactment has its basis in space, and space does not remain a physical entity, it becomes a 'social fact', a reality of life. No space, no cultural enactment. There is a clear space-status interactive nexus in Chanderi.

Correspondence between community spaces and public spaces is quite distinct in Chanderi. For example, Ansaris and Kolis are engaged in sari manufacturing since ages; Jains and Maheshwaris are pursuing trade and commerce; and Brahmins are overwhelming in teaching profession. Shopkeeping, salaried jobs and agriculture are the main occupations of the Pathans, and they consider weaving as a degrading pursuit. Barbers, potters, blacksmiths, sweepers, etc., continue to follow their traditional occupations, though not as per the *Chakarana deh*.

Thus, besides the caste and community-based segregation, the space-centred mode of living, adherence to traditional occupations and social ethics, ethics of economic behaviour and political dominance are quite strong in Chanderi. But, at the same time, people are very well aware of distinctions in terms of rich and poor, strong and weak, resourceful and resourceless, *bade adami* (great men) and *chhote log* (poor folk). Such a realisation means an acceptance of the reality of socio-economic and political inequalities and superimposition of 'cultural materialism'.

VII

No doubt, the Chanderi weavers have learned more the 'culture of silence' than that of protest, yet some of them are vocal in expression of their woes. The superior artisans have started working independently as they are highly skilled and earn substantially. A good number of them, nearly 50 per cent, have taken up marketing of their products, and some are aspiring to become master weavers as they are excellent weavers and designers. Some other indications of upward mobility of weavers and other groups of people can be discerned.

Chanderi has a unique economic formation and class structure. It has capital but no capitalism. There are entrepreneurs but no directly employed workers. Chanderi has industry (sari manufacturing), but no industrialisation. There are workers, but no fixed wages for them. Thus, 'proto-industrialisation' characterises Chanderi; it is a sort of 'pre-industrial city'. Several other economic activities, namely, *biri* (local cigarette) making (see, for example, Kriedt et al., 1981; Sjoberg, 1960), stone quarrying, pottery, basket-making are hardly noticed in Chanderi because of involvement of a few workers. Certainly, the white-collar workers are a notable addition to the class structure of the town in recent years without creating any perceptible antagonism and cleavages.

State intervention in terms of incentives, technical help, training of weavers, subsidies and loans has stimulated growth and benefited both the weavers and the master weavers. Chanderi is sustaining itself; it is moving forward. Everyone survives in Chanderi, hence no full unemployment, and no beggars. People are contended with the easily available means of survival in the town.

Akos Ostor's study (1984) of legend, theatre, bazaar and rebellion in a Bengal town has certain features in common with our study of Chanderi. We will make a reference to the bazaar of the Bengali town to compare and contrast with Chanderi. The town serves as a centre for the distribution and 'export' of local produce and of the 'imported' from outside. Like Chanderi, the Bengali town is a centre of administration. Some new wealth has come to the town in the form of contracts, expansion of offices, educational institutions, banks, government agencies, etc., like Chanderi. The occupants of the offices in the Bengali town are from outside like Chanderi. Both Chanderi and the Bengali town are centres of small, cottage and handicraft industries. Similar to Chanderi, the Bengali town has marked divisions of society and locality both in the sense of segmentary separation and hierarchical unification. Ostor considers bazaar as a living reality and as a cultural domain of action. "Bazaar denotes a set of relationships among persons and groups differentiated and mediated by various symbols and categories" (ibid.: 11–12). Further, Ostor observes: "We find a cultural form and a structure in the bazaar system of relationships". Hence, bazaar is not merely an idiom of 'economic' action (ibid.: 153–55). The Sadar Bazaar in Chanderi is an enactment of social relationships of more than the Bengali town because of its compactness, age-old ownership of the shops and residences, pre-eminence of trading castes and sari trade. Everything looks indigeneous in the Sadar Bazaar of Chanderi, and this alone makes it a cultural arena with economic strings and power politics. In such a situation, modernisation of the bazaar is not an easy task. Development does not take a jump, it lingers on. Chanderi is not an example of 'returning to culture' after witnessing the ills of modernisation, but it is a situation of postmodernity without having modernity, like 'deschooling' without schooling. Certainly, some people benefit from the continuity of tradition, and they often oppose innovations relating to trade and commerce and other economic and political ventures.

References

Bayly, C.A., 1980, "The Small Town and Islamic Gentry in North India: The Case of Kara", in Kenneth Ballhatchet and John Harrison (eds.), *The City of South Asia: Pre-modern and Modern*, London: Curzon Press.

——, 1992, *Rulers, Townsmen and Bazaars: North India in the Age of British Expansion, 1780–1870*, Cambridge: Cambridge University Press (Indian edition).

Bottomore, Tom, 1985, *A Dictionary of Marxist Thought* (paperback), Oxford: Basil Blackwell.

Bourdieu, Pierre, 1991, *Language and Symbolic Power*, Oxford: Polity Press.

——, 1995, "The Field of Cultural Production", (Editor's Introduction), Cambridge: Polity Press.

——, 1996, *Distinction* (paperback), London: Routledge & Kegan Paul.

Fazl, Abul, 1949, *Ain-e-Akbari*, Vol. II, translated by H.S. Jarrett, revised by J.N. Sarkar, Calcutta: Royal Society of Bengal.

Fox, Richard G., 1969, *From Zamindar to Ballot Box: Community Change in a North Indian Market Town*, New York: Cornell University Press.

Fussman, G. et al., 2003, *Chanderi*, (Three part in French, with a summary in Part III in English and Hindi), Paris: Edition – Diffusion De Boccard.

Gellner, Ernest, 1994, *Reason and Culture*, Cambridge: Blackwell.

Islam, M.S., 1980, "Life in the Mafassal Towns of Nineteenth Century Bengal", in Ballhatchat and Harrison, op. cit.

Kriedt, Peter, Hans Medick and Jurgen Schlumbohm, 1981, *Industrialization before Industrialization: Rural Industry in the Genesis of Capitalism,* New York: Cambridge University Press.

Lahiri, P.K., 1979, Chanderi me Hathkargha Udyog Adhyan Dal Ka Prativedan (Report of the Study Team of Handloom Industry in Chanderi), Government of Madhya Pradesh.

Lukacs, Gyorgy, 1920 (1970), "The Old Culture and the New Culture", quoted from Tom Bottomore.

Lynch, Kevin, 1977, *The Image of the City* (14th edition), (on culture and imagenery of three American cities), Cambridge: MIT Press.

Milner, Andrew and Jeff Browite, 2003, *Contemporary Cultural Theory* (Indian Edition), Jaipur: Rawat Publications.

Mines, Mattison, 1984, *The Warrior Merchants: Textiles, Trade, and Territory in South India*, Cambridge: Cambridge University Press.

Ostor, Akos, 1984, *Culture and Power: Legend, Ritual, Bazaar and Rebellion in a Bengali Society*, New Delhi: Sage Publications.

Schech, Susanne and Jane Haggis, 2000, *Culture and Development: A Critical Introduction*, Oxford: Blackwell.

Sharma, K.L., 2002, "The Social Organisation of Urban Space: A Case Study of Chanderi, a Small Town in Central India", *Contributions to Indian Sociology*, December, 2003.

——, 1999, *Chanderi 1990–1995*, Paris: Edition Diffusion De Boccard.

Sjoberg, G., 1960, *The Preindustrial City: Past and Present*, New York: Free Press.

Weber, Max, 1946, "Class, Status and Party", in *From Max Weber: Essays in Sociology*, edited and translated by H.H. Gerth and C.Wright Mills, New York: Oxford University Press.

8

The Social Organisation of Urban Space

A Case Study of a Small Town in Central India

Space and status are inextricably related to each other. Though space is a geographic entity, human society has a tendency to transform it into a socio-cultural phenomenon. Such a process of appropriation of space refers to trends of social change and status formation. Space segregation thus implies 'social distance'. Underlying a given space segregation, one can see the structure of society in terms of the ramifications of caste, class and ethnicity. Our study of Chanderi, a small town in Madhya Pradesh, shows that segregated *mohallas* (neighbourhoods) and *galis* (lanes) largely correspond with graded social divisions based on caste and community. Space segregation and commensurate social divisions do not obstruct the incorporation of modernity in the social fabric of the town.

> Our study also shows that space is not static. It is made and remade in accordance with the dynamics of social relations and status formation. Since space is social, it is appropriated by the privileged sections of society to their advantage. As such, tradition has a considerable hold in Chanderi. To a certain extent, tradition also prevails over modernity in Chanderi in terms of the patron-client ties between the master-weavers and weavers with regard to saree production and trade. *Mohallas* and *galis* continue to correspond with the ranking of the patrons and clients (master-weavers and weavers) or the upper and the lower castes/communities, including Muslims.

> Sociology has to include a sociology of the perception of the social world, that is, a sociology of the construction of the world-views which themselves contribute to the construction of this world (Bourdieu, 1990: 130).

The concept of 'space' is key to the understanding of how people conceive their social world. We may define space as a natural, non-cultural and purely geographic aspect of human existence. But this would not be a sociological definition of space. Human society invariably tries to translate, transform and appropriate geographical spaces such as land, locations, mountains, rivers, etc., into cultural objects, possessions and assets. The transformation of geographical 'space' into 'social space' is not only an ongoing and dynamic process, but involves also scientific, technical and political dimensions. The making and remaking of space implies a process of status formation and the appropriation of physical and cultural endowments. Ultimately, the delineation of social space affects individuals, families, groups, neighbourhoods, villages, cities and even nations in everyday life (Gupta, 2000). Thus, there is an omnipresent and ubiquitous process of space formation that is consequent upon social practices and that may have supralocal consequences. Each person knows his or her space in the social world but, on occasions, this may be at variance with how other people view it. 'Space segregation' prevails both at the subjective as well as the objective levels. Space segregation implies 'social distance' between people, including the semaphoring of social hierarchy. The recognition of distance, and also the negation of distance by way of political struggles, speak of both formal and substantive constructions of the social world. The question is: How does space segregation take place? A quick answer, anticipating our discussion, would be that the advantaged, upwardly mobile and highly motivated members of a society appropriate a given geographical space by converting it into socio-cultural space, using their skills and networks. At any given point of time a society can be seen as a socio-spatially divided structure stratified in terms of recognisable social groups, families and individuals. Bourdieu (1990: 128) writes: "In fact, social distances are written into bodies or more exactly, into the relationship to the body, to language and to time". This implies that distinctions of caste and class are significantly marked out in social space. In this case study we hope to exemplify this by examining a small town in Madhya Pradesh named Chanderi.

Space-Status Nexus

The town of Chanderi in Guna district of Madhya Pradesh is an early medieval town famous for its historical monuments and architecture, as well as for a traditional form of town planning. It is idyllic located on a hill surrounded by the Vindyanchal range on three sides. Today, it is well known as a manufacturing centre for fine cotton and silk cloth, particularly sarees, for urban middle and upper-middle class women. All of these factors are relevant for understanding the nexus between space and status in operational terms. Chanderi has clearly demarcated spatial segments commensurate with the graded social divisions among its inhabitants. The formal administrative divisions, namely, wards, do not reflect social divisions as clearly as do the *mohallas* (neighbourhoods) and the *galis* (lanes). These spatial divisions are not viewed by the people simply as territorial units in the town; they are accepted more as cultural sites and living marks of abodes and identities. Geographical demarcations thus amount to socio-cultural markers as well as insulations and inclusions, though in varying degrees.

It is interesting to note that those who have their houses located on the margins of *mohallas* and *galis* also become 'marginal' socially and culturally. On the other hand, such people have the advantage of serving as social bridges linking both sides of the *mohallas* and *galis*. This is particularly true of the walled city and the old walled-in-like *mohallas* in the outer city. Retaining tradition in the walled city and in the medieval parts of the outer city is an important concern, as status and honour are associated with and derived from it. The allocation of space to different castes and communities in Chanderi is a well-recognised aspect of status determination. This form of space segregation, with its explicit unevenness, is taken for granted because it is transmitted from generation to generation.

The perception of space segregation is formed largely because of underlying structural constraints, most notably, caste and class-based distinctions. The taken-for-granted social world is thus seen through 'mental structures' and these are in turn the product of an internalisation of structures of the social world (Bourdieu, 1990: 13). Edmund Husserl called this process a 'doxic modality' of apprehending the social world (quoted from ibid.: 125).

Simultaneously, Chanderi has also been absorbing modernity during the past one hundred years. Modernity not only creates a new space structure and thereby new patterns of status and honour, it also weakens traditional expressions of these themes. Since tradition and modernity are not absolute phenomena and the two could co-exist, one may think of a third paradigm of space and status in the form of a synthesis of tradition and modernity. Chanderi looks both old and new, as well as traditional and modern. If *mohallas* and *galis* represent tradition, new offices, shops, markets, institutions, residences, college, etc., symbolise modernity. As these exhibits of modernity have not wiped out traditional spatial and residential patterns, there is a co-existence of the two. This has contributed to a certain smoothness in Chanderi's social fabric.

In this regard, I go along with Dipankar Gupta's analysis of space and culture. Gupta (2000: 39) observes:

> Cultures are enacted in a space with all its dimensions. Cultures thus become palpable realities and ostensible facts. Cultures are not locked up in remote empyrean recesses but are enacted and need to be expressed in a variety of existential settings. This obviously presumes a space; no space, no cultural enactment. The longer the duration of a certain cultural space the greater is its identification with that culture. This also allows certain voices to consolidate themselves as regnant meanings of root metaphors. These voices have to do with the specifics of the cultural locale for the space. The specifics of the space and its diacritics are reflected in the various preferred innuendos and localities of the root metaphors.

For us, then, 'space' is both a physical entity as well as a cultural/social phenomenon. The people of Chanderi know the separation of one *mohalla* from another. Yet what is more significant for them is the name of the *mohalla* and the meaning and the message it gives to its members and to other inhabitants. This is how 'space' becomes a cultural construct and a determinant of status. People are well aware of the 'official classification' of wards and their actual delineations. In social life, however, it is the classification of *galis* and *mohallas* that is a more effective marker of identity and social ties. The following pages will dilate upon Chanderi's space-status interactive nexus.

Situating Chanderi as a Socio-cultural Space

Chanderi is an appropriate town for the study of the space-status nexus because it is both an extraordinary and an ordinary town. Populationwise, it is like any small town, but its rich cultural heritage, archaeological wealth and traditional craftsmanship make Chanderi unique. It is an ordinary town in some respects because it has all the features of a modern urban centre—banks, colleges, schools, roads, means of transport and communication, government offices, a police station, etc. But the effects of its long history are also discernible. Chanderi was not only the headquarters of a *suba* (province) in the reign of Akbar (1556–1605 AD), but also a substantially large town and cultural centre located at a strategic point on the trade route between north and south India. The urbanity of Chanderi was a matter of great pride in medieval times. Therefore, modern Chanderi cannot be judged solely on the basis of its size, or in terms of its recent history: this would not bring out its specific cultural ethos. Again, in spite of the fact that more than 50 per cent of Chanderi's population is dependent on weaving, Chanderi cannot be considered solely as a market/manufacturing town; nor is it a suburban or overgrown artisan village (Sharma, 1999).

Chanderi was always 'urban', and it was never a village in the garb of a town. Classifications like 'entrepot markets', 'regional entrepot', 'suburban artisan village' (Bayly, 1980: 21–24), and zamindari towns, European factory towns, or even transient mufassal towns, do not fit Chanderi. This is because Chanderi is not a town that lies between a village and a city. It is also not a residual entity, for village idioms and practices as well as a distinctive urbanity are to be found intermixed here in varying degrees.

What Akos Ostor (1984) says about a Bengal town applies to Chanderi as well. Local legends, rituals, bazaars, and memories of rebellion act as effective conceptual tools for probing into the cultural spaces within Chanderi, as well as Chanderi as a social space *sui generis*. The notions of *itihas* (history), *bazaar* (market), *sarkar* (government) and *andolan* (rebellion), as used by Ostor, can provide a convincing description of the dialectics of Chanderi's social formation. The description of Chanderi in *Ain-e-Akbari*, the vivacity of Sadar Bazaar with its *sahukars* and traders, the Mutiny of 1857 and the heroism of Tantia Tope in Chanderi, and the erstwhile power of the *rajas* and feudal lords have all left their traces over the entire gamut of Chanderi society.

The cultural heritage of Chanderi, which is evident in its natural endowments, historical monuments and objects and in the manufacturing of fine muslin fabrics,[1] has generated a strong sense of belonging and attachment to the town. The symbolic strength that people derive from Chanderi's cultural panorama is quite remarkable. Literary production and the cultural orientation of the people of Chanderi are dependent to a great extent upon what exists in Chanderi as a historical reality. The members of Chanderi's literati are aware of Chanderi's history and make positive references to it. Booklets, articles, reports, documents, etc., on Chanderi, are all known to a large cross-section of the people.[2] Chanderi has clearly an identity of its own and its people have a creative imagination rooted in memories, both mythic and historical, of the town.

Urbanisation, de-urbanisation and, lately, re-urbanisation characterise Chanderi's ups and downs. The *Ain-e-Akbari* gives us an idea of its past grandeur with mosques and caravanserais (Jarrett, 1949: 207, 212–14). The decline of Chanderi's administrative status to that of a sub-tehsil after 1857 indicated its downfall, but recent developments during the past two decades give evidence of its re-urbanisation. Chanderi's administrative status has been elevated to that of a tehsil and sub-divisional headquarters. This is in recognition of the fact that it has as many as forty offices, a postgraduate college, and a network of roads and bus routes within its confines. The expansion of markets, the establishment of telecommunication and trade links with major cities and towns, the emergence of a 'service gentry' and, finally, the commercialisation of saree manufacture and trade are recent developments. Interestingly, the manufacturing and selling of sarees are still carried out to a large degree in a traditional format. Production and trade continue to be family-based, though they are influenced by modern communication and technology. *Galis* and *mohallas* also retain traditional caste/community patterns, even as such forms of tradition are showing signs of accommodation with the present.

After Chanderi's rise to the status of a tehsil, and subsequently to the rank of sub-divisional headquarters, its population grew (during 1981–91) by as much as 64.63 per cent, whereas growth was only 21 per cent during the preceding decade. As the headquarters of a tehsil and sub-division, Chanderi has now become an important administrative town. It, therefore, has its complement of offices relating to block development, education, irrigation, forest, and so forth, which have given an impetus to Chanderi's population growth. An appreciable expansion in the handloom industry widened trade links and also encouraged outsiders (weavers) to visit Chanderi. Some of them even stayed on and settled down in Chanderi.

Chanderi's Urbanity

Is Chanderi 'urban' despite its small size? In 1911, the population of Chanderi was just 2,753 nearly half of what was in 1891. Up to 1951, Chanderi remained a type VI town—the smallest administrative category. Most of its inhabitants were dependent upon non-agricultural occupations. As per the 1991 census, Chanderi's population rose to nearly 20,000, and it was about 25,000 by 2001. During the decade of 1981–91, Chanderi was not only granted a higher administrative status due to the phenomenal increase in its population, but it also had the privilege of being chosen for development under the auspices of the Special Area Development Authority (SADA).[3] The SADA had the following aims: (i) to determine the use of land in future keeping in view situational, physical, natural and other related aspects; (ii) to renovate objects and places of archaeological significance, and to determine future plans of land use for their protection and development; and (iii) to promote and expand the traditional handloom industry by providing building, technical knowhow, quality improvement and provision for training facilities (Julka, 1985).

Two obvious outcomes of this plan were, first, the rejuvenation of Chanderi's rich cultural heritage; and second, the re-urbanisation of the town by way of new programmes and activities. The cultural revival of Chanderi was visualised as a complementary aspect of its re-urbanisation.

Urban life, as a cultural phenomenon, is visible in Chanderi in a variety of ways. Chanderi has many bazaars and a fairly diversified occupational structure, as well as several educational institutions, healthcare facilities, and other civic amenities. Even, the lifestyles of Chanderi residents are infected with consumer-oriented aspirations. But, this apparent urbanity has a village-like ethos and culture hidden within it. Social relations, intra-caste/community ties, spatial segregation, behavioural patterns and other forms of primary activities make Chanderi a rural-like settlement as well. On the other hand, Chanderi poses no difficulty as a town as far as its formal identification is concerned. From 1871 to 2001, Chanderi has been formally identified as a town, not so much because of its size as for its history, culture and architecture. However, urbanism as a way of life and idiom of social relations has not made major inroads in the interrelations between Chanderi's residents. The gestalt of family structure, and the adherence to certain socio-cultural values in interpersonal relations, remain traditional in many respects even today. For example, in Chanderi, the traditional values have remained largely intact as people often meet and interact in the bazaar and in *nukkads* (corners) of *mohallas* and *galis,* at *pan* shops and tea stalls. More than these common arenas of social interaction, community-specific festivals such as Teej, Gangore, Dussehera, Diwali, Holi, temples, *jagrans,* etc., for Hindus; and mosques, *namaz* (prayer), *madarsas, anjumans,* etc., for Muslims, provide opportunities for social intercourse. Some common activities, such as *mushairas* and *kavi sammelans,* involve a cross-section of people in Chanderi.

The social space of Chanderi is clearly observable to its citizens at two levels: (i) through popular literature; and (ii) through observation of the nexus between cultural ambience and social status. An examination of various popular writings, pamphlets, guides and historical texts reveals the importance Chanderi enjoys as a town *(nagar/nagari)* in these documents.[4] Since Chanderi was situated on the trade route between north and south India in the medieval period, its importance was considerable. The *Budhi* (old) Chanderi's ruins of Jain temples on the banks of the Urvashi river speak of its glorious past, and even today they are deemed to be architecturally very significant. The belief that Chanderi was a pre-Vedic town bearing the name Chandrapuram, which was later on known as Chedi in the Mahabharat period, or Chandragiri or Chandesh, creates another image of the town as one with a rich cultural heritage going back to very ancient times. The ruins of buildings, houses, forts, temples, mosques, etc., indicate the important cultural and political status that Chanderi enjoyed in the medieval period.

History and Cultural Imagery

More than the authenticity of the perceptions and images about Chanderi, the perception of Chanderi itself as a magnificent town has become an acknowledged reality. Rivers, fountains, lakes, *baolis* (step-wells), forests, hills, monuments, temples, mosques and *talabs* (ponds) provide existential evidence of the wonder that Chanderi was. Badal Mahal, Dilli

Darwaza, Koshak Mahal, Zami Masjid, Khandargiri, Jageshwari temple and numerous other sites make Chanderi distinctly different from other neighbouring towns in the region, such as Guna, Ashok Nagar, Mungaoli and Lalitpur. The people of Chanderi are also aware of the many historical inscriptions found in Chanderi. The post-10th century period is historically better known, and its historical records are taken to be more authentic than descriptions of the earlier period. As noted, the power dynamics of the later period and the cultural wealth of the earlier period are known to most of the enlightened residents of Chanderi. Most of the upper castes and middle class residents of Chanderi can knowledgeably refer to Alberuni, Ibn Battuta, Kirtidurga, Ghiyas-ud-din Balban, Ala-ud-din Khilji, Ghori, Rana Sanga, Medini Rai, Ibraham Lodi, Babur, Rudra Pratab, Sher Shah Suri, Akbar, Bundelas, Scindias, etc.

An apt example of this image is based on an account reported in the *Ain-e-Akbari.* After the fall of Malwa, Akbar took over Chanderi in 1569, and made it the headquarters of a *sarkar* in the *subah* of Malwa (Jarrett, 1949). The *Ain-e-Akbari* describes Chanderi in great detail as a large settlement, with 14,000 stone houses, 12,000 mosques, 384 markets and 360 spacious caravanserais. Besides these, Chanderi had 61 *mahals,* 5,54,277 *bighas* and 17 *biswas* of land, and maintained a cavalry of 5,970, an infantry of 66,085, and 90 elephants. Fourteen thousand houses were meant for a population of two lakhs. Whether such a description is accurate or not is not relevant. What is important is that people know of these descriptions and often glorify them. Even the intriguing and puzzling political biography of Chanderi is interpreted as an indicator of its strategic importance in the past. That it functioned once as the headquarters of a *sarkar* in Akbar's reign has added to its image and image-making.

The appreciation of Chanderi as a celebrated place for cultural wealth and the manufacture of muslin cloth has contributed to a romanticised image of the town. The establishment of the SADA in Chanderi in place of a Municipal Committee about two decades ago, and the elevation of Chanderi from a *tappa* (sub) *tehsil* to a full-fledged *tehsil* and sub-divisional headquarters, have not only given it a new administrative status, but have also led to the process of re-urbanisation and employment generation. The manufacturing of fine muslin cloth had generally been conducive to the multicultural character of the town, as it involved different communities and categories of people such as Muslims, Kolis, Jains, government functionaries, and outsiders (traders from major towns of India). Even the decline of the town as a manufacturing centre and the takeover by the British in 1857 after the defeat of Tantia Tope, the multicultural character of the town remained by and large intact. The economic revival of this town came by way of the introduction of weavers' cooperatives, and government subsidies and loans to the weavers. Nearly 25 per cent of the saree trade slipped from local traders and master-weavers to the cooperatives. The use of the Badal Mahal (a medieval palace, now a ruined monument), as an insignia on Chanderi sarees by the local administration, signifies harmony between economy and culture.

Today, despite numerous government offices and civic amenities and the level of social relations, Chanderi still retains many village-like characteristics. These are easily visible in the manner in which castes and communities interact, and also in the way spatial segregation is linked to status hierarchy. This is despite being a town for the past 1,000 years and more according to recorded history.

Caste/Community Structure and Space Organisation

A curious correspondence between caste/community structure and space organisation (that is, *mohallas* and *galis)* has upheld the diverse cultural character of Chanderi. The four main castes/communities of Chanderi, namely, Brahmins, Kolis,

Jains and Muslims, also constitute its three major religious communities, that is, Hindus, Jains and Musalmans. Together, they form approximately 75 per cent of the population of Chanderi. If we add to this castes like Chamars, Kachhis, Nais and Kumhars, then, these eight groups would make 90 per cent of the population of Chanderi. Though the Brahmins are at the top of the ritual hierarchy and ahead of other groups with regard to education and white-collar jobs, Muslims and Jains, who together form 50 per cent of Chanderi's population, control saree manufacturing, trade and commerce, and, in effect, the town's economy. The dominating numerical and economic presence of Muslims and Jains discourages the rigid observance of caste in everyday life. Some other castes, such as Chamar, Dhimar, Kachhi, Nai, Kumhar, etc., are reasonably numerous, but their presence in the affairs of Chanderi is minimal. On the other hand, though Rajputs are numerically a small caste, their overall status and dominance is even higher than that of Muslims, Jains and Brahmins. Some Rajputs are addressed even today as *Raja* or *Raja Bhaiya.*[5]

We have collected information about thirty five castes and communities (see Table 1).[6] All Muslim groups, including Pathans, Sheikhs, Momins, Kunjaras and Dhobis have been shown as one category. They constitute about one-third of the population of Chanderi.[7]

As Table 1 shows, there is a great degree of social and cultural diversity in Chanderi. This also has an impact on the allocation and distribution of space in terms of economic and cultural status. Muslims, Jains, Kolis and Brahmins still largely pursue their traditional occupations, viz., weaving, commerce, weaving, and teaching, respectively. Other castes also generally continue with their traditional occupations because, being numerically small, they find them viable even in the present situation. It needs to be mentioned that the *jajmani* system has never been a strong mechanism for regulating inter-caste relations in Chanderi. However, a considerable nexus between

Table 1
Chanderi Castes in 1992

Name of the Caste	*Number of Households*
Muslim	800
Jain	284
Brahmin	245
Koli (SC-Scheduled Caste)	301
Chamar (SC)	129
Dhimar (SC-fishermen)	98
Kachhi (vegetable growers)	59
Sihare (traders, formerly alcohol-sellers)	54
Nai (barbers)	47
Rawat (ST-Scheduled Tribe)	34
Soni (jewellers)	33
Basore (SC-basket-makers, band-masters)	31
Kumhar (pot-makers)	29
Khatik (SC-butchers)	29
Rajput	30
Mali (flower-growers)	19
Sahu or Teli (oil-makers)	19
Kayastha	18
Maheshwari (traders, Banias)	5
Mogia (ST-ex-criminal tribe)	10
Khangar, Mirdha (SC-watchmen)	9
Dakot (low-caste priests)	8
Punjabi	6
Jogi (OBC-beggars)	5
Katia (SC-former cotton-spinners)	5
Gadaria (herdsmen)	5
Shejwari (cot-makers)	4
Mehtar (SC-sweepers)	30
Ahir (herdsmen)	3
Darzi (tailors)	20
Lakhera (bangle-makers)	3
Kadera (cracker-makers)	3
Badai (carpenters)	4
Sikh	1
Barar (SC-like Basor)	1
Total Number of Households	2,381

Source: Sharma, 1999: 58.

caste and occupation is evident in the case of about twenty-one castes which continue to pursue their respective traditional occupations, as they did in 1921 in the Gwalior State (see Table 2). Though market forces may have changed the bases and modus operandi of occupational transactions, caste and occupation still largely coincide.

Table 2

Hindu Castes and their Traditional Occupations in the Gwalior State (1921) and in Chanderi (1992)

Name of Caste	*Traditional Occupation*
Ahir	grazing and dairy
Bania (including Jain)	trade and commerce
Brahmin	priesthood
Chamar	leather-work
Darzi	tailoring
Dhimar	fishing, palanquin-bearing
Gadaria	grazing and dairy
Kachhi	cultivation
Kayastha	office-work (white-collar)
Khangar	watchmanship
Khati	carpentry
Khatik	butchery
Koli	weaving
Kumhar	pot-making
Mali	cultivation, gardening
Mehtar	scavenging, sweeping
Mirdha	watchmanship
Nai	hair and nail cutting
Rajput	landholding
Sonar	goldsmithy
Teli	oil-pressing

Sources: Census of India, 1921, Gwalior, Report and Tables (Gwalior Aliah Darbar Press); Sharma 1999: 59.

Space, as a socio-cultural phenomenon, is evident in Chanderi's eighty-six *mohallas* inhabited by thirty-five castes and communities. Some of the *mohallas* are exclusively inhabited by a single caste or community. But, when *mohallas* have more than one caste or community of more or less the same social status, they are generally engaged in similar economic activities. In some single caste/community *mohallas* people are engaged in different economic pursuits because of intra-caste social differentiation. Traditional activities, such as pot-making, hair-cutting, priesthood, trade and commerce, manufacturing of clothes, etc., are pursued on a commercial basis by Kumhars, Nais, Brahmins, Banias, Kolis and Ansaris, respectively. However, there are a few *mohallas* with a plurality of caste groups and a corresponding diversity of occupations. Undoubtedly, in general, a close empirical connection can be seen between *mohalla* (space) and caste/community affiliation in Chanderi. This correspondence has effectively kept caste and community traditions intact. The location of temples, mosques and monuments in different localities also speaks of the spatio-socio-cultural character of the town.

Chanderi can be viewed as a social universe constituted by castes and communities defined by their relative status. The basic principles of differentiation and stratification demarcate boundaries within the universe. Despite socio-cultural homogeneity among the members of a caste/community in a designated social space *(mohalla/gali),* differences in economic and power relations are still discernible. Thus, the position of a given family in the social space *(mohalla)* is dependent also upon the position it occupies in different domains. So strong is the feeling of spatial attachment that people do not shift to other *mohallas* even if they have the opportunity of living in better conditions. The *mohalla* provides a sense of social security and social recognition.

Twenty-eight of the single caste/group *mohallas* are inhabited solely by Muslim groups. Another twenty are exclusively single caste *mohallas:* in three of them Kolis, in five Jains, and in three others only Brahmins reside, while the remaining nine are inhabited by other castes, singly.

Several of these *mohallas* are named after specific castes and communities. For example, only Chamars inhabit the Chamaryana *mohalla. Mohallas,* such as Khatikyana, Basoryana, Dhimaryana, Dhubiyana, Lalaji Ki Gali and Ghusyana, are eponymously named after castes such as Khatik, Basore, Dhimar, Dhobi, Kayastha and Ghosi. Besides these exclusively caste/community-based *mohallas,* in some *mohallas,* castes of nearly equal status reside. The Jogiyana *mohalla* is inhabited by Kolis, Chamars and Kasais with the exception of one Pathan family. Upper caste Hindus live in the Lakshmanji Ka Mandir *mohalla.* Ansaris and Bhangis live in Babaki Baoli, and in the Garmai Baoli *mohalla.* Ansaris and Ghosis reside together. However, there are some exceptions too. One or two upper caste families live in *mohallas* with a preponderance of lower castes and Ansaris. The reverse is also true. Finally, in *mohallas* such as Pancham Nagar Colony, Rajghat Road, Piran Chowk, Har Kund, Bala Khani and Kunjaryana, two or more castes/communities live together.

Map 1 clearly indicates that segregation is the hallmark of the social universe of Chanderi. Sayyids, Pathans and Mughals (upper stratum) and Momins (Ansari weavers) and other Muslims such as Kunjaras and Dhobis live in segregated enclaves. Brahmins, Thakurs and Maheshwaris live in exclusive *mohallas,* as do Jains and Kolis (weavers). Thus, the data of Map 1 and Table 3 substantiate the view that the people of Chanderi, across a wide range of lifestyles, from trade and commerce to weaving and worshipping, have a very strong and deep-rooted socio-spatial consciousness. Such a sense of belonging to a *mohalla* has geographical, social and psychological dimensions.

Map 1

Simplified Map of the Castes Drawn over an Intach Plan

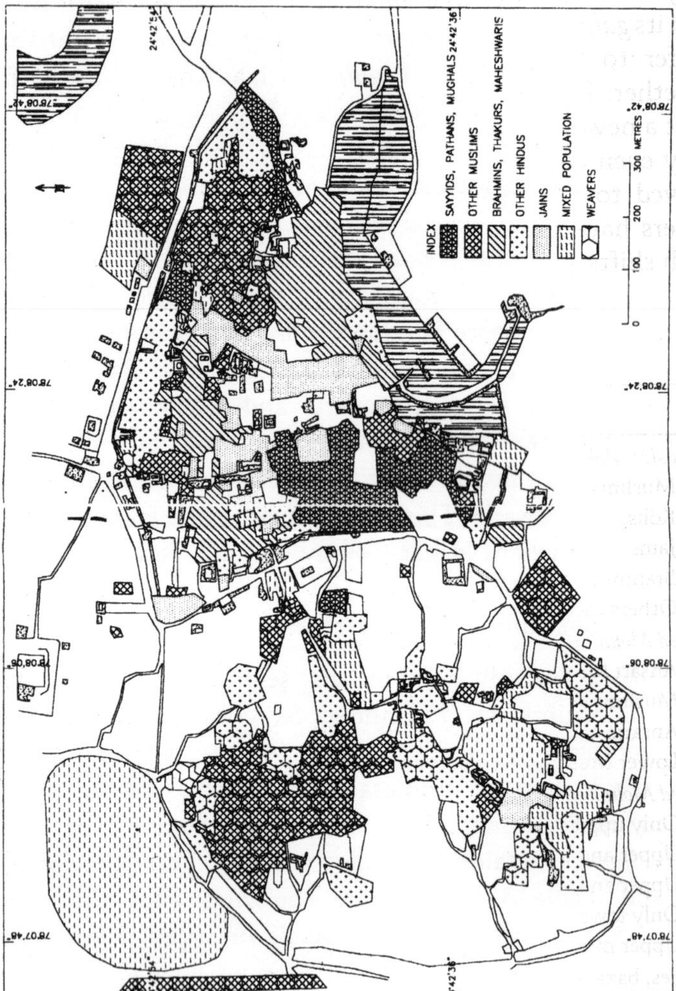

Jain and Maheshwari traders carry out their trade and commerce from their residential premises because it is both convenient and compatible with their lifestyles. They could very well shift their residences from the congested Sadar Bazaar and its *galis* to open areas on the outskirts of the town, but they prefer to keep family, community and economic activities together. However, when the people of Chanderi are certain that a new space will provide them higher status ranking, they may even compete to enter such locations. Some people have moved to the roadside market from the walled-in *mohallas;* others have started *dhabas* and hotels on the main road. But such shifts are still not frequent.

Table 3

Caste and Mohallas

	Number
Exclusive Mohallas	
Muslims	28
Kolis	3
Jains	5
Brahmins	3
Others castes	9
Mixed Mohallas (Muslims and other castes)	
Ansari Muslims and Kolis	4
Muslims (Pathans and upper castes)	4
Ansaris and other castes	5
Lower Muslims and other castes	1
Mixed Mohallas (without Muslims)	
Only upper castes	1
Upper and middle castes	1
Upper and lower castes	5
Only lower castes	5
Upper middle and lower castes	5
Offices, bazaars, etc.	7
Total number of mohallas	86

Source: Sharma, 1999: 40–42. (Though 96 *Mohallas* and *galis* have been counted, we have authenticated the social composition of only 86 of these.)

Chanderi is urban because of its recognition as a town in the census reports, and in terms of the existing civic amenities, bazaars, transport and communication networks, and educational institutions. Besides such infrastructural amenities, the historical and cultural significance of Chanderi has added to its urbanity. Chanderi has clear cultural boundaries drawn through *mohallas* and *galis,* a characteristic feature of small towns. Though *mohalla* identity is quite strong in a general way, what is more crucial is the specific space one enjoys within one's *mohalla,* in terms of caste, community and occupational group. Chanderi's cultural panorama is deeply imbued with traditional values and caste/community identities. All castes and communities observe their own specific celebrations and functions. For Brahmins, temples are a nodal institution. An old Jain temple and the Khandargiri caves are sites of religious activities for the Jains of Chanderi. For Muslims, the Zama Masjid is a sacred place for the Friday prayers. All castes participate in festivals like Gangore, Teej, Dussehera, Holi and Diwali, while *bhajans, kathas, kirtans, satsangs* and *havans* are normal activities in most Hindu temples. Then, there are activities such as *kavi sammelans, mushayaras, nataks, melas,* circus, etc., that are enjoyed by everyone irrespective of caste or creed.

Economy, Urbanism and Culture

Though Chanderi is 'urban', it is not 'modern'. Its current dynamics can be characterised by the term *proto-industrialisation* (Kriedte et al., 1981). The concept of proto-industrialisation aptly characterises the nexus between family, industry, technology and marketing in the manufacturing of silk sarees and muslin cloth. Weaving is what determines the regional and supra-regional importance of Chanderi. Feudalism extended a helping hand to Chanderi industry whenever it was facing a crisis of survival. Thus, Chanderi's proto-industrialisation can be perceived as 'industrialisation before industrialisation' (ibid.: 6). But Chanderi has so far not witnessed 'industrialisation' after proto-industrialisation, as there is no change in the technology and processes of saree production. After the eclipse of feudalism, the state came to the rescue of the industry in Chanderi, to some extent emancipating the weavers from the master-weavers and traders through weavers' cooperatives, loans and subsidies.

Weaving in Chanderi signifies 'family economy', the central feature of which is not to maximise profit and achieve a monetary surplus, but to maximise gross produce at the family level (ibid.: 40–41). This attitude rests on the structure of familial relations of production and consumption. Family's subsistence remains the main concern and the family continues to work until its subsistence is assured (ibid.: 66). Additional needs and contingencies, such as illness, birth, marriage, etc., are met by putting in more labour or by taking advance money from the master-weaver. In Chanderi one could see a close connection between production of cloth and socio-cultural reproduction. The observation made by Medick (ibid.: 66–67) aptly applies to the weavers of Chanderi. Weavers sang at their looms. A trip to the market combined business with social pleasures; exchanging news and courtesies with a craftsman or dealer introduced sociability into an economic or service transaction. Thus, the very nature of the textile industry in Chanderi substantiates our thesis of the space-status nexus. The amalgamation of non-capitalist features with the commercial and entrepreneurial modes of production characterises the economy and class structure of Chanderi. It is a situation of capital without capitalism, of industry without industrialisation, of workers without their organisations or trade unions (Sharma, 1999).

Generally, a weaver in Chanderi has three identities: (i) as a weaver; (ii) as a Muslim or Koli; and (iii) as a resident of a given *mohalla.* This pattern of identity is found among most of the social groups in Chanderi. All three identities, though internally further differentiated, make up a composite identity of a person/family/group as the case may be. While the semiotic or cultural approach of Nita Kumar (1988) assumes that the weavers have their own world, have control over their body, time and space, and have freedom in selection of the design and colour of their products as well as in the choice of instruments of weaving. Deepak Mehta (1992), on the contrary, observes that in the weaving of a highly ritualised cloth like a shroud, which is specific and outside the market economy, the weaver does not have freedom of selection. Our study of Chanderi weaving as a mundane activity shows that weavers are entirely dependent upon the master-weavers, even in the selection of design and colour; as such, weaving is a controlled activity. The existential condition of weavers determines their degree of autonomy and freedom, though state intervention has given them some relief from the bondage inflicted by the master-weavers. Certainly, the image of excellence in saree manufacturing has ensured continuity and perfection in this particular pursuit.

The major traditional occupation in Chanderi is weaving. This makes Chanderi a 'service *qasba'* for outsiders, but it also brings in a degree of commercialism which positions it in a nexus with the outside world, including big metropoles such as Delhi, Mumbai, Chennai and Kolkata. The revival of this traditional lifeline and of the process of re-urbanisation was initiated by the SADA. This significant step has stopped the de-urbanisation process which had started immediately after 1857. Re-urbanisation has created new cultural spaces in terms of the incorporation of offices, authorities, specialists and services. The new infrastructure has made a big difference to Chanderi, reviving the town after a lull of nearly 150 years.

Like many other small towns, Chanderi too has witnessed 'dependent urbanisation'. Dependence on state support and also on the wider economic order has largely determined the re-urbanisation of Chanderi. Small towns also suffer in competition with bigger towns and cities, because the latter corner the lion's share of the available infrastructure and resources. If Chanderi has survived as a town, it is more because of the twinning of its specific and unique cultural situation with SADA-inspired urban renewal programmes.

Though the *mohallas* of Chanderi are caste and community segregated, the municipal wards have a different character. Out of a total of twelve municipal wards, eight are named after modern leaders such as Gandhi, Nehru, Azad and Subhash Chandra Bose. The remaining wards are named after some significant religious symbols such as Jageshwari, Krishna, Hanuman and Bahubal. One can read in the naming of different wards a conscious effort to synthesise tradition and modernity. 'Space' is thus denoted by both tradition and modernity, separately as well as by way of a synthesis. Shops and residences are found together, the former on the ground floor and the latter on the first floor. Such an arrangement is not only convenient, but also eliminates contradiction between people's social and economic life.

A population of about 20,000 people (1991 census) engages in as many as ninety-five different occupations and economic pursuits. This indicates the diversified nature of the urban occupational structure and the 'mix' of traditional and modern occupations. Hair-cutting, shopkeeping, teaching, etc., are performed as non-traditional activities in a 'market situation'. Some new occupations have been almost monopolised by some castes and communities, for example, upper castes control modern trade and commerce, teaching and government jobs.

The social aspect of space is evident even in the commercial zones of the town. New markets do not have even one saree shop, while the old market does not have a single automobile repair shop. Weavers are mostly attached to master-weavers, but some of them are also independent weavers and small entrepreneurs. However, there is an inherent antagonism between the master-weavers and the weavers, though it rarely surfaces in the form of severing economic ties or in agitation for increased wages. Several weavers have emancipated themselves from the control of master-weavers by sheer hard work and superior skills. In the late 1970s and early 1980s, state intervention based on the Lahiri Committee's recommendations (1979) provided considerable relief to the weavers by way of subsidies and loans. About 25 per cent of the saree trade slipped from the master-weavers to the cooperatives, and to the new entrepreneurs who had sprung up from among the weavers themselves.

Concluding Remarks

A paradigm shift in our conceptualisation becomes necessary when people become conscious of their social space and status more than their material and existential conditions. Material objects and events alone do not create the social world in which people live. The natural and material worlds are transformed into the social world by way of social space and status. Our emphasis is on the recognition of the space-status nexus in a small town named Chanderi. Here is a town in which space is constructed on the basis of differentiation and ordered ranks of people in the form of *mohallas* and *galis*. Though Chanderi is a multifaceted town with diverse fields of activities, the space dimension appears in different domains of its social fabric.

In Chanderi, geographical space clearly indicates the space of social relations. Thus, geographic distances are social spaces. In the given situation of Chanderi's *mohallas* and *galis*, new social spaces or divisions may not easily come into being. Hence, a sort of stability characterises Chanderi. So entrenched is this space-status demarcation that even people's disquiet and anxiety do not stir the established cultural notions and their practices. The making and re-making of social space indicates a need for the reconceptualisation of social relations and space allocation.

Chanderi demonstrates a double contingency, a double game, in real life situations by way of a synthesis of tradition and modernity. Without dismantling boundary maintenance, it has accepted new classifications and social divisions. A new system of social recognitions and spaces, without severely attacking the existing hierarchies, characterises Chanderi's multiculturalism, that is, new meaning-strata and stratifications. Pride in the past and hope in the future speak of the co-existence of the old and the new, and traditional and modern in Chanderi. Proto-industrialisation continues in Chanderi despite the fact that the handloom industry has existed for 500 years. Caste/community remains at the centre stage in its affairs, though the presence of the state apparatus has always been abundantly visible. Various castes/communities continue to pursue their respective traditional occupations in a market situation. Even today, more than half of the eighty-six *mohallas* and *galis* are single-caste residential enclaves.

Chanderi characterises a unique conjunction of the ideal and actual social worlds in the enactment of socio-cultural activities. Caste/community no doubt remains a recognisable entity in festivals and social gatherings, the ideology and moorings of the people in general reflect space segregation, and social distance never remains hidden. At times competition for access to cherished social space is also observed. It indicates that no status is indisputable forever. Chanderi has not yet witnessed any effective struggle for creating new classifications of social classes, divisions and institutions. The deprived still hesitate to impose their worldviews on their superiors. Hence, geographic space remains commensurate with social space to a recognisable extent.

Acknowledgements

This study is based on an Indo-French research programme involving scholars from the College de France and CNRS, Paris, and

Jawaharlal Nehru University, New Delhi. Professor G. Fussman of the College de France and his associates were actively engaged in the research work. On the Indian side, I was involved in the project right from its inception in 1989–90. A study of Chanderi, a small town in Guna district of Madhya Pradesh, was a unique experience because of its interdisciplinary and holistic approach to the study of urban dynamics. I have already published a monograph on Chanderi (1999) using the data-base of our joint endeavour. I am grateful to my French colleagues for extending me cooperation and help. My sincere thanks are to Professor G. Fussman, who invited me to College de France in 1991–92, 1996 and 1997, and who undertook the responsibility for publishing *Chanderi, 1990–95* (Sharma, 1999). I am also extremely grateful to my colleague, Professor Dipankar Gupta, for offering constructive criticisms and for his painstaking editorial improvements to this. It goes without saying that responsibility for the data and analysis presented in this paper is entirely mine.

Notes

1. The fine silk fabric imported from China, Korea and Japan, and now also produced in India, used for manufacturing of sarees, is delicate, expensive and quite transparent. Women from ordinary families with meagre incomes cannot afford this expensive wear, which is also not considered desirable because of its transparency. However, urban middle class women appreciate the Chanderi saree as summer wear, particularly from March to September, because it is elegant, light, delicate, and a status symbol as well. Manufacturing of silk sarees began in 1940, and prior to this, fine muslin cloth was manufactured, including sarees.
2. Among booklets and guides to Chanderi are the following: M.B. Garde, *A Guide to Chanderi; R.* Nath, *The Art of Chanderi;* Government of Madhya Pradesh, *Chanderi* (1988, 1989); and

Kundan Lal Bharatiya, *Chanderi: Aikparichay.* Besides these popular booklets, educated Chanderi citizens are aware that the town has been mentioned in historical books and documents, and classics such as *Ain-e-Akbari.*

3. The Government of Madhya Pradesh replaced the municipal committees of some towns, which were of historico-cultural significance, by a Special Area Development Authority (SADA). Chanderi was one such town. A development plan for a period of seventeen years (1985–2001) was prepared with a budget of about Rs 5 crore. The SADA undertook several development projects and also repaired and renovated monuments such as Koshak Mahal, Badal Mahal, etc. SADA was supposed to be a non-political body. About two years ago the SADA was abolished and the municipality reinstated.
4. People in Chanderi indulge excessively in its glamorisation and glorification, calling it a *nagari* (beautiful city). Romanticisation, by way of counting the numbers of *baolis,* ponds, lakes, falls, hills, forts, palaces, temples, mosques, natural surroundings, etc., is not simply a metaphor. There are those who really believe in the magical charm of the town, dating from the pre-1857 period.
5. The title of 'Raja' among the dominant Rajput families is quite common. 'Raja Bhaiya' is often used to address politically influential young Rajput leaders. At times it is used for the local bullies as well, because people are scared of them. Generally, such a title indicates that the persons concerned belong to the traditional ruling caste of Kshatriya/Rajput. It is projected as a status symbol.
6. Caste and community-based spatial and social segregation is reflected in Chanderi by way of demarcated *mohallas* and *galis* and stratified social interactions. Clearly, three categories, namely, lower, middle and upper, are prevalent among the Muslims of Chanderi. For example, Faqirs, Dhobis, Ghosis and Kunjaras are lower than Momins (Ansaris), and the latter are lower than Pathans and Sayyids. Brahmins, Rajputs, Jains and Maheshwaris are the main upper castes. Each one of them is

internally differentiated. Jains have three sub-groups, whereas Brahmins have eleven sub-castes. Similarly, three sub-groups, namely, Chauhan, Bundela and Parmar, are found among the Rajputs of Chanderi. Kayasthas, Kolis, etc., also have sub-castes. The middle castes in Chanderi are Soni, Darzi, Ahir, Mali, Khati, Sihare, Kumhar, etc. Castes, such as Kachhi, Nai, Sahu, Dakot, Jogi, Gadaria, Shejwari, Lakhera and Kadera, are lower castes. Some castes, which were formerly 'untouchable', are at the bottom of the social pyramid. These are Koli, Chamar, Dhimar, Basore, Khatik, Khangar, Katia, Barar and Mehtar.

Comparing the Hindu and Muslim groups, it may be stated that Pathans are perceived as equal to the upper castes, while Ansaris and Kolis are seen as equal in terms of social hierarchy and common occupational status. Kunjaras and Dhobis are equated with lower castes, like Lakhera, Kadera, Shejwari, etc. These social perceptions are transmitted from generation to generation. Jati is used as a generic word for caste, sub-caste, gotra and community and for divisions within given communities. Ansaris are referred as a jati, as are the Pathans, Kunjaras, Fakirs, etc.

7. There are about 300 households of Sheikhs, Pathans, Mirzas and Moghols, and about 500 households of Momins/Ansaris and other Muslim groups.

References

Bayly, C.A., 1980, "The Small Town and Islamic Gentry in North India: The Case of Kara", in Kenneth Ballhatchet and John Harrison eds., *The City of South Asia: Pre-modern and Modern,* London: Curzon Press.

Bourdieu, Pierre, 1990, *In Other Words: Essays Towards a Reflexive Sociology,* Stanford, California: Stanford University Press.

Gupta, Dipankar, 2000, *Culture, Space and the Nation-state,* New Delhi: Sage Publications.

Jarrett, H.S., 1949, *Ain-e-Akbari of Abul Fazl-i-Allami* (transl. and ed., H.S. Jarrett, annotated by Jadu Nath Sarkar), Calcutta: Royal Asiatic Society of Bengal.

Julka, Vimal, 1985, Chanderi Vikas Yojna, 1985–2001 (Plan for the Development of Chanderi 1985–2001), Chanderi: Special Area Development Authority.

Kriedte, Peter, Hans Medick and Jurgen Schlumbohm, 1981, *Industrialization before Industrialization: Rural Industry in the Genesis of Capitalism,* New York: Cambridge University Press.

Kumar, Nita, 1988, *The Artisans of Banaras: Popular Culture and Identity, 1880–1986,* Princeton: Princeton University Press.

Lahiri, P.K., 1979, Chanderi Main Hathkargha Udyoga Adhyan Dal ka Prativedan (Report of the Study Team of Handloom Industry in Chanderi), Government of Madhya Pradesh: Department of Commerce and Industry.

Mehta, Deepak, 1992, "The Semiotics of Weaving: A Case Study", *Contributions to Indian Sociology,* 26, 1: 77–113.

Ostor, Akos, 1994, *Culture and Power: Legend, Ritual, Bazaar and Religion in Bengali Society*. New Delhi: Sage Publications.

Sharma, K.L., 1999, *Chanderi, 1990–1995,* Paris: Edition Diffusion de Boccard.

9

Some Reflections on Higher Education, State and Social Hierarchy in India

I

Undoubtedly, education brings about a desired type of social change, if other things remain equal. Since society is diversified and inequalitarian, social opportunities are also incongruent vis-à-vis education. Ranked people and unequal opportunities create stratified schools, colleges and universities. Hence, those who pass out are also ranked as high and low, superior and inferior. One can clearly see 'society in education' and 'education in society'. As such society adds to status quo and stability of the persisting structures. However, the fact that education is an instrument of social change cannot be overlooked. Under certain conditions education generates and strengthens the process of modernisation in a given society.

Does education become an agent of social change in Indian society, which is characterised by a complex of collectivities, differentiations, inequalities and specificities? Indian society is a sum total of continuity and change, absorption and assimilation, give and take, unity in diversities and vice versa, and it is also a grand synthesis of cultures, languages, regions and religions. At the same time, today's India has a comprehensive written constitution, central administration, civil services, fundamental rights and directive principles of state policy, provisions for protection and upliftment of weaker sections and women.

As continuity and change co-exist, so is the shape of rigidity and flexibility in Indian society. Resilience and adaptiveness of Indian society can be seen in more than one way. The Indian State has transformed itself by way of constitutional amendments and to meet new demands of the people of India. New forms of social relations have emerged with regard to individual, family and caste. A new middle class and a new power elite along with new issues and demands have taken up centre stage in Indian society and polity. Three factors, namely, education, migration and mobility, have played a vital role in such a process of social transformation of Indian society. Education is the foremost determinant of social change as it has created not only thinking people with heightened consciousness and conscientisation, but also a sense of civil liberties, civic society, public interest and judicial activism. In this way, education has strengthened democracy and has put a limit on regionalism, linguism, communalism, etc.

II

The above formulation is based on the assumption that education is a radical praxis, uniformly available and accessible to all members of the Indian society. It is free, compulsory and unfocussed at the elementary level. Because such a practice of education can provide equal footing to the children of socially diversified segments of society. The Marxist Educational Praxis (MEP) advocates free public education, compulsory and uniform for all children, abolition of cultural or knowledge monopolies of the privileged forms of schooling (see Entwistle, 1979, for a wholesome analysis of the MEP). The sociological reason of education is to weaken the role of family in social reproduction, to bring up children under less unequal conditions, and to utilise the socialising force of the community. Besides closing the gap between manual and mental work, between conception and execution, and a full understanding of the productive process, education has to assure the all-round development of the personality (Marx, 1964). The community is assigned a new and vast role in the educational process, a more open relation between school and society, a dialogical relation between the teachers and the taught.

In the MEP, emphasis is on auto-creation, and through this, on the transformation of the social division of labour. However, Emile Durkheim relates formal education to social structure and to the channels of socialisation in society. According to Durkheim, education is "an eminently social thing in its origins as in its function". The functionality of education lies in Durkheim's view that it (education) reflects and maintains the society, and can only partially change it (Durkheim, 1956). Education is an instrument to inculcate social ideals and cultural values, but there is no single ideal or perfect type of education for all men and women. This distinguishes the Durkheimian approach from the MEP. Moreover, education is an ever-changing social process. At the school level, today, we can see open schools, distance education, community/adult education, literacy mission, etc., and at the higher level professional and job-oriented programmes of study, internationalisation of education and its marketisation have been in vogue causing a setback to the classical and conventional studies and research.

The following four areas of research in education suggested by Durkheim are relevant even today:

1. Identification of the current social facts of education and their sociological function;
2. Identification of the relationships between education and social and cultural change;
3. Cross-cultural and comparative research in various types of educational systems; and
4. Investigation of the classroom and school (also university and college) as an ongoing social system (Durkheim, 1977, ch. 12–14).

Thus, education and society are interrelated at least in two ways: (i) in the preservation and development of culture, process of social control and the power system, i.e., as a mechanism of status quo or of sponsored mobility; and (ii) in promotion of social change and contest mobility being an instrument of new ideals and means for emancipation and equality.

As such, we may have to study higher education as a system conducive to social change and development keeping in view its ramifications vis-à-vis social diversities and inequalities. From this we would know the type of education and its condition that exist today in India. Can education in its present stratified form contribute significantly to the process of equalitarianism and modernisation? Is 'quality' education not a resource material in a few hands? Is education not power, a means of control in relation to the less educated?

The paradoxical nature of education in terms of the following makes it an ambivalent mechanism of social change. Because education is an instrument of social change on the one hand, and a means of status quo, on the other. Likewise, it contains equality/inequality, achievement/ascription, sponsored/contest mobility, etc. It is a double-edged weapon. Thus, it is paradoxical. If education brings about 'equality of opportunity' in true sense, the paradoxes of education can be minimised to a considerable extent. The equality of opportunity means benefiting to all those who have the ability and desire to be educated, and a longing for development of a scientific and objective outlook, and to work in a cohesive social environment without constraints of caste, class, language, region and religion. The fact is that today 'equality of opportunity' in true sense does not exist mainly because of uneven and inequalitarian social base of the students and their families. Colleges, universities and research institutes are also highly differentiated and ranked in terms of their location, size, resources, faculty and peer group evaluation.

III

In India, we have the central, the state and the deemed universities more or less in a ranked order with a few exceptions. Below the stratified university system are autonomous and private colleges. There are also government colleges. Some missionary colleges are known for their quality education. The universities of Bombay, Madras, Calcutta, Allahabad, Banaras Hindu University, Aligarh Muslim University and some other institutions were well known for their academic excellence. Today, barring the University of Delhi and the Jawaharlal Nehru University (JNU), and some colleges and research institutes, most of the universities have low standards of teaching and research. Why such a degradation? What about the question of autonomy?

Degradation is not uniform as Indian Institutes of Technology (IITs), Indian Institutes of Management (IIMS), Delhi University (DU), Jawaharlal Lal Nehru University (JNU), and some other institutes, universities and colleges are performing fairly well, particularly in metropolitan cities and towns. These select institutions meet aspirations of the socially privileged families and individuals. Pierre Bourdieu observes that very selection procedure legitimises 'unequal gifts', in other words, de facto has the seal of de jure. Economic and social differences are transformed into distinctions of quality, and this results into legitimisation of the transmission of the cultural heritage. Hence, elite perpetuation (Bourdieu, 1996). One can see a nexus between inequality, elite education and status retention. Social mobility through education is thus a myth; it is a sponsored phenomenon.

Education without appropriate policy and ethics is incomplete (Bottery, 2000). Education for what? Education for whom? No educational system can ignore its policy, ethics and relevance, because education implies philosophy, ideology and knowledge for both individual and society. Education is inevitable for a smooth interaction between the two. How education with policy, ethics and relevance can be made available in the wake of its privatisation and marketisation? Is it possible to ensure quality education in a situation of internationalisation/globalisation or as an export-import phenomenon? Can education be treated as a consumer service? 'Trade in services' (education, health) may mar its positive role in social integration, and it may be a part social stock of knowledge. It is obvious that education as a consumer product would call for a 'market situation' having buyers and sellers, loosers and gainers. And, thus, class and education can go hand in hand, making policy, ethics and relevance as redundant issues.

Marketisation of education brings in the element of class, and the latter produces and reproduces 'nobility' (intellectual/academic) (Bourdieu, 1996). How to check the lust for profit making in education through privatisation? One can suggest that 'intellectual public' in higher education can discourage such a tendency. Education is not an automobile or information technology industry. Knowledge is not a mechanical activity, it is a creative enterprise. It inheres dialogism. Education abhors managerialism. A good society is created by education, and therefore, education amounts to societal empowerment. It serves economic and political interests to a limited extent. Hence, education in true sense is antithetical to market. 'Civil society' and a desired type of citizenry are concomitant with quality education.

Export of higher education is being promoted by the Government of India, and its declared purpose is to increase our foreign exchange. At the same time, several foreign universities are opening up their centres in India with a view to propagate or market their education and related educational technology and other goods and services. So far as we are concerned in relation to export of our education, the main issues before us are, for example, institutional infrastructure, the quality of our programmes of study, global market for Indian education, quota for foreign students and admission without entrance test. It is not quite easy for us to enter the education market without having resources and competence to compete with the resourceful and well-equipped countries of the West. A reminder is not out of context here that the world's best institutions like the Cambridge, Oxford, London School of Economics, Chicago, Harvard, Stanford, McGill, Jawaharlal Nehru University, Delhi University, Indian Institutes of Technology, etc., have not given a message of trade and commerce, interest and cut-throat competition, and commercialisation of education. These universities and institutions have met the two objectives, that is, the cognitive—moral, and the practical—pragmatic, relating to higher education.

Education is thus not for 'reproduction'; it is for enlightenment. It is not for creation of nobility, but for creation of a new generation of thinking people. It is a mechanism of resolution of conflict and contradiction rather than a source of competition and rivalry. Education is a social sector, and it is responsibility of the Indian state not to allow education to become a matter of economic calculus and/or politics. Hence, education cannot be a commodity of global markets and that too in the hands of multinationals. Some of the educational entrepreneurs have their buildings, infrastructure, support systems, equal to seven star hostels, but they do not have qualified faculty to train young minds at par even with the poorly equipped colleges and universities. A university ought to have debates about the creation of a 'good society'. Educational systems cannot be handmade to provide human resources to the global markets. Nation and education can co-exist, but not the global market and education.

As stated above, education cannot be a commodity of global market in the hands of multinationals. Because it cannot simply be geared to economic and political imperatives. Marketisation of education would lead to the disappearance of debates and dialogues about the present and the further society. It would reflect the domination of the rich and developed countries and their ideology ignoring the specificities of the less developed and poor countries. In the hands of multinationals education would have contents conducive to the countries of the developed West. The WTO and multinationals do not contribute to the preservation of stability and legitimacy of nation-states, because marketisation of their resources leads to privatisation and then to the destruction of their national integrity. Hence, education cannot be a commercially competitive activity. Public education is antithetical to the principles of market and profit. It is a restraint on trade.

IV

However, it is a fact that education is highly stratified, and so is trade and currents of social change. Stratified education produces stratified individuals and families, and we would have thus stratified nations. In this way, education corresponds with the world order of national rankings. How India would compete with big powers or an Indian university would be equal to universities like Cambridge, Oxford, Harvard, Chicago, etc.? At times global forces constrain and direct the nation-state, and they would have profound effects upon the type and quality of education which it provides to its citizens. The question is: What should be the discourse of education by which conceptions of 'good life' and 'desired type of society' can be expressed? A clear answer is: No fragmentation of an individual's life be allowed. However, India needs to have (1) a greater global competitiveness, (2) a more skilled workforce, and (3) a greater legitimacy for the state's activities. Such a gospel of education is possible by way of complementary roles of the state and civil society. Citizenry and state, and civil society and society, have to act in closer proximity.

A controlled managerialist discourse, market competition, and a central direction can be ensured by a healthy interaction between state and society. Education can have a liberating, creative and ethical potential if it has policy management having balanced participation of state and society. We need to have a self-conscientious teaching profession, a fundamentally critical and self-reflective curriculum, and a clear perception of the private and the public good in education.

From narrow confines of nation-state, education has come to global market, that is, it is beyond nation-state. For a long time, education remained confined, for example, in the USA, the USSR and China, to their respective national boundaries, mainly due to ideological reasons. One could hardly know about the educational systems of the USSR and China. However, the USA tried to propagate its ideological and economic superiority by way of cheap textbooks and funding of research in India and other underdeveloped and developing countries. Such a situation did not allow a curriculum which could promote robust citizenship emphasising rights and duties, because education lacked choice, autonomy, epistemology and incentive.

In America, the notion and practice of saleability of education received fast speed, hence export of education to the vulnerable countries of the Third World. A claim was made to export superior intellect and cognitive apparatus. The question of its relevance in terms of the understanding of society, economy and culture of the receiving countries became dormant under the generalised hegemony of the USA and the countries of West Europe. India was thus 'imagined' and 'interpreted' from the viewpoint of the hegemonic West ignoring its ground reality, history and culture.

V

Barnett has listed four functions of higher education: (1) as a provider of quality personnel, (2) training for a research career, (3) management of teaching, and (4) better life-chances (Barnett, 1992). We should be more worried about the young people whom we enrol for higher education. The question is: Do we make them reflective citizens able to have independent thought and action in a coherent and articulate fashion? This is the main concern voiced by Barnett. No doubt, education is key to human development. But this cannot be achieved unless we transform education radically and relate it to the life of people, irrespective of their socio-cultural and economic backgrounds.

Opportunity to everyone for higher education is a prerequisite for making it an effective instrument of social change. Without ensuring quality, higher education becomes a superficial decoration of people with degrees and diplomas. Barring some universities and institutes, higher education is hardly empowering people in terms of human development despite the fact that higher education has increased manifold over the past 60 years since India's independence in 1947. Expansion of higher education is not only phenomenal; it has also participation of rural people and women across the country. But, the rural poor do not have access to good universities, colleges and institutes located in metropolitan centres and big cities and towns.

We have reviewed our educational system from time to time beginning with the S. Radhakrishnan Commission (1948–49) and subsequently we have the D.S. Kothari Commission (1964–66), National Policy on Education (1968 and 1986), and thc Ramamurthy Committee (1990). We had just eight universities in 1947, and today (2004) there are 307 universities in our country. We have today nearly one crore students whereas in 1947 there were just a little more than 2 lakh students. From nearly 600 colleges in 1947, today, there are 15,000 colleges. Today, we are next to the USA in terms of quantitative expansion of higher education. But, our participation is much less (nearly 7%) compared to the developed countries (UK 52%, France 50%, USA 81%, Canada 100%, Indonesia 11%, Brazil 12%, Mexico 14%, Thailand 19%) (*University News*, Vol. 41, Nos. 31, 41, 49; Vol. 42, No. 21). Even this 7 per cent participation is greatly differentiated in terms of quality and location of the institutions and performance of the students.

The recommendations of various commissions and committees remain either unimplemented or partially executed. Altbach observes that the Indian educational system remains to be a great monolith, inadequate and incapable for change. He also hammers on the role of a teacher as a catalyst and a change agent (Altbach, 2003). But, the question is that a very few teachers update their knowledge and skills to train the students.

In an issue of *Economic and Political Weekly* (Vol. XXXIV, No. 21, 2004, pp. 2151–84), a number of critical observations have been made based on deliberations in a workshop at Pune University on the state of higher education in India. Sujata Patel (2004) points out that higher educational institutions are now beset with new problems arising out of the uneven spread of such institutions in terms of lack of funds for infrastructure, research and salaries, outdated curricula and political interference in their day-to-day functioning. The changing character of the market is another additional factor having impact on the demand for particular subjects. In the current situation, a new debate on the learning process and commitment to it given by both teachers and students has taken over the conventional learning of fundamental sciences, social sciences and humanities. Patel's observation also implies degradation of quality of teaching and research in the traditional fields of knowledge. Another contributor to the workshop, J.B.G. Tilak (2004), perceives that the Government of India does not seem to have a coherent policy on the value and the plan for higher education.

Recently, two views have been articulated on higher education: (1) that the private control of higher education is acceptable because the state has no funds for it; and (2) that through private initiatives alone there could be an improvement in accountability and efficiency in the management of colleges and universities (Patel, 2004). The two views cannot be taken on their face value.

It is known that higher education is not an important concern and priority for the Government of India. Lately, it has put higher premium on primary education, hence neglect of higher education. Privatisation of higher education has resulted into trade in education by way of attractive publicity strategies and devices, undermining the quality of education and research. A large number of self-financing courses in medicine, pharmacy, engineering, information technology, computer applications, biotechnology, microbiology, management studies, food technology, film production, etc., have been initiated in private colleges with a view to extract maximum profit with least possible cost.

Sujata Patel (ibid.) raises two questions relating to this development: (1) Is liberal education based on humanities and social sciences not to be taught or is it because it has no commercial value? (2) Should commercial viability be the criteria for the promotion of higher education? We may add another question: Will social sciences, philosophy, literature, etc., become irrelevant and redundant?

Privatisation and marketisation of higher education have brought about migration of education from one country to another. Earlier, people from the less developed countries like India used to migrate to the world-class institutions, such as Cambridge, Oxford, Stanford, Chicago, Yale, Princeton, California, etc. One needs to see carefully the effects of privatisation and globalisation of higher education keeping in view a 'class situation' of buyers and sellers, loosers and gainers of trade in education. Who gets what? And, at what cost and quality? Obviously, there are at least three categories of the recipients of higher education: (1) who join best colleges, universities and institutions such as IITs, IIMS, AIIMS, etc., in India and abroad on the basis of their excellent performance, certainly having superior family background; (2) who do not have access to the institutions of the first order in India or abroad, but can afford to pay for professional education in private institutions; and (3) a general mass of students who join wherever they get admission without exercising choice either of a particular programme of study or of location and reputation of an institution.

Inter-regional and intra-regional disparities have also been reported due to demand-oriented educational delivery systems. For example, within Rajasthan, Jaipur has today maximum number of institutions of higher education compared to other cities. Differential costs and capacities of the clients (students) also reflect economic inequality in the country and then the stratified nature of higher education. Cut-throat competition has emerged among the educational entrepreneurs causing harm to policy and ethics in education. Capitation fee, admission of under-qualified students, recruitment of sub-standard teachers, malpractices in conduct of examinations and evaluation are some of the problems reported due to privatisation of higher education.

VI

Pierre Bourdieu (1996) acknowledges ranking by 'order of excellence' and associates with the notion of competitive examination, and also realises the role of considerable inherited cultural capital in this nexus. He also talks of 'safe' and 'profitable' tasks on the part of the competitor as one knows where to direct one's efforts and results are easily measured. This is a sort of actual normal situation. Bourdieu's concern is far more serious. His object is "the operation of social alchemy whereby a social hierarchy dis-simulates itself, to those it dignifies no less than to those it excludes, as a scale of human excellence, how a historically arbitrary social order rooted in the materiality of economic and political power transmutes itself into what displays every outward appearance of an aristocracy of intelligence" (ibid.). Such a system does not demarcate a before and an after so much as it differentiates—and elevates—those destined to occupy eminent social positions from those over whom they will lord. Such beneficiaries of degrees, diplomas and credentials acquired sacred reverence and legitimacy of a new form of class rule. This is a process of self-perpetuation in high positions manipulated by those who already monopolise them based on blood, diplomas and economic dominance.

Privatisation in higher education has added to this perpetuation of social hierarchy with considerable mediocrity. In this way, one can see correspondence between social structures and mental structures (ibid.). There is a need to explode the myth that education is a liberating force. Education, is therefore, not the triumph of 'achievement' over 'ascription' as Bourdieu observes. Ascription is transformed into achievement and then it is re-transformed into ascription. A vicious cyclical process is always there strengthening status quo. Such a process is characterised by Bourdieu as 'dualistic thinking' and the 'conciliation of opposites"(ibid.).

VII

Higher education must aim at a rediscovery of the humanising vocation of the intellectual, the power of thought. It has to be man's ontological vocation, a tool to encounter subjugation and a mechanism to know and assert one's own rights. Education must bring a new awareness of self, a sense of dignity, a new hope, conscientisation (to know contradictions), critical awareness and radicalism. Education cannot afford colonised mentality. Emancipation, freedom, dialogue and humanising pedagogy can demythologise the apparent positive face of higher education.

Characterisation of higher education in the above ideal sense may not be quite an easy task. However, ethos and organisation of higher education require urgent re-examination by way of policy management, development of a relevant teaching profession, critical and self-reflective curriculum and conciliation of the private and public good. I.L. Horowitz's understanding of the American situation in terms of the 'mainliners and marginals' applies largely to the universities in India. The mainliners are: (1) 'professionals' (pro-establishment professors), and 'occupationalists' (bright intellectuals but anti-establishment). The marginals are: (1) unprofessionals (subservient to the professionals) and the anti-professionals (followers of the occupationists)(Horowitz, 1967). Marginals do not read and teach; and professionals remain busy for power and fame, respectively.

The question is: How to reconcile these intra-systemic antinomies? Hence, a radical eradication of the maladies of higher education. There is no short-cut. Marketing of 'quality goods', which are useful, cannot be stopped. Such a globalisation has been in existence for a long time. Neo-imperialism in education in the name of privatisation and globalisation has serious manifest as well as latent dehumanising consequences.

References

Altbach, P.G., 2003, "Globalisation and the University: Myths and Realities in an Unequal World", *Journal of Educational Planning and Administration*, Vol. XVII, No. 2.

Barnett, R., 1992, *Improving Higher Education: Total Quality Care*, London: SRHE/Open University Press.

Bottery, Mike, 2000, *Education, Policy and Ethics*, London: Wellington House.

Bourdieu, Pierre, 1996, *The State Nobility: Elite Schools in the Field of Power* (translated by Lauretta C. Clough), Cambridge: Polity Press.

Durkheim, Emile, 1956, *Education and Sociology* (translated with an Introduction by S.D. Fax), New York: The Free Press.

——, 1977, *The Evolution of Educational Thought: Lectures on the Formation and Development of Secondary Education in France* (translated by Peter Collins), London: Routledge & Kegan Paul.

Entwistle, Harold, 1979, *Antonio Gramsci: Conservative Schooling for Radical Politics*, London: Routledge & Kegan Paul.

Horowitz, Irving Louis, 1967, "Mainliness and Marginals: The Human Shape of Sociological Theory", in Llewellyn Gross (ed.), *Sociological Theory: Inquiries and Paradigms*, New York: Harper & Row.

Marx, Karl, 1964, *The German Ideology*, Moscow: Progress Publishers.

Patel, Sujata, 2004, "Higher Education at the Crossroads", *Economic and Political Weekly*, Vol. XXXIX, No. 21.

Tilak, J.B.G., 2004, "Absence of Policy and Perspective in Higher Education", *Economic and Political Weekly*, Vol. XXXIX, No. 21.

University News (A Weekly Journal of Higher Education in India), Vol. 41, Nos. 31, 41 and 49, and Vol. 42, No. 21.

10

A Note on Modernity and Post-Modernism

Modernity refers to enlightenment of one or other sort as it implies a new state of structures and ideas leaving behind the bindings and regimentations of relations and norms and values. However, modernity is not replacement of the old by the new. It is a relative state of affairs involving ramifications of people and their cultures in varying measures. Today, modernity does not mean a subject-centred reason of enlightenment nor is it an absolute form of knowledge. It is relational. Reason is basic to modernity, but unreason never disappears completely from human mind or from society and culture. Impurity of reason is in history and tradition, society and power, practice and interest, body and desire. Hence, modernity is not synonym of reason. One can see a radical critique of reason in contemporary thought. J. Habermas (1987) observes that reason is social and inter-subjective. He talks of the determinate negation of subject-centred reason by reason understood as communicative action.

Modernity is not a matter of aesthetic discourse. It is a philosophic discourse, clearly identifying and marking out a road for action and interaction. There is no place for romanticism in the discourse on modernity. Modernity emanates from radical experience, which is free from the constraints of morality and utility, religion and science. A sovereign rational subject is nowhere in such a discourse. Modernity provides a critique of the subjective rationalism. Rational speech and action are core elements of modernity at any given time and place. Differentiated systems of signs mediate universally speech and action. Hence, language is a social phenomenon. Words are worlds, hence power. A new language reflects modernity as it is mediated by a new value system.

Thus, modernity is not rhetoric and poetics. It is also not to be seen in terms of logos and mythos, logical and rhetoric, literal and figurative, concept and metaphor, argument and narrative, etc. Tradition and modernity are misplaced polarities. The two are not only relative phenomena, one is found in the other in some measure. Therefore, openness to critique and revision and their internal relation to inter-subjective recognition refers to modernity.

Habermas has thus reconceptualised the concept of modernity in terms of its historical, social, embodied, practical, desirous assertive nature of the knowing and the acting subject—and to record according to over-received humanistic ideals. Habermas rejects the paradigm of consciousness and its associated philosophy of the subject in favour of the through and through inter-subjectivist paradigm of 'communicative action'. In his thinking, there is no putative ontological difference between Being and Beings, between worldview structures and what appears within these worlds. Modernity is empirical. It uproots prepositional truth and devalue discursive, argumentative thought. There is a dialectical interdependence between a historically shaped understanding of the world and the experience and practice possible within its horizon. This is life-world.

Meaning cannot be separated from validity. Enlightenment is not an end product—it requires further enlightenment. Thus, one has to think of the totalised critique of reason. When reason becomes practice, old structures transform giving way to new formations.

Do we have such a meaning and construction of Indian modernity rooted into rational inter-subjective communicative action? Let us have a brief survey of the construction of modernity in the Indian context. In the recent times, G. Myrdal in his monumental work, *Asian Drama* (1968, Vol. I), talks of a new man, the modern man, the citizen of the new state, the man in the era of science, the industrial man, etc., in terms of 'modernisation ideals' relevant for India as an independent nation. 'Individual' is at the centre stage in Myrdal's analysis of the countries of Asia. The 'rational subject' or the 'subjective rationalism' and man's consciousness are the main considerations in Myrdal's understanding of India. He refers to efficiency, diligence, orderliness, punctuality, frugality, honesty, rationality, etc., as the main attributes of 'modernisation' and of a modern 'man'. Obviously, Myrdal talks of 'individual' and not of 'society'. This is undoubtedly subjectivistic determinism, a peculiar western notion of modernisation. Myrdal's vehement attack on institutions such as caste, family, religion, etc., supports his eurocentric construction of modernity.

Contrary to Hebermas' view, the Indian tradition is resilient and adaptive in the sense that it changes itself pragmatically, and also external forces of change adapt in tune with the force of the tradition. Milton Singer (1972) in particular has advocated such a view in his work, *When a Great Tradition Modernizes*. This is with regard to modernisation in the field of industry, trade and commerce. A slightly different view is held regarding modernisation by M.N. Srinivas (1966), who characterises social change as a result of cultural role of the British in India in the form of westernisation. Srinivas looks at westernisation as a value having humanistic impact on Indian society. This is basically a cultural explanation with regard to the passing of the traditional Indian society through the process of external forces and factors. A somewhat different view is held by Yogendra Singh in his seminal work, *Modernization of Indian Tradition*, where he talks of a synthesis of both ontogenetic and heterogenetic changes in Indian society at cultural and structural levels. He talks of both specific and historical contexts of modernisation affecting micro and macro structures and the little and great traditions, respectively. Based on Yogendra Singh's integrated approach, we can understand cultural renaissance and pattern recurrence, elite circulation, etc., as ontogenetic changes, and Islamanisation, westernisation, role differentiation, new legitimations, and political and bureaucratic structures in terms of heterogenetic changes.

Interestingly, the viewpoint advocated in Dipankar Gupta's *Mistaken Modernity* (2000) implies 'multiple modernities'. According to Gupta, modernity is not unadulterated good, at the same time, he likes Yogendra Singh's construction of modernisation. He also acknowledges the fact that genesis of modernity lies in India's traditions. Gupta's experiment with some new words and phrases refers to the 'westoxicated' elite and gentlemen or 'gentoos'. Are they really modern? However, Gupta defines modernity in terms of the dignity of individual, adherence to universalisation of norms, elevation of individual achievement. According to Gupta, privileges or disprivileges of birth, accountability in public life, trust in institutions and not in individual must be the basic elements of modernity. Gupta looks at modernity as relations between people because modernity refers to inter-subjective phenomena. It implies to sharing of all societal resources and institutions. Thus, one has to examine modernity as a genuine course of social change. It cannot be judged by a shallow middle class because such a class refers to a superficial modernisation.

In one way, modernity can be simply based on indicators, such as cars, refrigerators, washing machines, colour televisions, etc. However, if one compares some of these electronic gadgets with that of the USA, India remains far behind. Modernity is more of a way of life and mode of thinking. We talk to intellectuals on secularism and degendering vis-à-vis modernity. We are not just traditional nor are we modern in the sense of the US. We are somewhere in-between the two. Modernity implies innovation no doubt, but tradition does not imply necessarily static binding, because its continuity may be seen in terms of its logic, rationale and relevance.

The excess of dependence on industry, technology and modern devices has resulted into the realisation of getting away from the suffocation created by such a modernity. For some time now the advanced countries are talking of coming out of the syndrome of consumption and commodification. An attitude of distance towards automisation and scientific differentiation speaks of limitations of modernity. This is being referred as post-modernity. Post-modernisation is a realm of signification. It is a concept which refers to a new cultural paradigm implying spatio-temporal configuration. Post-modernisation is an exercise to bring back in 'culture'. It refers to cultural economy and specific relations of production of cultural objects. Emphasis is on collectivity.

In fact, the emphasis is on specific mode of signification. One can say that excessive industrialisation and technology have disturbed the stability of society, and therefore, post-modernism has been initiated as programme of action for re-stabilisation of society and culture. Culture is seen as an economic fact. One can refer to emergence of 'cultural markets' as a result of post-modernism. Such a formalisation of post-modernisation can be questioned, but it certainly refers to a new condition of society and economy. It refers to a new concern for creation of a social, cultural and political condition free from the melodies of an industrial society. It refers to a new form of life as it implies a possible social future, a condition, alternative form of sociality away from ill-effects of modernity. In this way, post-modernity implies reconstruction. This is why one can see today increased emphasis on a number of new areas such as art, literature, cinema, music, fashion, communication, expansion of subjects and at times aspects of identity and sexuality. It is philosophical, political and sociological recreation relating to broad questions on social life. A new meaning of progress and development is intrinsic to the idea of post-modernity. One can say that under post-modernist regime there is prodigious expansion of culture throughout social realm—economic value, state power, practice and physique. If social roles have become 'cultural', somewhere 'cultural' has become all pervasive, and post-modernism has become 'cultural dominant'.

Post-modernism is not an unadulterated mode of thinking. It results into the status quo because there is an affirmative post-modernism as well. A critical post-modernism for all reaction and resistance is yet to come. Freedom against the discourse of male domination has not made deep roots. Post-modernism can be seen therefore as a philosophy of action in terms of relations, and therefore, post-modernism implies post-structuralism as well. One has to think of both textual and worldly strands in the contemporary thought constructions.

References

Gupta, Dipankar, 2000, *Mistaken Modernity: India between Two Worlds*, New Delhi: Harper Collins.

Habermas, J., 1987, *The Philosophical Discourse of Modernity*, Cambridge: Polity Press

Myrdal, G., 1968, *Asian Drama*, Vol. I, London, Allen Lane: Penguin Books.

Singer, Milton, 1972, *When a Great Tradition Modernizes*, New York: Praeger Publihers.

Singh, Yogendra, 1994, *Modernization of Indian Tradition*, Jaipur: Rawat Publications.

Srinivas, M.N., 1966, *Social Change in Modern India*, Berkeley: University of California Press.

11

Explicating Amartya Sen's Concept of 'Social Opportunity'

Professor Amartya Sen's concern for sociological causation in economic and political development makes him a class apart from most other social scientists. Freedom is social, and so is economic and political development. The concepts of 'individual', 'development', 'freedom', 'opportunities', 'market', 'state', etc., are formulated in Sen's writings in search of the 'social' behind all human endeavours. Such an integrated approach of Sen combines the classical messages of welfare economics on the one hand and of the modern theories of development, on the other. Since my main emphasis in this paper is on the construction of the notion of 'social opportunity' by Sen, I will concentrate on the explanation of this very important conceptual innovation and its extrapolation. Let me state here that the notion of 'social opportunity' is not a narrow socio-centric construction, germane to social moorings, in fact, it covers a wide range of societal dimensions having implications for Indian polity, economy and culture. I wish to discuss this focal theme after a brief presentation of Prof. Sen's seminal thesis on 'development as freedom'.

Development as Freedom

While introducing the thesis on 'development as freedom', Sen observes that freedom of individual is qualified and constrained by the social, political and economic opportunities that are available to us. He writes: "There is a deep complementarity between individual agency and social arrangements" (Sen, 2000; XII). Social arrangements include opportunities, which are given or made available to its members by state and society for livelihood, education, health care, etc. If an individual has built capacity to make choices out of available structure of alternatives, he enjoys a great deal of freedom. This is why, Sen writes: "We have to see individual freedom as a social commitment" (ibid.). Freedom is 'social', and implicit in it is political and economic freedoms. Sen (ibid.) refers to five distinct types of freedoms, namely, political freedoms, economic facilities (ibid.), social opportunities, transparency guarantees, and protective security. Availability of such freedoms would imply development of an individual, and ultimately of the society as a whole.

The Constitution of India enshrines the idea and practice of freedom of an individual in the form of the 'fundamental rights', but at the same time a great emphasis on 'collectivity' (generally a supposed one) is also placed in the Constitution and its amended versions. Such a duality has caused an ideological or rather philosophical ambivalence with regard to connectivity between individual and society. The basic idea of the development of society through its individual members emanates from the western notion of freedom and action, and the idea of collectively as a unit of action emerges from the philosophy of submergence of individual into group (*sangh*).

Caste, tribe, ethnicity, etc., become the nodal agencies for implementing welfare policies and programmes.

Freedom is seen by Sen as a very broad instrument of action for development. He (ibid.: 4) observes that expansion of freedom is now both as the primary end and as the principal means of development. Sen writes: "Development consists of the removal of various types of unfreedoms that leave people with little choice and little opportunity of exercising their reasoned agency" (ibid.: 15). Thus, the removal of unfreedom is constitutive of development. Sen talks of instrumental effectiveness of freedoms. One freedom substantiates other freedom. Withdrawal of sanctions relating to women, 'untouchables', tribals, etc., would imply 'social freedom' for these sections of Indian society. Such a situation of social freedom would mean opening up of opportunities for education, health care, employment, etc., for these deprived groups like other traditionally privileged castes and communities.

The main thrust of Sen's thesis is that the linkages between different types of freedoms are empirical and causal. For example, between economic and political freedoms, positive linkages are well recognised (ibid.: 9–10). Sen explicates these linkages by using the idea of social opportunities, which refer to education and healthcare, in particular, and they further complement individual opportunities of economic and political participation and overcoming of deprivations. Sen's 'integrated analysis' analysis (ibid.: 10) refers to the linkages between economic, social and political activities along with 'instrumental freedoms' (five types) as referred above. Effective social arrangements alone can ensure freedom leading to development. These include the state, the market, the legal system, political parties, the media, public interest groups, and public discussion forums, etc. (ibid.: 35–41) Real freedoms that people enjoy come through these arrangements, and more and more expansion of the real freedoms would mean development of individual and society. Freedom is not thus a political phenomenon, it is shaped by social and economic arrangements (education and health care), political and civil rights (ibid.). Sen observes: "Development requires the removal of major sources of unfreedom: poverty as well as tyranny, poor economic opportunities as well as systematic social deprivation, neglect of public facilities as well as intolerance or over activity of repressive states" (ibid.: 3).

Freedom is also a yardstick to make assessment of progress and achievement of development. As such, freedom is more than entry into market; it also means interchange of words, goods, gifts, etc. What Sen observes is: "Economic unfreedom can breed social unfreedom, just as social or political unfreedom can also foster economic unfreedom" (ibid.: 4). Thus, freedoms to enter markets or of labour contract are just not economic phenomena, it can breed social and political freedoms as well. Sen (ibid.: 4–5) convincingly argues that development process is to be seen in inclusive terms that integrate economic, social and political considerations.

Unfreedom as Inequality

Four different examples have been cited by Sen to show how critically important is freedom. Various forms of labour bandage, the failure of bureaucratic socialism in Eastern Europe and the Soviet Union, child labour and the unfreedom of women are the major examples of the unfreedoms. Except the bureaucratic socialism, all the other three exist in India. Let us recall that for nearly twenty years after India's independence in 1947, various models of planning and development were worked out, including the Soviet path of development. Today, it is difficult to discern a clearly chartered path of development and change in terms of either capitalism or socialism (the American and the Russian). The 'mixed economy' approach to development too is invisible, particularly in the wake of recent madness for 'privatisation' and selling off the public sector undertakings and institutions. State is no more 'statist', it has become an unchartered and eclectical instrument in the hands of power elite and political agents and brokers.

The idea of 'coupling of disadvantages and inequality of freedom' by Sen (ibid.: 19) refers to what he calls 'the perspective of substantive freedoms'. The equity of outcomes or the equity in the distribution of freedoms is not simply an outcome of 'efficiency'. More important is curbing of enormous inequalities in the distribution of utilities and of freedoms (ibid.).

In the seminal work *Asian Drama*, though Gunnar Myrdal (1968: 49–69) confesses the significance of valuations of ideas and interests specific to the South Asian countries, but after articulating the difficulties in identifying such valuations, turns to a set of value premises, namely, the 'modernisation ideals', experientially rooted into the western path of development and change. While referring to the colonial legacy and the influence of the Soviet Union, Myrdal states that "they (modernisation ideals) have become the 'official creed', almost a national religion, and are one of the powerful strands of the 'new nationalism' (ibid.: 54). The radical creed of the sixties is no more on the Indian political scene. However, Myrdal's following observation even refer nearly four decades ago is quite relevant. He writes: "The modernization ideals are mainly the ideology of the politically alert, articulate, and active part of the population—particularly the intellectual elite. The judgments that follow refer to the opinions of these groups" (ibid.: 55).

Myrdal (ibid.: 57–59) refers to the set of 'modernisation ideals' constitutive of rationality, development and planning for development, rise of productivity, rise of level of living, social and economic equalisation, improved institutions and attitudes (including efficiency, diligence, orderliness, punctuality, frugality, scrupulous honesty, rationality in decisions on action, preparedness for change, alertness to opportunities, energetic enterprise, integrity and self-reliance, cooperation, and willingness to take the long view), national consolidation, national independence, political democracy, democracy at the grassroots, social discipline vs democratic planning, and derived value premises. The listing of the modernisation ideals by Myrdal makes his claim for a South Asian angle merely a pretence, as these attributes of modernisation have not emanated from the experiential reality of Indian society. However, Sen's analysis of 'development as freedom' brings out the genuine concerns of India's development in relation to the poor and the deprived sections of Indian society.

Sen's realisation about the inequality in the distribution of substantive freedoms and, capabilities is based on his understanding of some 'coupling' of income inequality with unequal advantages in converting incomes into capabilities. The relationship between income earning ability and income spending ability is an empirical reality (ibid.: 119–20). Market, being a competitive arena, is a test-ground for capabilities to converge one into other. No doubt, the problem of inequality can be gauged in the market-situation to a considerable extent, provided market is a well-developed institution for convergence and articulation of capabilities which would ultimately take upon persisting inequalities. An unchanging nexus between caste and class, gender and stratification, and caste and empowerment are some of the crucial issues, reflections on which may carry further discourse on Sen's seminal thesis on 'development as freedom'.

Caste, Development and Freedom

Today, one has to go beyond the conventional meanings and interpretations of caste and class to understand both caste-class nexus and encounters based on the experiential inputs. Dipankar Gupta's (2000: 225–64) that caste needs to be seen in the context of its settings and surroundings. However, in all situations, "caste refers to inequality, difference, discrimination, in both theory and practice. Theoretically, caste is more a state of mind of an individual, rather than an ideology dictating collective actions. However, in practice, individual members of a caste may appropriate their caste identities in their own favour or against the interests of others"(Sharma, 2001: 11). Today, contingent appropriation of caste identity and mobilisation have acquired more significance than the pre-given ideology of the 'pure and impure' (see Dumont, 1970) or of 'sanskritisation' (see Srinivas, 1962). In fact, casteism has surfaced in a major form without accompanying resurgence of caste system.

Thus, mobilisation is for extracting systematic as well as situational/contingent gains from the state and the society by a select band of mobilisers. Such 'custodians' of casteism have acquired abilities to transform their private ambitions into public concerns, and also public issues as their own troubles. Caste is reduced, by way of casteism, as a political or cultural or economic entity on the one hand, and it is projected as a 'sacred' phenomenon, irreducible to class, culture and power, on the other. Such a flexibility has no concern with relaxations with regard to connubiality and commensality—the two cardinal principles of regulating the caste system. 'Individual'—in caste, as Gupta (2000) observes, would demythologise the rigid and closed hypersymbolisations, typifications and binary oppositions. Elsewhere, I have pleaded that 'individual' was always present in caste, family and larger society (Sharma, 1974). However, Gupta's observation, that individual's sensuousness has increased considerably, which has enabled him to decide for himself rather than being guided by the received knowledge and socio-cultural recipes, is of immense value to know the weakening of caste and the new form of casteism, caste-based encounters and cooperative endeavours and coalitions.

Caste, bereft of inter-caste relations, does not become a system of ideas and values and consequent hierarchy of caste groups, locally or regionally. Resurgence of the exclusiveness of 'caste' creates vote banks and seeks a share in the scarce salaried jobs, and it is nothing but casteism. In fact, 'casteism' is practised as a social opportunity. The provision of reservation for the SCs and the STs in the Indian Constitution in 1950 could be seen as a social opportunity for the age-old deprived groups. In the wake of a countrywide agitation, making the B.P. Mandal Commission Report as the basis, decision of the Supreme Court of India for caste-based reservation to the OBCs in 1991–92 could be considered another step in creation of 'social opportunity' for the socially and educationally backward castes.

Discourse on caste remains incomplete without two major points, namely, the constitutional provision for the SCs and the STs, and the verdict of the Supreme Court granting caste-based reservation for the OBCs. In a way, caste consciousness has acquired a new vitality, very different from the traditional one, which was based on the notions of 'pure' and 'impure'. Today, the discourse centres around the notions of status and honour (*izzat*) of the backward, the poor, the deprived and the womenfolk (Kolenda, 1978). Three clear formulations can be made out based on the recent developments in the states of Bihar, Uttar Pradesh and Rajasthan.

In the late 1970s, Bihar witnessed sharp divisions between the 'forwards' (upper castes) and the 'backwards' (middle and lower castes) (Blair, 1980: 64–74). Brahmins, Kshatriyas, Bhumihars, Kayasthas, etc., enjoyed high status based on landownership and lucrative white-collar jobs. The 'backwards', which were further divided into the 'upper backwards' and the 'lower backwards', were engaged in agriculture as tenants and artisans, and manual and agricultural labourers, respectively. Such a differentiation was initially socio-economic in both letter and spirit, but in course of time, it was transformed into a means of political mobilisation. As such, the SCs, the STs and the minorities also transformed themselves into sorts of political entities. Today, Bihar is projected not in terms of linear caste precedence, it is seen mainly as a society having the forwards, the upper backwards, the lower backwards, the minorities, the SCs and the STs. Women do not constitute a distinct social and political entity so far.

Caste clusters, such as AJGAR (Ahir, Jat, Gujjar and Rajput), had surfaced even before independence, mainly for socio-cultural mobilisations and social status in the countryside. Political twisting of such a constructed entity was done by political leaders after independence. The late Choudhary Charan Singh, (Jat-Kisan leader), was one of the main architects of the caste-coalition thesis, though he did not succeed much in achieving a political mileage out of it. The results of the 1967 elections for the state legislatures were quite astonishing as the Congress lost its single party hegemony in more than half of the provinces. Such a situation marked the beginning of 'coalition politics' which had predominantly rural base, representing anti-Congressism led by dominant agricultural castes and communities. One could see clearly an initiation of decline of the upper castes, on the one hand, and neglect of the lower castes on the other. The lower and 'untouchable' castes had carved out some space in the first one and half decades partly because of the vote bank politics of the Congress which patronised Muslims, the SCs and the STs. It is another matter that no political party has ever opposed the patronage extended to the weaker sections by the Indian State.

The state of Uttar Pradesh is a distinct contrast compared to Bihar. Bihar can be characterised by Laloo Yadav's social justice plank to a considerable extent, but Uttar Pradesh has three distinct paths of political activities and mobilisation. These are: (1) BJP's Mandir Kamandal; (2) Mulayam Singh Yadav's Samajvad, which is easily reducible to the OBC politics, and that too, mainly concerning the Yadavas; and (3) Mayawati's Bahujan Samaj model of politics and change. Substantively, all the three have been engaged in creation of their respective social bases. The BJP is busy in effecting the 'Hindutva' card, hence all out efforts for construction of the Ram Temple at Ayodhya. The

Samajvadi Party of Mulayam Singh Yadav, though swears by socialism and secularism, is busy in consolidation of the backward castes, particularly the Yadavas. Mayawati is discarding the upper and the upper-middle castes in her gospel. Her Bahujan Samaj Party (BSP) is wooing the 'lower' and the 'untouchable' castes by advocacy of the rejection of 'Manuvad', that is, socio-cultural and political hegemony of the upper castes, particularly Brahmans.

An alert and articulate section has emerged from amongs the SCs. Since independence, the state-sponsored legislations, programmes and actions have transformed the 'untouchables' into today's 'dalits'. Mahatma Gandhi designated 'untouchables' as 'Harijans', who became the 'Scheduled Castes' as per the constitutional provisions, and the SCs turned into 'dalits' as a consequence of their struggle to gain more respectability and an identity of their own (Sharma, 1997: 107–32). Let me state here that the word 'untouchable' implies despise, remorsefulness and unseeable distance. The word 'Harijan' indicates a pre-given, unchangeable mass of people who need compassion for their upliftment. The word 'Scheduled Caste' refers to a legal and exclusive entity at the bottom of social ladder. However, the word 'dalit' implies resistance and rejection of the 'pre-given' value system and acquisition of ones own 'knowledge' and 'power', which means a new social language, conveying new meaning, strategies, situations and status parameters (Sharma, 2001: Ch. 3). Incorporation of class and status in caste is the main message of dalitism.

Traditionally, Rajasthan has not witnessed a caste-based turmoil (except the recent one) due to pre-eminence of feudalism because in everyday life the 'priest' was subservient to the 'king'. However, the effective abolition of the *jagirdari* system facilitated quick surfacing of the peasant castes on Rajasthan's political scene. Within fifteen to twenty years one could feel an effective process of equalitarianism. Commensality started loosing ground. Even violation of connubial norms became somewhat acceptable without punitive actions. The decision of the Supreme Court for a provision of reservation for the OBCs and the crude 'appropriation, of caste in Bihar and Uttar Pradesh have motivated castes like Jat, Brahmin and Rajput in Rajasthan to mobilise themselves for a share in jobs, services and other sectors. Since the Jats of Rajasthan mobilised themselves against the Congress in the 1999 Lok Sabha elections, the party suffered heavy losses. The Congress had a landsliding victory in the last Vidhan Sabha elections because it had support of the Jats as they had been included in the OBC category for reservation. Today, Brahmins and Rajputs too are making a similar demand. Both the castes have organised several rallies and congregations. Rajput leaders have even obstructed several public meetings of the BJP Chief Minister Vasundhara Raje to get their demand accepted by the government. Political leaders, including those in power, are participating in their respective caste councils and rallies. Both Brahmins and Rajputs have pronounced that they would vote for those parties which could ensure them reservation.

Such a casteism-centric development implies appropriation of 'caste' as a source of social placement and as an instrument of identity. The questions which emanate from the practice of casteism are: Has caste simply become an interest group? How far the modalities being practised to appropriate caste as an instrument of political mobilisation are in tune with the conventionally accepted norms of the caste system? Are caste conflicts also class conflicts and vice versa (ibid.: 53)? The question by E.R. Leach (in Leach, ed., 1960: 1–10) posed more than forty years ago, though with a somewhat different connotation, seems to be quite relevant even today to know about the nature of caste-class nexus, its continuity and change. The question is: "What should we mean by caste?" This question is before us today also in the wake of resurgence of 'casteism'. There is 'definance of caste principles', hence, there is no caste system. Inter-caste relations, which ensured organic ties between different castes, are no more the basis of division of labour and of participation on occasions like birth, marriage and death.

In one of the six villages, which I had studied in the mid-sixties, today, people identify themselves as very rich, rich, well-off, not so poor, and poor (Sharma, 1974). According to another mode of perception, families and persons are assessed as 'powerful' and 'weak', and 'superior' and 'inferior'. People also identify others as those who are engaged in prestigious jobs, and those who are businessmen, men of big, middle and small standings.

More important to note is that in everyday life every time people do not recognise themselves as castes. Caste identities have become increasingly personalised realisations rather than public expressions. However, in the wake of the demand for reservation in jobs, recently, the upper castes such as Brahmin and Rajput in Rajasthan, have mobilised themselves as *biradaris* (caste councils). In such a new situation, inter-caste relations do not find a platform to stand on for articulation of caste identities and related perceptions of status.

The notion of 'social opportunity' thus needs to be carefully viewed in terms of (1) the absence of inter-caste relations, and (2) the rejuvenation of caste identities and perceptions without inter-caste relations. In the new situation, the main actors of the enactment of the 'caste drama' are alert and articulate sections having prudence in presentation of the thesis of 'relative deprivation', in relation to the beneficiary castes, by way of reservation. Thus, caste is no more an end in itself. Caste is for casteism, for a constructed cause, may be of the entrenched middle class, made out of the upper castes like Brahmin and Rajput. The demand for being clubbed with the castes, which have the privilege of having reservation in elections, jobs and services, if realised, may bring about 'new opportunities' for the upper castes. A share in the resources is being asked for by the so far deprived castes.

Women and Social Opportunity

Another important point refers to 'social opportunity' for women across the ramifications of the Indian society. Some questions may be posed here. Have women been subsumed in men? What is patriarchy? How maleness becomes a different 'object' compared to femaleness? Why reproduction, sexuality and socialisation of children are viewed as obligations and duties of women? What are the visible and the invisible aspects in everyday life of a woman which makes her subordinate to a man? What is the real and the imagined nature of man-woman relations? Why reforms, legislations and movements have not produced results towards equality of women with men (Sharma, 1997: 135–56)? These and many other questions refer to a legitimising mechanism of biophysical differences and unequal access to resources, opportunities, rights and rewards between men and women. Almost every act relating to women implies a distinct institutionalisation of the functioning of gendering, derived status of women, superiority of patriarchy, and gendered division of labour. Michael Mann (in Cromption and Mann, eds., 1968: 40–56) observes that "stratification is gendered and gender is stratified".

This is why, there is no distinct 'female reason'. 'Male reason' makes women passive and invisible in understanding of human behaviour and thought, and in structures and processes of human societies. Further, it results into a controlled access of women to education, employment, property, decision-making, etc. Hence, invisibility of women. Gender hierarchies are thus created and recreated by persisting 'male reason' in one or other form. 'Deconstruction' of gender hierarchies by way of negation of gendering and sexing of biology seems to be the best solution to mitigate gender inequalities (Kabeer, 1955). Attack on overgazed male identity, negation of derived status of women, rejection of male mindset, and dominance of men on women are the main points of the women's question. R.W. Cornell (1994: 29–40) holds 'gender regime' responsible to dichotomy between man and woman. Gender regimes refer to a complex of institutions (family, work, state) that create and substantiate gender inequalities. Gender is reproduced within these institutions through 'male reason' and through the dichotomy of 'maleness' and 'femaleness'. A given gender regime is a cluster of practices in a particular social context, and acts to construct images of masculinity and feminity, hence, gender inequality (ibid.).

It is suggested that women should be in human 'gaze', they should be actors and subjects and agency of actions (Sharma, 1997: 133–56). But, then, the question is: How to go about with such a praxis of knowledge and power for men? We know that reforms, legislations and movements have not brought about desirable egalitarian results in making the hidden and invisible women as open and visible persons, equal to their menfolk. Bina Agarwal (1998: xv and 11–45) advocates against the top-down approach, namely, 'statisation' and patronage. She is for rights of women in property because rights in land/property would ensure more equal gender relations. Hence, we do not plead any more for a 'reform theory', rather, we demand for a 'resource theory' for equalitarian gender relations. Land rights are an instrument of women's empowerment (ibid.: xv).

Let me refer to two different situations. Education of girls has speeded up in the recent years in rural Rajasthan. Once during my visit to a village school in Sikar district, I found that girls were nearly 40 per cent of the total students and they were ahead of boys in their studies and extra-curricular activities. They even fondly mentioned about Indira Gandhi and Kiran Bedi, India's most known women celebrities. But, when they were asked what was their view on their own education, all of them told that it was upto their families and parents whether they would be sent for higher education or allowed to take up jobs or would be married after school education (Bourdieu, 1988). Thus, women's education is family-centric, rather than concerned with individual's own development and personality formation. Individual is in society.

However, reforms, legislations and movements have brought about some visible results. Age of girls at marriage has gone up because of their education. Today, women are quite conscious about their subordinate status in family and at workplace. They know about legislations relating to marriage, divorce, dowry, rape, etc., and also realise that not much has been achieved in liberating women from oppression and subjugation. The 73rd Constitutional Amendment, which provides one-third seats for women in Panchayati Raj and civic bodies, despite the phenomenon of 'Pati-Sarpanch', has initiated a process of social transformation of men-women relations. While attending a public function on July 14, 2003, along with a senior minister, in a village in Nagaur district of Rajasthan, I happened to interact with a woman Pradhan of a Panchayat Samiti. She belonged to political families on both sides—consanguine and affine, and she was educated up to 8th standard only. I found her quite alert, articulate and vibrant. She was quite conversant with local political culture idioms and tactics. Her traditional attire did not synchronise with the issues she dealt with in her speech relating to development, education and family welfare.

Such a change is quite restrictive in its scope and impact, but it sends a message of optimism for transformation of inequalitarian gender relations. No more women can be treated as 'half-men'. They ought to be seen as equal to men. Controlled access to essential domains of life, such as education, mobility, employment, property, income and decision-making, has to go and inclusion of women with men needs to be ensured in these domains.

Marginality and Social Opportunity

Lastly, a look at marginality and marginalised groups would also reflect upon the question of 'social opportunity'. Marginality is both a historical reality and a context-specific phenomenon. Structure and variants of marginality would indicate a general character of socio-cultural dominance of some groups and individuals and weak and ineffective social standing of a large number of people at the same time. In other words, it would mean dominance of a minority of people and subjugation of a large majority in specific given societies. In fact, patterns of injustice and inequality characterise the phenomenon of marginality all over the world. However, meanings and expressions of marginality are numerous. A self-alienated person is also a marginal one (see for example, Horowitz, 1975: 358–83). Our concern is with denial of social opportunity based on marginality, which is historically produced and socially structured in terms of the deprived huge mass of people, and certainly there would be the privileged few. Thus, marginality is not a question of numerical preponderance or of small size of a given population.

Marginality refers to a situation of the people which is far away from the mainstream. Restrictions and impediments created by a given social system and its 'guardians' make marginality as a pregiven reality for the marginalised. Marginality is thus not a matter of violation/attitude or of a belief system. It implies a critique of those historical forces and socio-cultural bindings, which have reduced a large number of people to an insignificant position. As such, marginality implies: (1) deprivation from a legitimate share in resources and opportunities by a large number of people; and (2) socio-cultural alienation of people in spite of their apparent participation in political processes (elections, etc.). Here, we neither deal with the ideologue who condemns the mainline precepts and behavioural patterns, nor on the marginality of the immigrant groups and individuals. The question in this paper is of the marginalised masses and their deprivations vis-à-vis the privileged ones. The point is: What can make the deprived to move up, or in other words, how to mutilate the fortunes of the privileged to provide viable support to the underprivileged?

Pierre Bourdieu's observation is quite apt in this context. He writes: "Indeed, there exists a correspondence between social structures and mental structures, between the objective discussions on the social world—especially the decision into dominant and dominated in the different fields and the principles of vision and division that agents apply to them" (1988: 49). Bourdieu's study of 84 institutions selected on the basis of students' social origins and on the scale of a structured sample of 21 schools of differing status shows differentiation according to a cumulative index of social and academic prestige. The academic capital required and on the degree of autonomy of the criteria and the stakes of the competition two other patterns emerge: (1) an academically dominant but economically and socially dominated scientific and intellectual pole; and (2) an academically dominated but socially and economically administrative and economic pole. Thus, clearly, a double structured homology emerges: the homology between the fundamental opposition of higher education, separating the grand schools/ universities from the petty schools and the universities. A distinct and definitive social boundary between the grand pole (gate) and the small pole, or in other words, between the upper and the petty bourgeoisie, between top-level executives and so-called mid-level managers, etc., can be made out based on these two academic universes. These function as structures, as systems of academic differences, giving way to systems of social differences.

Bourdieu finds a high degree of correspondence between the occupations of the families of the students in the different establishments, the structure of the distribution of these occupations in social space, the hierarchy of institutions, based on the social status of their students and the general social hierarchy, selection of the educational institution, etc. More than pure academic value, the market value determines the selection of the institution. For placing both students and institutions, Bourdieu uses both in the space of positions and the space of stances which include the student's social trajectory, parents' education and occupation, grandfather's education, size of family, place of residence, academic trajectory, and academic capital (schools and tracks, baccalaureate results), and involvement in sports and cultural activities, respectively.

If the state remains as it is in the above description, the nobility continues to maintain its status quo. In a highly diversified and inegalitarian Indian society, the state cannot be left free to the dictates of the privileged at the cost of the age-old deprived social groups. The question is: How to assign weights to the deprived groups/families/individuals to enable them to come close to the entrenched sections of Indian society? Rawls (1999) observes: "The assignment of weights is an essential and not a minor part of a conception of justice. If we cannot explain how these weights are to be explained by reasonable ethical criteria, the means of rational discussion have come to an end." The principle of fairness applies to those who have remained deprived for a long time and the existing mechanisms have proved futile in ensuring actual equality of opportunity and achievement.

Empowering the socially and educationally marginalised groups and individuals is the prime motive in providing special consideration in the field of higher education and research. India ranks very low in the Human Development Index. Nearly 35 per cent of India's population is suffering from absolute poverty and other allied problems, such as illness, unemployment, illiteracy, etc. Plight of the rural people is more pathetic than that of the urban people. The deprived groups constitute about 76 per cent (52% OBCs and 24% SCs and STs) of the total population. The SCs who are 16.48 per cent are found in 25 states and five union territories (UTs) and only 37.41 per cent of them are literate. The STs are 8.08 per cent and are found in 25 states and 4 UTs, and 29.60 per cent are literate among them (India, 2003). Socio-economic condition of the minorities is also quite pathetic. Various commissions have been set up from time to time to protect and safeguard interests of the marginalised groups, consisting of the SCs, the STs, the OBCs, the minorities, women, disabled, etc. The Government of India and other agencies have to implement effectively some schemes by providing funds, subsidies, scholarships and training facilities to secure distributive justice for the marginalised groups. Past experience shows that such facilities have been cornered by small groups of people from among the officially deprived groups, denying the same to the deserving ones.

It is evident that about the three-fourths of people belong to the deprived/marginalised groups. But, the fact is that they are highly differentiated in terms of their social origins and access to education, employment and positions of prestige and power. For example, the 'upper backwards' like the Jats, Yadavas, Kurmis, Sainis, Gujars, etc., are ahead of the 'lower backwards' like the Nais, Telis, Lohars, etc. Similarly, generally speaking, tribals who have converted to Christianity are ahead of the non-converts in the field of education and white-collar employment. The same applies to the SCs as well. For example, Mahars in Maharashtra have concerned most of the benefits based on the reservation policy. The Meenas (an ST in Rajasthan) have extracted maximum mileage out of the reservation policy.

In comparison of these ascending groups, a large number of other groups have also remained marginalised and deprived. The lower backwards and the deprived SCs and the STs can be identified without much difficulty. For example, the forward families from amongst the backward castes and the lower backward castes are being identified and notified in case of

Bihar. The Commission for the Scheduled Castes and the Scheduled Tribes has identified in its various reports that the castes/tribes, which have extracted maximum benefits, have deprived a large number of other castes and communities.

It may be desirable to earmark a number of resources for each region based on its size and presence of the marginalised groups. For each region a fixed number of benefits may be decided for minorities depending upon their population and separately for women. A list of resources and benefits may be prepared regionwise, and the deprived groups from amongst the OBCs, the SCs, the STs, the minorities and women may be made aware about resource allocation. Since the 'forwards' from amongst them have already been benefited for nearly 60 years, the disadvantaged from these categories need to be considered for resource allocation. Members of the deprived communities may be encouraged to have access to Class I and II services, and professions, such as law, medicine, engineering, etc.

The above diagnosis should help in working out an outline of social opportunity for the marginalised groups and individuals. This would minimise their inequality of opportunity as well as their inequality of competitive capability.

To sum up, we have identified three entities, namely, caste, gender and marginality, to understand and analyse the question of 'social opportunity' in India. Our main thrust is to look at creation of social opportunity as a process of development. Social mobility of groups and individuals would depend upon available and equitable social opportunities for the deprived sections of people. Thus, freedom emanates from structure of relations and process of change. 'Development' needs to be seen as a liberating mechanism for those who suffer from inequities of caste, creed, illiteracy, poverty, unemployment, etc. Cure of a disease is not just in pills. Food, water, shelter, etc., are rather more important for the poor who are suffering from tuberculosis and other deadly ailments.

Creation of social opportunities would weaken the entrenched monopolists of societal resources and agencies. A lot more is required to equalise the iniquitous path of mobility, change and development.

References

Agarwal, Bina, 1998, *A Field of Ones's Own: Gender and Land Rights in South Asia* (paperback), New Delhi: Foundation Books.

Blair, Harry W., 1980, "Rising Kulaks and Backward Classes in Bihar, Social Change in the late 1970s", *Economic and Political Weekly*, Vol. XV, No. 2.

Bourdieu, Pierre, 1988, *Homo Academicus*, Cambridge: Polity Press.

Cornell, R.W., 1994, "Gender Regimes and the Gender Order", in *The Polity Reader in Gender Studies*, Cambridge: Polity Press.

Dumont, Louis, 1970, *Homo Hierarchicus: The Caste System and Its Implications*, London: Weidenfeld and Nicholson.

Gupta, Dipankar, 2000, *Interrogating Caste: Underlying Hierarchy and Difference in Indian Society*, New Delhi: Penguin Books.

Horowitz, Irving Louis, 1975, "Mainliners and Marginals: The Human Shape of Sociological Theory", in L. Gross (ed.), *Sociological Theory: Inquiries and Paradigms* (Indian Edition), Bombay: Allied Publishers Private Ltd.

Kabeer, Naila, 1995, *Reversed Realities: Gender Hierarchies in Development Thought*, New Delhi: Kali for Women.

Kolenda, Pauline, 1978, *Caste in Contemporary India: Beyond Organic Solidarity*, California: Benjamin Cummings Publishing Co.

Leach, E.R., 1960, "Introduction: What Should We Mean by Caste?" in E.R. Leach (ed.), *Aspects of Caste in South India: Ceylon and North-West Pakistan*, Cambridge: Cambridge University Press.

Mann, Michael, 1986, "A Crisis in Stratification Theory? Persons, Households/Families, Lineages, Genders, Classes and

Nations", in Rosemary Crompton and Michael Mann (eds.), *Gender and Stratification*, Cambridge: Polity Press.

Myrdal, Gunar, 1968, *Asian Drama*, Vol. I, New Delhi: Penguin Books.

Rawls, John, 1999, *A Theory of Justice* (revised edition), Oxford: University Press.

Sen, Amartya, 2000, *Development as Freedom*, New Delhi: Oxford University Press.

Sharma, K.L., 1974, *The Changing Rural Stratification System*, New Delhi: Orient Longman.

——, 1997, *Social Stratification in India: Issues and Themes*, New Delhi: Sage Publications.

——, 2001, *Reconceptualising Caste, Class and Tribe,* Jaipur and New Delhi: Rawat Publications.

Srinivas, M.N., 1962, *Caste in India and Other Essays*, Bombay: Asia Publishing House.

12

Society, State and Development

The Indian Dynamics

I

In one of his perspective essays "Man and Plan in India", D.P. Mukerji (1958: 30–76) observes: "Two questions vex thinking men at the time of major social changes: what is the new society, and what is the new man?" These questions can be asked at any point of time in the history of a society. Mukerji raised these questions in a seminar in 1948, just after India achieved independence on August 15, 1947. At this juncture of our infant democracy, Mukerji wrote: "India's social order, which is both a fact and an act, has not had the benefit of a clear or a systematic theory or design of new society behind it. Nor was the outline of the new man which could be filled in by the movement towards the new society ever firmly sketched" (ibid.: 31). In the same essay, Mukerji outlines assumptions of a new social order (ibid.: 49–52). These are: (1) harmonious social order, (2) a moving order, (3) a technology savvy order, (4) higher standard of living, (5) a mixed economy, (6) equal opportunities, (7) comprehensive development, (8) democratic process as the basis of the new social order, (9) a band of honest, efficient, knowledgeable administrators with social imagination, and (10) the state as a welfare state.

Such unambiguous questions relating to "man" and "society" and relationship between the two provided a stimulating vivid sketch for searching answers to these questions in the forms of the assumptions of the new social order. Such a sketch is for us the baseline to see what has happened since then in the six decades. We have a well-framed Constitution, and intellectually and pragmatically vibrant eleven Five-Year Plans till date, beginning from 1951. Several legislations and constitutional amendments have facilitated new programmes of action for the benefit of the people of India. The million-dollar questions are: Where do we stand today in terms of the state of our society, state and development? Do we have logical and pragmatic coherence between these three vast components of India? Have we resolved contradictions in their functioning which have occurred between them from time to time? What are the impediments in reducing the social inequalities among the people which are still persisting in an alarming proportion?

What Frantz Fanon (1971) has written about Algeria, at the age of 27 in the book—*The Wretched of the Earth*, is considerably relevant to the Indian downtrodden. In a long "preface" (ibid.: 7–26), Jean-Paul Sartre brings out the salient features of Fanon's revolutionary thesis. Sartre writes: "In short, the Third World finds *itself* and speaks to *itself* through his voice. We know that it is not a homogenous world; we know too that enslaved peoples are still to be found there, together with some who have achieved a simulacrum of phoney independence, others who are still fighting to attain sovereignty and others again who have obtained complete freedom but who live under constant menace of imperialist aggression. These differences are born of colonial history, in other words of oppression" (ibid.: 9–10). Fanon, a man of medicine (psychiatry), a patient of leukaemia, died at the age of 36, in 1961. He was a fearless revolutionary and a man of profound thinking and reflection. What he says is that some have attained complete freedom, but they live under the shadow of imperialist ideology and praxis. India belongs to this category. It has not been able to establish a smooth nexus between society, state and development.

Another interesting critique of the system and culture of the "oppression", the "oppressor" and the "oppressed" is given by Paulo Freire (1973) in the book—*Pedagogy of the Oppressed*, which is an inspiring analysis of the educational system. Richard Shaull (ibid.: 9–14) in his "foreword" observes that Freire's sharing of the life of the poor led him to the discovery of the "culture of silence" of the dispossessed. "He (Paulo Freire) came to realise that their ignorance and lethargy were the direct product of the whole situation of economic, social, and political domination and of paternalism – of which they were victims." Critical awareness and response about the concrete realities of life were not encouraged. This was done through the educational system which led to the culture of silence. To create a new social order, a new unity of theory and praxis is the most essential prerequisite. Such a theory could be formulated by redefining the prevailing notions of society, state and development, and by creating coherent parameters of interaction between these three dimensions.

Freire considers "conscientization" and "critical consciousness" as genuinely liberating means for men from all sorts of enslavement. "The term 'conscientization' refers to learning to perceive social, political, and economic considerations, and to take action against the oppressive elements of reality" (ibid.: fn. 1–15). Freire is against the notions of "false generosity", "false charity" and "false consciousness". He is for realisation of the oppression by the oppressed. The oppressed must know the oppressive society, the effects of oppression, and the necessity of liberation. He need not to be "fearful of freedom".

II

Drawing from D.P. Mukerji, Frantz Fanon and Paulo Freire, we find three different views: relationship between man and society, oppression by the state, and the culture of oppression, in the contexts of India, Algeria and Brazil, respectively. India has a distinct civilisation, and quite different socio-political and economic contours compared to Africa and Latin America. Its vast and multifaceted labyrinth of religious, linguistic, regional, racial, tribal and caste allegiances largely shape its polity and economy, and in turn, compulsions of the latter have also made the socio-cultural structure quite resilient and adaptive. Despite being such a diversified social conglomerate, India has followed the path of equality and democratic politics with considerable efforts (Fallers, 1971: 15–219).

After independence, the first decade of India is seen in somewhat two different ways. Charles Bettelheim (1968: 358–371) observes that India did not make a rapid start towards economic development. Growth was slow. Society as a whole did not gain equally from its industrial expansion. The richer classes cornered the fruits of development. Bettelheim observes: "Social and regional inequalities have increased" (ibid.: 360). The standard of living among the majority of the population has remained stationary and sometimes it has even deteriorated. The wealth and the power of the big bourgeoisie have increased rapidly, hence class has also become evident. "Semi-feudal" relations persist. However, Bettelheim seems to toe the erstwhile Soviet path of planning and development for India. According to him, India's social and economic structures, including "semi-feudal" relations, the power of commercial and moneylending capital and foreign capital in industry and banking are responsible for its economic backwardness.

Landless peasants are suffering at the hands of the big bourgeoisie and the richer urban and rural classes. "The contradictions inherent in a capitalist society will also develop and cause further social tensions" (ibid.: 366). Radicalisation of the working classes, including the industrial proletariat and the exploited rural classes, would emerge.

Another approach, at the same time, was advocated by Gunnar Myrdal (1968), though at a significant variance compared to that of Bettelheim's analysis in the first one and half decades of Indian independence. Myrdal puts forward "a plea for an institutional emphasis" to the development problems in South Asia. This is done because the basic social and economic structure of South Asia is considerably different from that of the advanced Western countries. Social matrix of the Western countries does not hinder economic development. The problem of development in South Asia requires induced changes in the social and economic structure, because it hinders economic development. Myrdal says: "So our approach is broadly institutional." Such an approach implies understanding of attitudes, institutions, modes, and levels of living, and broadly, *culture*, seen in the process of economic development. The title, *Asian Drama*, thus, is indicative of all the complexities and dissimilarities, a clear-cut set of conflicts and a common theme as in a drama. The following statement by Myrdal (ibid.: 34) makes clear the main aim of his study:

> Thus drama has its unity in a set of inner conflicts operating on people's minds: between their high-pitched aspirations and the bitter experience of a harsh reality; between the desire for change and improvement and mental reservations and inhibitions about accepting the consequences and paying the price. Such conflicts are a part of human life in all times and places; but in the countries under study, they have an exceptional, mounting intensity and assume a unique form.

Myrdal chooses a set of value premises, which he calls—*The Modernization Ideals* (ibid.: 49–69). These value premises have become the "official creed", almost a national religion, and are one of the powerful strands of the "new nationalism", observes Myrdal (ibid.: 54). The creed is radical, the leftward in public declarations, though hardly in practical politics. This, however, implies a drastic change in India's economic, social and political conditions. Myrdal writes: "The modernization ideals are mainly the ideology of the politically alert, articulate, and active part of the population – particularly the intellectual elite" (ibid.: 55). These ideals are as follows:

1. Rationality
2. Development and planning for development
3. Rise of productivity
4. Rise of levels of living
5. Social and economic equalisation
6. Improved institutions and attitudes with following elements:
   (i) efficiency
   (ii) diligence
   (iii) orderliness
   (iv) punctuality
   (v) frugality
   (vi) scrupulous honesty
   (vii) rationality in decisions on action
   (viii) preparedness for change
   (ix) alertness to opportunities as they arise in a changing world
   (x) energetic enterprise
   (xi) integrity and self-reliance
   (xii) cooperativeness
   (xiii) willingness to take the long view
7. National integration
8. National independence

9. Political democracy, in a narrow sense
10. Democracy at the grass roots
11. Social discipline versus "democratic planning".

Myrdal candidly admits that "among the articulate groups there is unanimous support, on a very general plane, for changing institutions and attitudes, but there is also much escapism, particularly in regard to specific issues" (ibid.: 63). India made a significant beginning by having a composite Constitution, Five-Year Plans, land reforms, elections, adult franchise, etc. Considerable progress was made in agriculture, industry and administration during the Nehruvian era. Consolidation of India as a new nation-state was the remarkable achievement despite defeat at the hands of China in 1962. Myrdal observes that India, being a "soft state", could not effectively reduce social inequalities and impediments obstructing distributive justice.

Indicators of inequality chosen by Myrdal include food and nutrition, clothing, housing and sanitation, health facilities, information media, energy consumption and transportation. These are closely interrelated manifestations of inequality. The disparity is evident between agricultural and non-agriculture income commensurating to the rural-urban differential. Myrdal writes: "The entire structure of inequality is bolstered by the caste system, the color line, ethnic discrimination, nepotism, and the general set of social and religious taboos" (ibid., 579). There is a vicious circle of cumulative interrelation and causation. The present institutional arrangements impede the rise of social, regional and occupational mobility, and encourage the persistence of multidimensional segmentation of social and economic life, which is a major obstacle to economic growth (ibid.).

Soviet Union had a decisive influence on India's Five-Year Plans in the Nehruvian era, in particular. However, India has considered planning as a necessary means of democracy and people's welfare. Myrdal is a strong advocate of the institutional approach to planning, development and democracy. He abhors the Marxist approach. He writes: "Marxism is a most confused concept and will not be used as a technical term in this book" (ibid., fn. 1: 726). Further, Myrdal observes: "Marx was not a planner, and his ideology in its more undiluted forms was not a planning ideology" (ibid., fn. 2: 726). Lenin's theory of imperialism is seen more relevant by Myrdal in the context of South Asian countries.

Myrdal's observation regarding equality and democracy is quite perceptive (ibid.: 747–49). The main points are as follows:

1. Economic inequality is typically the outcome of social inequality, and the reverse is also true.
2. A large part of the population suffers from malnutrition and from the lack of elementary health and educational facilities. This deters labour input and efficiency.
3. People in the higher income brackets indulge in conspicuous investments that do not contribute to raising the national product.
4. The independent value of greater economic and social equality has to be weighed on the scales. Inequality means much greater suffering in the poor countries.

Can the upper-class state alternative be feasible for India to have a reasonable level of equalisation? Myrdal answers through this poser: "A quasi-democratic upper–class state cannot be created once universal suffrage has been conceded and political, social, and economic equality has commonly been accepted as a moral imperative and a goal for planning" (ibid.: 783). Since Myrdal's monumental work appeared in 1968, wide-ranging social, political and economic changes have occurred in India, including green revolution, privatisation, liberalisation and globalisation, political and social transformations. The existential conditions have changed considerably, new players have entered into social, political and economic arenas. The "institutional approach" of Myrdal has become quite ineffective to understand the new dynamics of the 1970s and thereafter.

III

One may not confer with John Stuart Mill's thesis that aristocracies and democracy are not antithetical, rather they could be complementary and mutually supportive (Williams, 1985: 179–185). Mill wrote in 1835 that identification of interest between the rulers and the ruled cannot be realised. Therefore, the government may be run by a select body, not by the public collectively. "That political questions be not decided by an appeal, either direct or indirect, to the judgment or will of an uninstructed mass, whether of gentleman or of clowns; but by the deliberately formed opinions of a comparatively few, specially educated for the task" (ibid.: 180). Mill further asks: "How best to conciliate the two great elements on which good government depends; to combine the greatest amount of the advantage derived from the independent judgment of a specially instructed few, with the greatest degree of the security for rectitude of purpose derived from rendering those responsible to the many"?(ibid.: 181).

The majority of people should be sensible of the value of superior wisdom. The people should know what things are done by the select few, that is, the judges. This is the idea of a *rational democracy*. It means that the people do not govern themselves, but they have security for good government. "This security they cannot have by any other means than by retaining in their own hands the ultimate control. If they renounce this, they give themselves up to tyranny" (ibid.: 182). If a governing class is not accountable to the people, not to the good of the people, but to their own good, their very virtues are class virtues. Their rulership becomes questionable. However, Mill does not approve of unnecessary interference in the functioning of the government.

Like Mill's view on democracy, Alexis de Tocqueville has discussed various properties and tendencies of democracy. He has ascertained the separate relations in which it stands towards the different interests of society, and the different moral and social requisites of human nature (ibid.: 188–189). Tocqueville talks of the political effects of democracy, its influence upon society, upon the relations of private life, upon intellect, morals, and the habits and modes of feeling which constitute national character. The following statement defining democracy by Tocqueville is quite revealing:

> That Democracy, in the modern world, is inevitable; and that it is, on the whole, desirable, but desirable only under certain conditions, and those conditions capable, by human care and foresight, of being realized, but capable also of being missed.

Democracy is a tendency of a progressive civilisation. It is like a law of nature. By democracy Tocqueville understands equality of conditions. Democracy is towards equality between man and man. Equality of conditions often tends to produce a popular government. Equality may be equal freedom or contrarily equal servitude. Democracy ultimately tends to have no distinctions of political rights, no great or very permanent distinctions of hereditary wealth.

IV

India is considered as world's largest and effective democracy. Regular elections for the provincial legislatures and parliament and civic bodies have been held during the past six decades. Planning as a mode of development has been institutionalised. Programmes for the needly, hapless, disabled, poor and downtrodden, rural, urban and tribal people have been implemented at least partially. Dominance of upper castes has declined. A section of the middle castes has emerged over the years politically strong and influential. To some extent, a small segment of the lower castes too has come up politically and socially.

Since some select groups, families and individuals have been benefited, it is clear that distributive process is lacking. The state's unrealistic but manipulated policies and actions on the one hand, and the liberalisation and privatisation of economy on the other, have distorted the twin systems of democracy and development. The nature of politics in India is largely responsible for socio-political and economic unevenness as a result of inappropriate linkages between society, democracy and development.

Rudolph and Rudolph (1987:1–15) rightly characterise the Indian scene by the "the weak-strong state and the rich-poor economy" as a political and economic paradox. Rudolphs are of the view that "class politics" is marginal. A variety of social formations and identities organise and represent society in India. These even shape Indian economy, industrialisation and democracy. They write: "Of the many cleavages that animate Indian politics, class usually matters less than other social formations, such as caste, religious and language communities, and regional nationalisms. Other cleavages rival or surpass class in political silency because the consciousness and commitment focused on them are usually more transparent and accessible than those focused on class" (ibid.: 396).

Democracy and reorientation of tradition (caste, religion, region) have appeared at the same time after 1947, and therefore, class and industrialisation have lagged behind compared to the association of electoral politics and socio-cultural revivalism. Such a situation has also led to the emergence of "demand groups", emphasizing specific interests of the groups and entities such as peasants, artisans, students, communities, trade unions, etc. "Demand politics" implies "pluralism", and opposite to this is the "command politics" – the centralisation of authority and power. One would see only a lopsided direction of change and development due to irreconciliation between society, development and politics. However, in our view, the situation has changed considerably since 1987 when Rudolphs advocated that class-politics was less than politics of caste, religion, etc. We have reflected on this point later on in this essay. Certainly, during the post-liberalisation period, the nature of class politics has changed, and new pattern of nexus between politics and society has also emerged.

There are contradictions between Indian politics and society (Brass, 2004: 1–28). Firstly, there was a massive contradiction between the rhetoric of Indian public discourse and the reality of political practice. Secondly, there is a contradiction between rhetoric and reality in contemporary Indian politics regarding the disjunction between the language of planning, equality, socialism, and social justice and the practices of day-to-day politics.

V

Who control land, resources and people (castes and communities)? Who get elected to legislatures and local bodies? Who are caste leaders or leaders in villages or of factions thereof? Who make the mafia in politics? Who decide about public spending? What are the priorities for resource allocation and public spending? Who are benefited by the development programmes relating to transport, communication, education, healthcare, etc.? What is the structure and hierarchy of political leadership? What are the linkages between different layers of leadership? What is the modus operandi of political mobilisation? How funds are raised by political parties and their leaders? Who are the financial supporters? What do they get in return for funding the political parties and contestants in elections?

The listing of such questions can be unending. More important is to understand the substance of these questions and then to understand and analyse the nexus between society, state and development.

A large number of people are of the view that the pace of economic development has been considerably slow, and India is far behind from being a modern, industrialised power, comparable with the advanced countries of the Western world. India has the legacy of its pre-independence national leaders, including Gandhi and Nehru. It has become an established democratic country. Planned development and public institutions have taken deep roots. Its economic growth is also not discouraging, but it has not been transformed into "development", "distributive" and "fair justice". Unevenness of the consequences of growth has hampered human and social development. Success in ending of poverty, ignorance, disease and inequality of opportunity has not been encouraging. Reproduction of "good things" in life by a select few, including prosperity, quality education, good health and manipulation for availing opportunity, has thwarted human progress and development. The Indian State has failed to a large extent in ensuring a minimum level of living for the poor, deprived and common men. Who is "capable" for availing opportunity for suitable employment, a proper healthcare, a roof over his head, etc.? Or, who is not "capable" for all this?

Jean Dreze and Amartya Sen (1996: 179–204) talk of Indian economy like that of the *caged tiger*. It is caged because of its "ever-proliferating bureaucracy" and its "licence raj", and the "fiscal crisis" claimed by every newly elected government on an interval of five years. They observe that India's overall growth rate is not disappointing, but it does not have corresponding reduction of poverty, social backwardness and sectional deprivation, as India lacks *participatory* economic expansion. We have "radical needs", but our reforms are "moderate". Both state and people (public) need to play effective role in this process of development. "Private" cannot be free from the state, and the state cannot function without participation of the public (people). This is what we mean by public-private partnership. Who are the people who could be engaged in participatory economic expansion? Who are the people managing educational institutions and healthcare agencies as private actors? What is their modus operandi? The state needs to have a constant vigilance, keeping in view the interests of those who pay to them for these institutions.

In the book *Development as Freedom*, Amartya Sen (2000) argues that individual freedom is a matter of social commitment. Development is freedom because it removes unfreedoms or impediments which an individual encounters in seeking opportunity for better avenues. Freedom in one sector of human endeavours facilitates freedom in some other sphere. Freedoms or for that matter unfreedoms are interrelated phenomena. Social opportunities require public action, to complement individual's efforts for economic and political participation. Thus, Sen sees development as a process of expanding the real freedoms that people enjoy (ibid.: 3). He writes: "Development requires the removal of major sources of unfreedom: poverty as well as tyranny, poor economic opportunities as well as systematic social deprivation, neglect of public facilities as well as intolerance or overactivity of repressive states" (ibid.: 4). Freedom is related to development for two reasons, says Sen: (1) the evaluative reason; and (2) the effectiveness reason (ibid.).

VI

Basing on Pierre Bourdieu's viewpoint (1996), we can look at our political situation. While referring to Marx and Engels,

Bourdieu mentions that there are no painters but at most people who engage in painting among other things. And based on this, Bourdieu observes that there are no politicians but at most people who engage in politics among other things. A true politician needs to extract good from bad, truth from false. He is required to recognise a political question as political, and to treat it as such by responding to it politically based on political principles, and not ethnically. Bourdieu says that this is "political competence" and "political culture". What is required, according to Bourdieu, is a clear demarcation between "electoral democracy" and "technocratic aristocracy". The two should avoid interfering with each other (ibid.: 405).

Bourdieu discusses politics as a practice in relation to socio-economic condition. Indicators of social origin need to be accounted for given political practices. Even media, including "sensational press" and "informative press" need to be seen in terms of political space and political language. Sensational press implies *politics*, and informative press denotes *policy*, and the two are two sides of political space and political language. In politics, there is an intense tendency of *distrust*. The question is often like this: "Are your friends' friends your friends"? Generally, a politician is a *dexosopher*, who never teaches anything other than the difficulty of taking sides; he generates only *distance*. Along with deep distrust, there is deep form of recognition. Both constitute political language. Thus, politicians are the master of the art of packaging and of fobbing off with words. The following quote from Bourdieu (ibid.: 464–65) is quite relevant:

> Everything combines to reinforce the deep distrust – not incompatible with an equally deep form of recognition – which the dominated feel towards political language, broadly identified, like everything symbolic, with the dominant, the masters of the art of packaging and of fobbing off with words. This suspicion of the political state; a 'theatre' whose rules are not understood and which leaves ordinary taste with a sense

> of helplessness, is often the source of 'apathy' and of a generalised distrust of all forms of speech and spokesmen. And often the only escape from ambivalence or indeterminacy towards language is to fall back on what one *can* appreciate, the body rather than words, substance rather than form, an honest face rather than a smooth tongue.

Besides being dexosophers, Indian politicians have made politics a *family business*. Vir Sanghvi (*Hindustan Times*, 27 September 2009) writes: "Sons follow their fathers into Parliament with a depressing regularity." They owe their prominence less to any merit and more to their fathers. They remind us that in a dynastic system, the past becomes the future – it just speaks better English, because some of them are educated at Doon School, at an American University or Delhi's St. Stephen's College. Another journalist, Manas Chakravarty (*Hindustan Times*, 27 September 2009) labels such a trend as *Family Democracy*. Chakravarty cites examples of Indira Gandhi, Sharad Pawar, Stalin, Farooq, etc. Some families represent alliances between political and business empires. The Deshmukhs, the Chavans, the Shekhawats, the Yadavs, Mundes, Badals, Mahajans, Scindias and many more at the local level can be added to this list of dynasts. Can we relate family, politics and development in such a situation? Is this not a step more, in a negative sense, than the "caste democracy"? Glamourisation of family has become a political creed. The protagonists from Devi Lal to Badal, to Karaunanidhi, to Farooq do not see anything wrong in this political tendency of intergenerational continuity of family in politics. This happens in education, professions, cinema, and it used to be so in good old days based on *jajmani* system. Why it cannot happen now based on democratic process of adult franchise? The argument seems to be ridiculous, but the fact remains that such people are in the political field generation after generation.

VII

In the famous work *India After Gandhi: The History of the World's Largest Democracy*, Ramachandra Guha (2008) brings out a comprehensive analysis of eventful six decades after India's independence in 1947. A history of events is presented in four Rs, that is, Rights, Riots, Rulers, and Riches (ibid.: 605–719). These refer to constitution and law, conflicts, political power, and economy, respectively, during the post-independence period. I am particularly impressed by Guha's analysis of our democracy. He says that there is the "hardware" and "software" of our democracy. "Hardware" implies freedom of expression and of movement, and right to vote. The "software" implies that "Most political parties have become family firms. Most politicians are corrupt, and many come from a criminal background". The "hardware" is merited, and the "software" is less cheering. Thus, Indian democracy is successful upto 50 per cent only.

Another eminent scholar, Dipankar Gupta (2009) holds Indian democracy in high esteem, based on political representation, urbanisation, education and scholarship, science, technology, etc. However, the statesmanship and vision of Gandhi and Nehru are no more visible, except chanting of their names at chosen times. Indian politicians are to be blamed because they have become a class in themselves, away from the masses. They have caged the phoenix (Indian democracy). India has become an *undelivering* democracy. No more we can blame caste, religion, ethnicity, etc., for such a malaise. There is, no doubt, growth, but not commensurate with development. Amartya Sen has also argued, why, despite growth, corresponding development is not there. Besides blaming the state and politics of the day, Gupta holds intellectuals also responsible for the hiatus between growth and development as they do not call a spade, a spade.

The latest work, *The Idea of Justice* by Amartya Sen (2009) addresses questions of enhancing justice and removing injustice. Sen heavily draws from John Rawls (1999) regarding "fair justice" or "perfect justice". According to Sen, a theory of justice must serve as the basis of practical reasoning for ways of judging how to reduce injustice and advance justice. Resolutions about the nature of perfect justice are generally abstract and philosophical propositions rather than publicly reasoned ways and means to reduce institutional bottlenecks.

Reasoned argument is essence of reducing injustice. The remedial injustice should be the focal point in a reasoned philosophical explanation of justice. Through public reasoning, several ways and means may emerge for reducing injustice, and this is in tune with democracy as "government by discussion", as argued by John Stuart Mill, about which we have mentioned earlier in this essay.

Sen emphasizes on both the institutions right and the actual societies that ultimately would emerge. Indignation and argument, frustration and ire alone are insufficient as resistance to inequality, what one needs include both assessment and effectiveness, based on reasoned scrutiny for a plausible and sustainable understanding of the basis of injustice and its solution. This is the way we can interrelate society, state and development.

VIII

I have reasoned earlier (Sharma, 2001) that we need to understand structures and their interrelations to bring about an effective and desired social transformation. The conventional categories, such as caste, ethnicity, religion, ritual distance, etc., have considerably lost their value and significance. The emergent categories are related to divides between the rich and the poor, the strong and the weak, the privileged and the deprived, the resourceful and the resourceless, the well-employed and the unemployed/underemployed, etc. Such structural categories are not bound to a given caste, community, religion, language, region, etc.

At this juncture of our post-independence history, we have to locate people as rich and poor, etc. And ask why this is happening? Why there is no doctor in a Primary Health Centre? If there is a doctor, why the Centre is ill-equipped or does not have medicine required for the needy and poor? Democracy for whom? State for what? Whose development? IITs/IIMs are for whom? Who get into lucrative services? Who go abroad for higher studies/jobs?

If a large majority of our people remain deprived of nutritious food, proper healthcare facilities, quality education, suitable employment, then we have to diagnose, in a specific manner, this malady and strike at it by institutional transformation, actual living conditions, and patterns of relations and behaviour.

Dipankar Gupta argues that we need a *new* (emphasis added) sociology rather than a culturology. We have had enough of return of cultural conceptualisations or reconceptualisations. Postmodernity is not our cup of tea, because we never reached the stage of full industrialisation. Our problems are not that of an *industrialised society*. We are a country where 40 per cent of our people do not get adequate food and drinking water. Hollow cultural imaginations would not solve our problems. Such an intellectual luxury and hedonism are a plaything for a select so-called intellectuals of the West, who have a superficial concern for Indian civilisation and culture.

References

Bettelheim, Charles, 1968, *India Independent*, London: Macgibbon & Kee.

Bourdieu, Pierre, 1996, *Distinction: A Social Critique of the Judgment of Taste* (Reprint), London: Routledge & Kegan Paul.

Brass, Paul R., 2004, *The Politics of India since Independence* (second edition), Cambridge: Cambridge University Press.

Chakravarty, Manas, 2009, "Family Democracy", in *Hindustan Times*, New Delhi, September 27.

Dreze, Jean and Amartya Sen, 1996, *India: Economic Development and Social Opportunity*, Delhi: Oxford University Press.

Fallers, Llyod, 1971, "Equality, Modernity, and Democracy in the New States", in Clifford Geertz (ed.), *Old Societies and New States: The Quest for Modernity in Asia and Africa* (Indian edition), New Delhi: Amerind Publishing Co., pp. 158–219.

Fanon, Frantz, 1971, *The Wretched of The Earth* (preface by Jean-Paul Sartre and translated by Constance Farrington), Harmondsworth: Penguin Books.

Freire, Paulo, 1973, *Pedagogy of the Oppressed*, Harmondsworth: Penguin Books.

Guha, Ramchandra, 2008, *India: After Gandhi* (paperback), London: Pan Books.

Gupta, Dipankar, 2009, *The Caged Phoenix: Can India Fly*?, New Delhi: Viking/Penguin Books.

Mill, John Stuart, 1976, *John Stuart Mill on Politics and Society*, selected and edited by Geraint L. Williams, Glasgow: Fontana Press.

Mukerji, D.P., 1958, *Diversities*, New Delhi: People's Publishing House.

Myrdal, Gunnar, 1968, *Asian Drama: An Inquiry into the Poverty of Nations*, Harmondsworth: Penguin Books.

Rawls, John, 1999, *A Theory of Justice* (revised edition), Oxford: Oxford University Press.

Rudolph, Lloyd I. and , Susanne Hoeber Rudolph, 1987, *In Pursuit of Lakshmi: The Political Economy of the Indian State*, New Delhi: Orient Longman.

Sanghvi, Vir, 2009, No Room for Outsiders in Indian Politics", in *Hindustan Times*, September 27.

Sen, Amartya, 1995, *Inequality Reexamined*, New Delhi: Oxford University Press.

——, 2000, *Development as Freedom*, Delhi: Oxford University Press.

——, 2009, *The Idea of Justice*, London, Allen Lane, an imprint of Penguin Books.

Sharma, K.L., 2001, *Reconceptualising Caste, Class and Tribe*, Jaipur and New Delhi: Rawat Publications.

Shaull, Richard, 1973, "Foreword" and "Preface" in *Pedagogy of the Oppressed,* by Paulo Freire, op. cit.

Tocqueville, Alexis de, 1990, *Democracy in America*, translated into English by George Lawrence, Chicago, Il: Encyclopaedia Britannica.

Williams, Geraint L., 1985, "Introduction", in *John Stuart Mill on Politics and Society*, op. cit.

Index